Chaucer: The Basics is an accessible introduction to the works of Geoffrey Chaucer. It provides a clear critical analysis of the texts, while also providing some necessary background to key medieval ideas and the historical period in which he lived. Jacqueline Tasioulas gives a brief account of Chaucer's life in its historical and cultural context and also introduces the reader to some of the key religious and philosophical ideas of the period. The essentials of the language and pronunciation are introduced through close reading in a section dedicated to demystifying this often alien-seeming aspect of studying Chaucer.

Including a whole chapter devoted to poetry, the book also discusses key works, such as:

- *The Book of the Duchess*
- *The House of Fame*
- *The Parliament of Fowls*
- *Troilus and Criseyde*
- *The Legend of Good Women*
- *The Canterbury Tales*

With glosses and translations of texts, a glossary of key terms and a timeline, this book is essential reading for anyone studying Chaucer and medieval literature.

Jacqueline Tasioulas is a Lecturer in English at the University of Cambridge and a Fellow of Clare College, Cambridge, UK.

The Basics

The Basics is a highly successful series of accessible guidebooks which provide an overview of the fundamental principles of a subject area in a jargon-free and undaunting format.

Intended for students approaching a subject for the first time, the books both introduce the essentials of a subject and provide an ideal springboard for further study. With over 50 titles spanning subjects from artificial intelligence (AI) to women's studies, *The Basics* are an ideal starting point for students seeking to understand a subject area.

Each text comes with recommendations for further study and gradually introduces the complexities and nuances within a subject.

TRANSLATION
JULIANE HOUSE

FINANCIAL ACCOUNTING
ILIAS G. BASIOUDIS

GERONTOLOGY
JENNY R. SASSER AND HARRY R. MOODY

GENDER (SECOND EDITION)
HILARY LIPS

WOMEN'S STUDIES (SECOND EDITION)
BONNIE G. SMITH

EDUCATION RESEARCH
MIKE HAMMOND WITH JERRY WELLINGTON

For a full list of titles in this series, please visit www.routledge.com/The-Basics/book-series/B

CHAUCER

THE BASICS

Jacqueline Tasioulas

Routledge
Taylor & Francis Group

LONDON AND NEW YORK

First published 2020
by Routledge
2 Park Square, Milton Park, Abingdon, Oxon OX14 4RN

and by Routledge
52 Vanderbilt Avenue, New York, NY 10017

Routledge is an imprint of the Taylor & Francis Group, an informa business

British Library Cataloguing-in-Publication Data
A catalogue record for this book is available from the British Library

Library of Congress Cataloging-in-Publication Data
Names: Tasioulas, J. A. (Jacqueline A.), author.
Title: Chaucer : the basics / Jacqueline Tasioulas.
Description: Abingdon, Oxon ; New York, NY :
Routledge, 2019. | Series: The basics |
Includes bibliographical references and index.
Identifiers: LCCN 2019013270 |
ISBN 9781138667709 (hardback : alk. paper) |
ISBN 9781138667716 (paperback : alk. paper) |
ISBN 9781315618852 (ebk)
Subjects: LCSH: Chaucer, Geoffrey, –1400–Criticism and interpretation.
Classification: LCC PR1924 .T28 2019 | DDC 821/.1–dc23
LC record available at https://lccn.loc.gov/2019013270

ISBN: 978-1-138-66770-9 (hbk)
ISBN: 978-1-138-66771-6 (pbk)
ISBN: 978-1-315-61885-2 (ebk)

Typeset in Bembo
by Newgen Publishing UK
Printed by CPI Group (UK) Ltd, Croydon CR0 4YY

For Con and Gregory

CONTENTS

PREFACE

This book is the essence of many years spent teaching the works of Chaucer at the University of Cambridge and, before that, at Stirling and at Oxford. My thanks first of all, therefore, must go to my students for making that such a joyful experience. The University of Cambridge has been an inspiring place in which to work, and Clare College has been a model of what an academic community might hope to be, for which great thanks is owed to the Master and Fellows, particularly my teaching colleagues Tamara Follini, Fred Parker, and Anne Stillman. I'm also conscious of how many people it takes to create such a workplace for others and I'm grateful to all the staff for everything they do on a daily basis. As Senior Tutor, I have relied heavily on the knowledge and wisdom of many people, but particularly upon Jonathan Goodman, Jamie Hawkey, and Paul Warren, each of whom has lightened the load considerably. It remains to say that the book would not have seen the light of day at all without the tremendous kindness and scholarly generosity of Barry Windeatt, who has been supportive from beginning to end, and to whom I am forever grateful. Finally, thanks must go to my family for being the people they are and for helping always: Richard and Rosemary; Michelle, Gareth, Kurt, and Ethan; and my two wonderful sons, Con and Gregory, to whom this book is dedicated with love.

ACKNOWLEDGEMENTS

All quotations have been taken from *The Riverside Chaucer*, ed. Larry D. Benson. My debt to other scholarly and critical work is given in the various lists of 'Further Reading' and in the Bibliography.

ABBREVIATIONS

B	*Boece*
BD	*The Book of the Duchess*
CCP	'The Complaint of Chaucer to his Purse'
CT	*The Canterbury Tales*
CWA	'Chaucer's Wordes unto Adam, His Owne Scriveyn'
GP	*The General Prologue* to the *Canterbury Tales*
HF	*The House of Fame*
LGW	*The Legend of Good Women*
PF	*The Parliament of Fowls*
TA	*A Treatise on the Astrolabe*
TC	*Troilus and Criseyde*

GEOFFREY CHAUCER
A LIFE IN TIME

Bubonic plague, the 'Black Death', reached England in the autumn of 1348. It was a disease that had already claimed the lives of an estimated hundred million people, and it would go on to wipe out perhaps a third of the population of England. The ports of Weymouth, Southampton, and Bristol saw the first outbreaks of what the Middle Ages simply called 'the Death', carried by trading ships from mainland Europe and the East. London outbreaks quickly followed, and soon only the most isolated parts of the country remained untouched by the plague. Geoffrey Chaucer was only a boy, perhaps five years old, but he would live through several more outbreaks of the Black Death in his lifetime. The swift, all-encompassing nature of the disease is captured by him in one of the *Canterbury Tales*, as some young revellers hear a bell toll as a corpse is carried through the streets for burial. They are told it is the body of their friend, killed as he sat in the tavern by 'a privee [sneaky] theef men clepeth [call] Deeth' (*CT* VI 675), a silent criminal who has already claimed a thousand lives. Unlike some authors of the time, Chaucer does not dwell on the horrors of the plague, but what he conveys here is the speed with which it killed – the number so vast that it defies comprehension (in a time when most villages did not have a population of more than two hundred) – and the familiar sight of plague victims being carried through the streets.

The horror and terror are difficult to imagine, and for many it seemed that the plague was a judgement on sin and a prelude to the end of the world. For those who survived, however, fortunes were at least mixed. Chaucer's Physician in the *Canterbury Tales* dresses himself in fine red and blue silk, the result of the profit he has made from the 'pestilence' (*GP* 442). As for Chaucer's own family, in spite of living in Southampton, his immediate relations survived the plague. The London relatives, however, were not so fortunate, and several members of the family died during the 1348 outbreak, among them Chaucer's great uncle, a wealthy 'moneyer' at the Mint in the Tower of London. It was to his uncle's London house that the Chaucer family returned once the immediate threat of death had receded, Geoffrey's mother having inherited the house together with an impressive legacy of 24 shops.

The Chaucer family was already relatively prosperous, its status having risen steadily throughout the fourteenth century. Early records show that they were previously named de Dynyngton, or le Taverner and, as the name suggests, had been tavern keepers and vintners. The medieval tavern is vividly conveyed in the description of Southwark's Tabard Inn at the beginning of the *Canterbury Tales*, as the genial Host, Harry Bailley, a 'right a myrie man' (*GP*, 755–7), calls for a story-telling competition from the assembled pilgrims. A more riotous side of tavern life is seen in the tale of the drunken Miller, who can heave any door off its hinges, or 'breke it at a rennyng [running] with his heed' (GP 551). In fact, it was following a fatal brawl that the family changed its name. Geoffrey's grandfather inherited property from a merchant who was killed in a brawl and they then took on the name of their dead benefactor: Chaucer.

Some of the considerable property owned by Chaucer's parents was in the Vintry Ward, one of the wealthiest parts of medieval London, where even Queen Philippa owned a residence. Geoffrey's father was a very successful wine merchant (a vintner), supplying wine to the king's cellars. He was influential and heavily involved in not just the business affairs of the city, but also in its politics. That a merchant should have done so well and occupy a position in society that took him beyond the affairs of trade was not surprising at this point in the fourteenth century. The merchants formed a powerful group, organising themselves into societies known as guilds, with the craftsmen soon following and organising into similar bodies. Indeed, in 1381 one of the members of the craft guilds became Lord Mayor of London, removing the merchants temporarily from this position of power. There was, therefore, the opportunity for movement and advancement in fourteenth-century England. The old feudal order, in which a small number of nobles and members of the Church were supported by a vast population of land-tilling peasants, was becoming a thing of memory. Famine and population decline had started the process at the beginning of the fourteenth century, and the ravages of the Black Death then shifted the balance forever. Old laws binding the remaining peasants to the land of ancestral lords could not be sustained. With labour in short supply, there was a shift in power, and with it came freedom of movement, throughout the country and into the emerging towns.

Of course, old orders tend to resist new orders, and this showed itself in a number of ways. Laws were introduced, for example, to attempt to regulate the kinds of clothes that various ranks of society could wear, and even the kind of food they could eat. Those who worked with animals, such as ploughmen and carters, were supposed only to wear coarse cloth, with belts of linen. Servants were not permitted to eat meat more than once a day. Craftsmen and their wives were forbidden to wear any precious metals and were limited to the fur of rabbits, foxes, or cat. Squirrel fur was reserved for those with higher incomes, the wives of less lowly knights being permitted this, together with silver and silk. This so-called 'sumptuary' legislation did not last long, but shows a society attempting to order itself in terms of wealth rather than nobility. In the *Canterbury Tales*, Chaucer supplies us with a small subgroup of pilgrims who proudly wear their guild livery and display with a certain ostentation their elaborately carved silver daggers. Consisting of a haberdasher (who would have dealt in hats and similar goods), a carpenter, a weaver, a dyer, and a tapestry maker, they are part of a parish guild, keen to imagine themselves as 'an important and great fraternity', out enjoying their newfound status and the chance to wear their guild finery:

And they were clothed alle in o lyveree	one livery
Of a solempne and a greet fraternitee.	important; parish guild
Ful fressh and newe hir geere apiked was;	their; adorned
Hir knyves were chaped noght with bras	mounted
But al with silver, wroght ful clene and weel	made; splendidly

(GP 363–7)

Such rules, however, were nothing compared to the laws put in place to keep the peasants on the land and in the same positions they had been in before the plague led to a shortage of labour. Parliament attempted to enforce the old laws, while attempting to set wages at pre-plague levels, with fines and imprisonment for those who would not comply. It was an explosive situation, needing not much more to fan the flames. In the event, what was added was a lengthy war and a boy king.

EDWARD III AND THE HUNDRED YEARS WAR

At the time of Chaucer's birth in the 1340s, Edward III had been king of England for more than a decade. He was crowned in 1327 and reigned for 50 years, almost all of them spent at war with France. Indeed, the series of conflicts with the French that began with Edward, has come to be known as the Hundred Years War. The earlier years of the conflict saw some considerable English successes in battle, English skill with the longbow being credited with bringing about several crucial victories. Chaucer's portrait of the Yeoman (a free servant) in the *Canterbury Tales* is one of his most complimentary portraits. Such men would have been required by law to practice archery every Sunday, and to be ready to fight for their king when called upon. Chaucer depicts a shaven-headed, armed man in camouflage green, with arrows at the ready and a bow as tall as himself:

A <u>sheef</u> of <u>pecok</u> arwes, bright and <u>kene</u>,	sheaf; peacock; sharp
Under his belt he <u>bar ful thriftily</u>	carried very properly
(Wel koude he dresse his takel yemanly;	he knew how to care for his equipment as a good yeoman should
His arwes <u>drouped noght</u> with fetheres lowe)	did not fall short
And in his hand he <u>baar</u> a myghty bowe.	carried
	(*GP* 104–8)

With a claim to the French throne on his mother's side, and with several decisive victories behind him, Edward led his army to Rheims, the site of French coronations since the tenth century. He even carried with him a crown, ready to have himself proclaimed King of France. However, events conspired against him, and he failed to take the city. In retreat, a number of the English forces were captured, among them a young Geoffrey Chaucer.

The wealth and connections of the Chaucer family had enabled them to enrol the child Geoffrey as a page in the royal household. By 1359, Chaucer was serving as a member of the household of Edward's second son, the Duke of Clarence, which is how he came to be captured near Rheims. His period of captivity was not long. It was the medieval convention to ransom higher-ranking prisoners, and the king paid £16 towards the release of Geoffrey within a few months. Nevertheless, there are occasional glimpses of battlefields in Chaucer's work; scenes that are very dark in tone. *The Knight's Tale*, for example, in addition to its pageantry, describes the business of those scavengers who searched through the dead after a battle, stripping them of their belongings:

To ransake in the <u>taas</u> of bodyes dede	pile
Hem for to <u>strepe</u> of <u>harneys</u> and of <u>wede</u>,	strip; armour; clothes
The <u>pilours diden bisynesse</u> and cure	scavengers took great care
After the bataille and <u>disconfiture.</u>	defeat

(*KT*, 1005–8)

War exacted a great cost, both in terms of lives and of money. After Rheims, Edward faced growing opposition to the length and expense of the conflict. It continued, but it would never again be so close to English success in Edward's lifetime, and it ultimately cost him the life of his own eldest son, the 'Black Prince'. A hero of the earlier war years, the Black Prince fell not to the sword but to illness, contracted while on campaign in Spain. He died in 1376, leaving his son, Richard, as heir to the throne. Edward III died the following year, and Richard, aged ten, became king of England.

RICHARD II AND THE PEASANTS' REVOLT

King Richard inherited a country that had been ravaged by plague and impoverished by protracted war. Sensing weakness, the French landed on the Isle of Wight and held it to ransom. There were other French raids on Hastings and Winchester. The realities of war were literally brought home to the English in a way that they had not endured for hundreds of years. Parliament's response was to raise as much money as it could as quickly as it could in order to defeat the French. Its efforts took the form of a poll tax, a 'head' tax, levied on every man and woman over the age of 15. Rich and poor were required to pay the same amount, a law that inevitably led to suffering and unrest among those least able to pay. The tax was levied in 1377, 1379, and again in 1380. In 1381, the people finally revolted. What is popularly known as the 'Peasants' Revolt' in fact involved not just those who worked the land, but many townspeople. The uprising began in Essex, but quickly reached London, the city workers swelling the ranks of the rebels. Richard II, still only 14 years old, rode out to meet them at Mile End. Initial promises from the king came to nothing, however, and the heads of the rebel leaders were soon displayed on London Bridge.

By this point, Geoffrey Chaucer had served his country on various military campaigns and diplomatic missions in France and Italy, some of them with John of Gaunt, the king's uncle. Chaucer had returned to London and was appointed controller of customs, ensuring the proper duties were paid on England's major export: wool. With this post came a new home, and he leased the dwelling over Aldgate, one of the six gates into the walled city of London. It was through this gate that thousands of rebels poured. It is not known whether Chaucer was there when the uprising began, but his home literally overlooked the scene of rebellion. The victims of the mob included his former neighbours and associates, and the headless bodies of Flemish merchants were left piled up in the area in which he had lived as a boy. John of Gaunt, Chaucer's patron, was not in London, but his magnificent palace was destroyed by the rebels, who systematically eradicated the trappings of luxury and wealth that they found there.

In Chaucer's *Nun's Priest's Tale*, an animal fable in which a fox snatches a chicken, the farmyard fracas of barking dogs, stampeding cattle, and swarming bees is compared to the Peasants' Revolt:

So <u>hydous</u> was the noyse – a, benedicitee! –	hideous
<u>Certes</u>, he Jakke Straw and his <u>meynee</u>	certainly; followers
Ne made nevere shoutes half so <u>shrille</u>	loud
Whan that they wolden any <u>Flemyng</u> kille,	Flemish person
As <u>thilke</u> day was maad upon the fox.	that

(NPT, 3393–7)

It is perhaps a surprising reference for someone who experienced the events of the Peasants' Revolt first hand, but there is a lot hidden behind the farmyard façade of the *Nun's Priest's Tale*.

CHAUCER AND JOHN OF GAUNT

A particular focus of the rebels' anger was John of Gaunt's Savoy Palace (now the site of the Savoy Hotel in London). Gaunt was the third son of Edward III and one of those who acted as an advisor to the boy king, Richard II. He was the wealthiest and most powerful landowner in England, the king's uncle, and father of the man who would later become Henry IV. He was also Chaucer's patron. That does not mean, however, that he paid Chaucer to write poetry. The kind of patronage he gave enabled its recipient to move up the ranks of those who served the court as clerks or diplomats. Chaucer did write poetry that connected him to Gaunt – for example, *The Book of the Duchess* is thought to commemorate the death of Gaunt's first wife, Blanche – but he was not a 'court poet', paid for his verse. He was, from 1389, Clerk of the King's Works, in charge of overseeing the building and repair of the royal properties, and he would have been in and out of the court in the course of his duties. His life was a varied one. On the one hand, he had close connections to power, even to the extent that his wife's sister, Katherine Swynford, became Gaunt's mistress and, eventually, his third wife; but at the same time he was responsible for supervising the royal labourers and ensuring that such things as the jousting scaffolds were ready at Smithfield to entertain the king.

WORDS AND PICTURES

Chaucer's work, like all literature at the time, would have been read aloud: a shared performance rather than a solitary act of reading. Only a small percentage of the population would have been able to read, and while the court circle could read several languages, the ordinary people would largely not have been able to read at all. Chaucer's Wife of Bath in the *Canterbury Tales* is assailed by stories of wicked women, but they are all read to her by her student husband from his 'Book of Wicked Wives' (*CT* III 685). Also, the printing press had not yet been invented, so all books had to be copied out by hand. This was a long and expensive process, and books were, therefore, very valuable. Depending on the scribe doing the copying, it could also be a process full of errors. Chaucer writes a little poem to his own scribe, the long-haired 'Adam', cursing him with a scabby scalp if he does not learn to copy the work more carefully (*CWA*, 3–4).

More expensive manuscripts were often illustrated. In a society in which the written word was the reserve of a learned few, images were found everywhere, taking the place of texts and presenting stories and commentaries in visual form. The interior walls of medieval churches were often densely painted with scenes from the Bible and pictures from popular devotion, and there were carvings on almost every available surface. The invention of stained glass allowed for further image making and storytelling in those churches that could afford it. Not all the images were pious, however. Among the crucifixes and depictions of saints there are often simple domestic details: carvings of cats catching mice, or of children playing. These can, of course, be interpreted in religious terms, but the same cannot be said of the sometimes obscene or erotic images that find their way into church carvings or the illustrated margins of prayer books. What would be deeply shocking in the modern world, was not necessarily so in the Middle Ages, partly because religion was the foundation on which medieval existence in its entirety was built. Time itself was measured in terms of the Church. The key events in the year were those of the religious feast days, not just Christmas and Easter, but a whole calendar that recorded saints' days and periods of fasting and festivity. The hours of the day and night were marked by the chiming of church bells that called some to prayer and signalled the hours of work for others.

THE MEDIEVAL CHURCH

Essentially, England in the fourteenth century was aligned with the Church of Rome. The beginnings of religious change were starting to be felt, with reformers such as the Lollards calling for the Bible to be available in English rather than Latin, but real change was a long way off, and religious belief was secure, so secure that Chaucer's work contains many jokes that centre on Christianity. His *Miller's Tale*, for example, has a seduction plot that exploits simple-hearted belief in the story of Noah and the Flood, and a student lodger who uses a hymn to the Virgin Mary as a prelude to his sexual approaches to his landlord's wife. None of this is critical of religion in itself; it is, instead, testimony to a confident faith that allows for laughter and play.

That does not mean, however, that Chaucer is uncritical of the religious world of the later Middle Ages. Of the six church figures who appear in the *General Prologue to the Canterbury Tales*, five are the object of satire. Gentle fun is poked at the pretty Prioress, 'Madame Eglantyne', who, more lady than nun, sings through her nose and is praised for the way in which she wipes food from her top lip and refrains from dipping her fingers in the sauce. She is, we are told, all 'conscience and tendre herte' (*GP* 150), but her pity is reserved for her lapdogs and for mice caught in traps. Her portrait contains all the words we would expect to describe a nun – 'charitable', 'pitous', 'semyly' – but they are applied to her feelings for animals, the refinement of her table manners, and the cut of her headdress, rather than to any religious impulses or observances. The same can be said of the Monk, an avid hunter with the animal vitality of one of his own horses: 'He was a lord ful fat and in good poynt [condition];/ His eyen stepe [bulging], and rollynge in his heed' (*GP* 200–1). His jingling bridle is compared to the sound of church bells, but otherwise he is not in any way a religious figure. In the Parson, however, we encounter an ideal man of the Church. Faced with parishioners who cannot afford to pay their dues, he not only refuses to excommunicate them, but supports them instead with his own meagre earnings (*GP* 486–9). He travels widely across his country parish in order to support his flock, leading them by example, for there is no point, as the text bluntly puts it, in 'A shiten [defiled] shepherde and a clene sheep' (*GP* 504). The Parson embodies everything that fourteenth-century religion aspired to be: he teaches the Bible, 'but first he folwed it hymselve' (*GP* 528).

CHAUCER'S UNIVERSE

Medieval science, too, had a firm religious foundation. The sun and the planets were thought to revolve around the earth in a universe that moved because it was made to do so by God, himself the Unmoved Mover. Tiny in comparison with the heavens, the earth was nevertheless at the heart of a system of concentric spheres, each planet's orbit enclosed by the orbit of the next planet until heaven itself was reached. The cosmos was filled with the sound of perfect music, created by the spheres as they turned, and signifying the harmony of all creation. Chaucer makes references to this planetary system throughout his work, though the guide in *The Parliament of Fowls* gives the clearest account:

Thanne <u>shewede</u> he hym the lytel erthe that here is,	showed
<u>At regard</u> of the hevenes <u>quantite</u>;	in comparison to; great size
And after shewede he hym the nyne <u>speres</u>;	spheres
And after that the melodye herde he	
That cometh of <u>thilke</u> speres <u>thryes thre</u>,	those; three times three
That <u>welle</u> is of musik and melodye	source
In this world here, and cause of <u>armonye</u>.	harmony

(PF 57–63)

The heavens were, therefore, thought to be full of music and also a wonderful golden light, with the stars thought to be holes in the shifting firmament that separated us from heaven, but which allowed heavenly light to show through. As such, the Middle Ages believed that truth was contained in their movement across the night sky.

Astronomy was one of the four key subjects studied in medieval universities, and all educated people in the Middle Ages had some knowledge of its basic principles. Chaucer takes that further than most in writing an instruction manual for his son, 'Lyte [little] Lowys' (*TA* 1), aged ten, in the use of the astrolabe, a scientific instrument, the name of which literally means 'star catcher'. This *Treatise on the Astrolabe* provides us with a clear working example of how the Middle Ages approached astronomy, and of the links with what it viewed as the sister science of astrology. After explaining how the word 'zodiac' comes from the Greek for 'beasts', Chaucer explains that, 'whan the planetes ben under thilke signes [signs of the zodiac] thei causen us by her influence operaciouns [behaviour] and effectes like to the operaciouns of bestes' (*TA* I. 21. 59–62). The planets, therefore, have a role to play in our daily lives though, significantly, it is one of 'influence' and not of direct causation. We see this distinction throughout Chaucer's work. The Wife of Bath might claim that her Venus and Mars horoscope means that she has strong sexual desires, but it is her own choice whether or not to follow them. There is a certain ambiguity in her declaration that

I folwed ay myn <u>inclinacioun</u>	astrological inclination
By vertu of my <u>constellacioun</u>	horoscope
(*CT* III.615–6)	

The term 'inclinacioun' is a technical one from astronomy, but there is a strong suggestion that what is really at stake is the Wife's own inclination to do whatever she pleases. References to the stars, therefore, abound in Chaucer's work. Whole poems, such as *The Complaint of Mars*, have astronomy at their core, and horoscopes make frequent appearances, though often with less than serious intent.

THE DEATH OF CHAUCER

On Christmas Eve 1399, Chaucer took the lease on a house within the confines of Westminster Abbey, on the site of what is now the Chapel of King Henry VII. The last decade or so had been turbulent, with Richard II taking action against those who had acted against him as a boy king, and in Chaucer's work we catch a haunting glimpse of a pale face sent to execution:

Have ye nat <u>seyn</u> somtyme a pale face,	seen
Among a <u>prees</u>, of hym that hath be <u>lad</u>	crowd; led
Toward his deeth, wher as hym <u>gat no grace</u>,	received no mercy
And <u>swich</u> a colour in his face hath had	such
Men myghte knowe his face that was <u>bistad</u>	in trouble
Amonges alle the faces in that <u>route</u>?	crowd
(*CT* II 645–50)	

But 1399 saw the deposition and death of Richard himself, and John of Gaunt's son, Henry of Bolingbroke, become king. Chaucer had written a memorial to Henry's mother (see *The Book of the Duchess*) as well as having close ties to his father, and the new King Henry IV increased the grants that Chaucer received.

The slow arrival of such necessary gifts prompted many poets of the time to write verses addressed to their benefactors, and the last work that we know to have been written by Chaucer is 'The

Complaint of Chaucer to his Purse', the kind of poem traditionally directed towards a cruel mistress and inclined to lament the 'heviness' [sadness] the speaker feels. For this speaker, though, there is not enough 'heaviness' associated with his purse, and the traditional 'yelownesse' (*CCP* 11) for which he longs, is that of golden coins rather than golden hair. The final lines, however, are not in jest: a call to Henry, as one who was, 'by lyne and free eleccion / … verray kyng' (*CCP* 23–4). On 5 June 1400, there was a final payment made to Chaucer. It is the last mention of him in the records. The date of his death is traditionally held to be 25 October 1400, or, at least, this is the date on his tomb in Westminster Abbey. He was buried there because his house was within the precinct walls and because of his work as a clerk for the crown, not on account of his fame as a poet. Nevertheless, that fame would eventually lead to Poets' Corner being established around his tomb, as his works were preserved and brought to the masses by the printing presses of William Caxton, set up just a stone's throw from Chaucer's final resting place.

FURTHER READING

For an informed and balanced account of Chaucer's life and works, see Derek Pearsall (1992). *The Life of Geoffrey Chaucer.* Oxford: Blackwell. For a succinct account, see Douglas Gray, 'Chaucer, Geoffrey (ca. 1340–1400)', in the *Oxford Dictionary of National Biography.* A generously comprehensive and discerning account of Chaucer's literary career can be found in Derek Brewer (1998). *A New Introduction to Chaucer,* 2nd edn. Harlow: Longman, while a richly documented introduction to Chaucer in the context of his times is provided in Derek Brewer (2000). *The World of Chaucer.* Cambridge: D.S. Brewer. In Paul Strohm (1989). *Social Chaucer.* Cambridge, MA: Harvard University Press is an historicised interpretation of Chaucer's social relations and the social implications of his styles and forms. Paul Strohm (2014). *The Poet's Tale: Chaucer and the Year that Made the Canterbury Tales.* London: Profile explores the implications of the pivotal year of 1386, when Chaucer's fortunes changed, with lasting effect on his subsequent career as a poet. On Chaucer's work in the context of social and professional dispute and conflict in the London of his day, see Marion Turner (2006). *Chaucerian Conflict: Languages of Antagonism in Late Fourteenth-Century London.* Oxford: Oxford University Press. See also David R. Carlson (2004). *Chaucer's Jobs.* Basingstoke: Palgrave Macmillan. For briefer introductions to questions posed by the biography of Chaucer, see Ruth Evans, 'Chaucer's Life', in *Chaucer: An Oxford Guide* (2005). Ed.

Steve Ellis. Oxford: Oxford University Press, pp. 9–25, and also Christopher Cannon, 'The Lives of Geoffrey Chaucer', in *The Yale Companion to Chaucer* (2006). Ed. Seth Lerer. New Haven: Yale University Press, pp. 31–54. On a lighter note is the highly speculative historical whodunnit Terry Jones et al. (2003). *Who Murdered Chaucer? A Medieval Mystery*. London: Methuen, which deploys rich resources of intriguing documentation in order to suggest that Chaucer's poems put him on the wrong side of ruthless authorities, with fatal consequences. For a lively introduction to the period, try Ian Mortimer (2008). *The Time Traveller's Guide to Medieval England: A Handbook for Visitors to the Fourteenth Century*. London: Bodley Head with information on eating and drinking, health and hygiene, clothes, law, landscape, and much else. The essential and authoritative archive of documentary sources for Chaucer's biography is collected in *Chaucer Life-Records* (1966). Ed. Martin M. Crow and Clair C. Olson. Oxford: Clarendon Press. No documents are translated but there are helpful headnotes.

On the plague, see the classic study, Philip Ziegler (1970). *The Black Death*. London: Penguin. For an account through contemporary sources, see *The Black Death* (1994). Ed. and trans. Rosemary Horrox. Manchester: Manchester University Press. Other studies include Colin Platt (1996). *King Death: The Black Death and its Aftermath in Late-Medieval England*. London: UCL Press, and John Aberth (2005). *The Black Death: The Great Mortality of 1348–50: A Brief History with Documents*. New York: Palgrave Macmillan, together with John Hatcher (2008). *The Black Death: An Intimate History*. London: Weidenfeld and Nicolson.

See also B.L. Grigsby (2004). *Pestilence in Medieval and Early Modern Literature*. London: Routledge.

On the Peasants' Revolt, see R. H. Hilton and T. H. Aston, Eds. (1987). *The English Rising of 1381*. Cambridge: Cambridge University Press. For translated contemporary sources, see *The Peasants' Revolt of 1381* (1983). Ed. R.B. Dobson. 2nd edn. London: Macmillan. For how the events became the subject of writing, see Steven Justice (1994). *Writing and Rebellion: England in 1381*. Berkeley: University of California Press.

On the Hundred Years War, see the classic study: Jonathan Sumption (1990–2009). *The Hundred Years War*. 3 vols. London: Faber. See also Desmond Seward (1996). *The Hundred Years War*. London: Constable, together with Christopher Allmand (1988). *The Hundred Years War: England and France at War, c.1380-c.1450*. Cambridge: Cambridge University Press. On the war during Chaucer's earlier life, see Clifford J. Rogers (2000). *War Cruel and Sharp: English Strategy under Edward III, 1327–1360*. Woodbridge: Boydell, supplemented by Clifford J. Rogers (2010). *The Wars of Edward III: Sources and Interpretations*. Woodbridge: Boydell.

On Edward III, see W. M. Ormrod (1990). *The Reign of Edward III: Crown and Political Society in England 1327–1377*. New Haven: Yale University Press, and also Scott L. Waugh (1991). *England in the Reign of Edward III.* Cambridge: Cambridge University Press. For Edward III's eldest son, the Black Prince, see Richard Barber (1978). *Edward, Prince of Wales and Aquitaine: A Biography of the Black Prince.* London: Allen Lane. For Edward III's son and Chaucer's brother-in-law and possible patron, John of Gaunt (i.e., Ghent, where he was born), see

Anthony Goodman (1992). John of Gaunt: The Exercise of Princely Power in Fourteenth-Century Europe. Harlow: Longman.

On the character and troubled reign of Richard II, see Nigel Saul (1997). *Richard II.* New Haven: Yale University Press, along with Chris Fletcher (2008). *Richard II: Manhood, Youth, and Politics 1377–99.* Oxford: Oxford University Press, and also

Richard II: The Art of Kingship (1999). Ed. Anthony Goodman and James Gillespie. Oxford: Oxford University Press. For succinct accounts, see Laura Ashe (2016). *Richard II.* London: Penguin, and also James Simpson, 'Richard II', in *A New Companion to Chaucer* (2019). Ed. Peter Brown. Oxford: Wiley-Blackwell. For an overview of the cultural ambience around Richard II's court, see Gervase Mathew (1968). *The Court of Richard II.* London: John Murray, and for an account of contemporary political discourse, see Lynn Staley (2005). *Languages of Power in the Age of Richard II.* University Park: Pennsylvania State University Press.

See the sections in the Bibliography for further reading on Audiences and Reading, Visuality, Structures of Belief, and Science and Philosophy.

2

CHAUCER'S LANGUAGE OF POETRY

There are a few historical differences between Chaucer's language and Modern English that are particularly worth noting.

STANDARD ENGLISH

English had not yet become standardised in the fourteenth century. The two Cambridge students in the *Reeve's Tale*, for example, come from the north of England, and we can hear in their pronunciation of words such as 'home' ('ham') and goes ('gas'), and in their use of unfamiliar words such as 'wanges' (teeth) and 'howgates' (how) that Chaucer is signalling a difference in their speech from his own (*CT* I 4029–39). Chaucer himself uses the London English of the king's court that would become the basis for standard English, and for that reason his language is largely familiar, but in the fourteenth century it had not yet become the dominant form. Spelling was not standardised either, and words are spelled differently from work to work, and often even within a text.

WORD ORDER

There is greater flexibility in medieval English than in Modern English when it comes to the order of words. Modern syntax is relatively fixed, but in the fourteenth century word order was more fluid, allowing for greater adaptability in terms of rhyme and also emphasis. When the Wife of Bath, for example, wants to stress that the source of her vaunted experience in marriage is down to her high number of husbands, the important word can be loaded at the front of the sentence to make the point: 'Housbondes at chirche dore [door] I have had fyve' (*CT* III 6). Similarly, words can be held off to suit the poet's needs. The final word of *Troilus and Criseyde*, for example, is an adjective:

> For love of mayde and <u>moder</u> thyn <u>benigne</u>   mother; gracious
> (*TC* V 1869)

This could not naturally be accomplished in Modern English, but for Chaucer it is permissible and allows for a final emphasis, not on 'mother', but on a defining graciousness and kindness in love.

NEGATIVES

Unlike in Modern English, two negatives do not make a positive. Extra negatives are used for emphasis and it is possible to allow them to accumulate in order to make the point. When the husband in the *Franklin's Tale*, for example, decides that the power in the marriage will not be his alone, his determination is signalled by a quadruple negative form:

> Of his free wyl he swoor hire as a knyght
> That *nevere* in al his lyf he, day *ne* nyght,
> *Ne* sholde upon hym take *no* maistrie
> (*CT* V 745–7)

As for the devout and faithful Parson in the *General Prologue* – 'A bettre preest I trowe [believe] that nowher noon ys' (*GP* 524) – his unparalleled goodness is emphasised by the double negative in 'nowhere' and 'none'.

'YOU'

There is a different form for the singular and plural of 'you'. The singular form is *thou* and the plural is *ye*. As with some modern languages, an individual can be addressed using the singular form to show familiarity, or the plural to signal respect. The Host in the *Canterbury Tales*, for example, switches between pronoun forms depending on the social status of the pilgrims. He addresses the Knight as 'ye' throughout, and then shows the Monk similar respect as he invites him to tell the next tale: 'Now telleth *ye*, sir Monk, if that *ye* konne [know] / Somwhat to quite [match] with the Knyghtes tale' (*CT* I 3118–19). When the drunken Miller interrupts, however, he is dismissed by the Host using the more familiar form: '*Thou* art a fool; *thy* wit is overcome' (*CT* I 3135). Courtly lovers such as Troilus and Criseyde address one another using the formal *ye* throughout the poem, even at moments of greatest intimacy, while the friends Pandarus and Troilus are almost always *thou* to one another.

OLD FORMS AND NEW

Older language forms and the newer ones exist side by side in Chaucer's English. The first-person pronoun *I* and the older *ich* coexist, for example, being used interchangeably, as in this declaration by Criseyde:

> And <u>nameliche</u>, my deere herte, ye,   especially
> Whom that *I* <u>nolde leven</u> for to se   would not wish to cease
> For al this world, as wyd as it hath space,
> Or ellis <u>se *ich* nevere</u> Joves face!   may I never see
> (*TC* IV 1334–7)

Similarly, the older plural noun form *-en* (as in modern *oxen*) keeps company with the simple *-s* ending, so that the Wife of Bath wears scarlet red 'hos*en*' and new 'shoe*s*' (*GP* 456–7). As for verbs, the same is true. Dorigen's oath in the *Franklin's Tale* is referred to using both the older form (with a *y-* prefix) and its more modern counterpart: 'my lady hath my deeth *ysworn*' (*CT* V 1038); 'thus have I *sworn*' (*CT* V 1464). Chaucer makes no distinction in using these. In the linguistically fluid fourteenth century all forms are available to him and he employs them interchangeably, though it is clear that he is often moved to use one or other by the demands of the verse.

PRONUNCIATION

CONSONANTS

All consonants are sounded, even those that would not normally be sounded in Modern English. This means that the *k* would be pronounced in a word such as 'knyght', where the *gh* would also sound a little different, more like the sound in Scots 'lo*ch*'. Other examples are the sounded initial *w* in a word like '*w*rite', or the *g* in '*g*nof', the word used to describe John the Carpenter in the *Miller's Tale* (*CT* I 3188) and all the more evocative when given its fourteenth-century pronunciation. The letter *l* should also be sounded before *f*, *k*, and *m*, for example, 'fo*l*k'.

VOWELS

Vowel sounds are a more complicated matter and have changed more significantly since the fourteenth century. They are divided into 'short' and 'long' sounds.

Short vowels

Vowel	Fourteenth-century word	Modern sound
a	al, can	French 'patte' (not bat)
e	set,	set
i	with, sitten	with, sit
o	toppe	top
u	but	put (not but)

Long vowels

Vowel	Fourteenth-century word	Modern sound
a	cas, name	father
e	lene, sweete	air, there (not sweet)
	eek, teche	French é,
I	I, child	feel (not while)
o	gon	broad
	goode	go
u	aboute	boot

Diphthongs

Diphthong	Fourteenth-century word	Modern sound
ai / ei	dai	die
au / aw	lawe	now
ou / ow	ought,	thought,
	showres	shoe

Final -e, -ed, -es

Final -e, as in 'kinde', sounds like the final syllable of modern English *China*. When the next word begins with a vowel or the letter h, final -e is not sounded. In medieval English, word endings such as -ed and -es are regularly pronounced, so that words like *showres* and *lakked* will almost always have two syllables.

CHAUCER'S VERSE

The vast majority of Chaucer's works are in rhymed verse of various kinds. There were two different poetic traditions in England in the fourteenth century. The older form, known as the alliterative tradition, tended not to rhyme, but had three or more words in any given line that alliterated. This is the kind of verse that is dismissed by Chaucer's Parson when he declares that he cannot tell a story, '"rum, ram, ruf" by lettre' (*CT* X 43).

The other tradition did not rely on alliteration but was instead attentive to the number of syllables in a line, which were then rhymed in pairs (known as couplets) or other configurations. This is the kind of verse form used by Chaucer. In a basic line there will be an unstressed syllable (x) followed by a stressed syllable (/):

```
x     /     x     /    x     /    x  /  x     /
A  Knyght  ther  was,  and  that  a  worthy  man,
```
                                                        (*GP* 43)

The stress will fall naturally on the 'important' words, and it is crucial that this natural emphasis of the words in English should be retained. While the pattern above stays in the background as the 'norm',

Chaucer will expect his reader to retain the rhythm of natural sense and speech.

Chaucer might choose to introduce an extra unstressed syllable, or perhaps begin the line with a stressed syllable instead of an unstressed one (known as a 'headless line'):

```
 /    x  x    /    x  / x   / x    /
Love  is  a  thyng  as  any  spirit  free.
```

(CT V 767)

This is sometimes used for emphasis or to introduce a new line of thought.

THE FOUR-STRESS LINE

The dominant poetic form in southern England towards the end of the fourteenth century had lines with four stresses (usually, therefore, eight syllables), often arranged into rhyming couplets. These 'octosyllabic couplets' are the basic form that Chaucer uses in his earlier works: the *Book of the Duchess* and the *House of Fame*. The opening of the *Book of the Duchess* is metrically very regular and even uses some of the redundant phrases ('by this light', 'neither day nor night') that would have been common in the English metrical romances that used the four-stress rhythm:

I have gret wonder, <u>be</u> this lyght,	by
How that I lyve, for day ne nyght	
I <u>may</u> nat slepe <u>wel nygh noght</u>;	can; scarcely at all
I have so many an <u>ydel</u> thought	futile
<div align="center">(BD 1–4)</div>	

However, while the opening keeps steadily to the x / x / x / x / pattern, Chaucer inevitably goes on to disrupt the rhythm and privileges the natural cadences of speech so that the poem does not 'jogtrot' along too easily. Had he not done this, then the effect would have been monotonous, as it becomes in the *Tale of Sir Thopas*, the only one of the *Canterbury Tales* to employ the four-stress form. Chaucer chooses to enhance the steadiness of the rhythm by making it a tailrhyme romance. What this involves can vary slightly, but here it is a rhyming pair of longer lines with a shorter line (the 'tail'), gathered in six-line stanzas:

<u>Listeth</u>, lordes, in good entent,	listen
And I wol telle <u>verrayment</u>	truly
Of myrthe and of <u>solas</u>,	entertainment
Al of a knight was fair and <u>gent</u>	elegant
In bataille and in tourneyment;	
His name was sire Thopas.	

(CT VII 712–7)

The narrative rattles along unremittingly until the Host feels compelled to interrupt 'Chaucer' with a disparaging verdict on his poetry as 'drasty [crappy]' (*CT* VII 923) and urges him to tell another tale.

The *Book of the Duchess* and the *House of Fame* are far less regular than *Sir Thopas*, and their octosyllabic structure is overlain with the natural rhythms and irregularities of speech, though there are also moments when the structure is exploited. The *House of Fame*, for example, is very much concerned with authorship as a theme, and the beginning of Book III offers a tongue-in-cheek comment that the work's, 'rym ys lyght and lewed [unsophisticated]' (*HF* 1096) and occasionally likely to 'fayle [lack] in a sillable' (*HF* 1098). Of course, it rarely lacks any syllables, though one obvious moment when it does is worth examining. Faced with the ingratitude of 'Geffrey' the dreamer – who is claiming that he has not yet seen or heard anything that he did not already know – his guide the Eagle appears flummoxed:

'Whych than be, loo, these tydynges,	
That thou now [thus] <u>hider</u> brynges,	here
That thou hast herd?' <u>quod</u> he to me;	said

(HF 1907–9)

The [thus] has been supplied by modern editors who feel the gap when an expected eight-syllable line can only muster seven; but this may be the point. The irrepressible Eagle has been brought up short, just for a moment, and the verse conveys the splutter.

THE FIVE-STRESS LINE

After the *Book of the Duchess* and the *House of Fame*, Chaucer began to develop a longer line that contained five stresses instead of four. This was not a form that had been much in use in England until this point, and it is possible that he was influenced by longer lines in French and Italian. Initially, he used five-stress lines in seven-line stanzas, a form that came to be known as *rime royal*. This is the form he employs for the *Parliament of Fowls*, *Troilus and Criseyde*, and some of the *Canterbury Tales* (those of the Clerk, the Man of Law, the Prioress, and the Second Nun). The rhyme-scheme becomes *a b a b b c c*, as in this stanza from the *Clerk's Tale*:

Therwith he was, to speke as of <u>lynage</u>,	lineage
The <u>gentilleste</u> yborn of <u>Lumbardye</u>,	most noble; Lombardy
A <u>fair</u> persone, and strong, and yong of age,	handsome
And ful of honour and of curteisye;	
<u>Discreet ynogh</u> his contree for to <u>gye</u>,	with sufficient prudence; govern
Save in somme thynges that he was to blame;	
And Walter was this yonge lordes name.	

(CT IV 71–7)

The rhyme scheme behaves as we would expect it to. As for the sense of the final couplet, it often summarises the five lines that have gone before but, sometimes, as here, serves to undercut what has just been said. In this case, the 'name' of the fine young lord is bound by rhyme to 'blame' as soon as it is mentioned.

The rime royal form can also be exploited and certain lines foregrounded when Chaucer chooses not to follow the expected rhyme pattern. *Troilus and Criseyde* contains many examples of this, including a stanza from Book I, where Troilus finally declares to Pandarus that it is love that is making him ill:

Love, <u>ayeins the which</u> <u>whoso</u> defendeth	against which; whoever
Hymselven most, <u>hym alderlest avaylleth</u>,	fares the worst
With <u>disespeyr</u> so sorwfulli me <u>offendeth</u>,	despair; assails
That streight unto the deth myn herte <u>sailleth</u>.	sails
Therto desir so <u>brennyngly</u> me assailleth,	ardently
That to ben slayn it were a <u>gretter</u> joie	greater
To me than king of Grece <u>ben</u> and Troye.	to be

(TC I 603–9)

It is a stanza crammed with syllables, so many that words have to be compressed in order to make them fit the syllable count. Moreover,

the rhyme scheme has become *a a a a a b b*. It is Troilus's first con-
fession of love, and the intensity of the moment is signalled by the
packed, rather convoluted stanza, and the single-minded sounding
of the same rhyme as the fixated Troilus opens his heart to Pandarus.

In his later works – *The Legend of Good Women* and most of the
Canterbury Tales – Chaucer moved away from *rime royal* and devel-
oped a style, instead, of rhyming couplets and five-stress lines. The
natural rhythm of speech continues to overlay the expectations of
the basic form x / x / x / x / x /. This can be seen in action in an
example from the *Nun's Priest's Tale* in which the poor widow's farm
and her rooster are described:

```
x   /     x    /     x / x    /    x / x
A yeerd  she  hadde,  enclosed  al  aboute
x   / x    /    x  / x  /    x  /  x
With stikkes, and  a  drye  dych withoute,       palings
x  /    x    /    x  /      /    /  x  /
In which she hadde  a  cok, hight Chauntecleer.   named
x  / x  /    x  / x    /    x  /
In al the  land, of crowyng  nas his peer.        there was not
```

(*CT* VII 2847–50)

As final -*e* is not pronounced when the next word begins with a vowel
and final -*ed* is usually pronounced (See *Final -e, -ed, -es*, p. 19), the
first 2 lines here each have 11 syllables (which is one more than the
norm, but very common). The rhythm, however, changes in the third
line as three stresses in a row signal the arrival of the great bird that
is the rooster Chauntecleer. The line ends strongly on a stressed syllable (known as a masculine line) that is then echoed by the 'peer' that
completes the couplet. It is not elaborately signalled by Chaucer, but
the cluster of stresses slows the line down and subtly signals that this is
a bird and a name to be reckoned with. Of course, we primarily know
that Chauntecleer is a prince amongst birds because of the language
used about him, but the verse, too, is doing its work.

FURTHER READING

For a guide to the principal features of Medieval English spelling, pronunciation, grammar and vocabulary, see Simon Horobin and Jeremy Smith (2002). *An
Introduction to Middle English*. Edinburgh: Edinburgh University Press.

For an introduction focussed on Chaucer's dialect, sound system, lexicon, use of grammar and sentence structure, discourse and pragmatics, see Simon Horobin (2007). *Chaucer's Language*. Basingstoke: Palgrave Macmillan. Analysis of such issues as tense, negation, vocabulary, register and propriety, and levels of style is found in J. D. Burnley (1983). *A Guide to Chaucer's Language*. Basingstoke: Palgrave Macmillan. For a literary study of Chaucer's language, attending to questions of plain style, churls' terms, oaths, and uses of scientific and specialist terminology, see Ralph W. V. Elliott (1974). *Chaucer's English*. London: André Deutsch. On the question of Chaucer's linguistic innovation, its nature and degree, see Christopher Cannon (1998). *The Making of Chaucer's English: A Study of Words*. Cambridge: Cambridge University Press.

On metre and versification, see Alan T. Gaylord, Ed. (2001). *Essays on the Art of Chaucer's Verse*. New York: Routledge. For briefer studies, see Tauno F. Mustanoja, 'Chaucer's Prosody', in *Companion to Chaucer Studies* (1979). Ed. Beryl Rowland. Oxford: Oxford University Press, pp. 65–94, together with Donka Minkova, 'Chaucer's language: pronunciation, morphology, metre', in *Chaucer: An Oxford Guide* (2005). Ed. Steve Ellis. Oxford: Oxford University Press, pp. 130–57, and also Donka Minkova, 'The Forms of Verse', in *A Companion to Medieval English Literature and Culture c. 1350-c.1500* (2007). Ed. Peter Brown. Oxford: Blackwell, pp. 176–95.

For some examples of more literary analyses of aspects of Chaucer's style and rhetoric, see Amanda Holton (2008). *The Sources of Chaucer's Poetics*. Ashgate: Aldershot, and also J. D. Burnley (1979). *Chaucer's Language and the Philosophers' Tradition*. Cambridge: D. S. Brewer.

An indispensable resource for understanding Chaucer's vocabulary is Norman Davies et al. (1979). *A Chaucer Glossary*. Oxford: Oxford University Press.

3

THE CANTERBURY TALES

The Tabard Inn in South London is the chance gathering place for a group of travellers making their way to Canterbury. The convivial Host, Harry Bailley, is delighted with his customers and proposes to travel with them, leading a story-telling competition as they go. Technically, they are pilgrims, but some are more serious in this than others, and their stories range from pious tales of decapitated virgins, to farmyard tales of nearly decapitated chickens; from tragic death to comic celebrations of life and love. Story collections were popular in the Middle Ages, but *The Canterbury Tales* is unusually wide-ranging in content, with an unusually diverse group of narrators. They differ in age, rank, and opinion, arguing with their neighbours and interrupting one another as they go.

Satirical portraits of 'types', such as the dishonest miller or the hunting monk, were popular in the Middles Ages, often in lists that brought together various professions and classes. Chaucer's group does not quite encompass all of medieval society: there are no real noblemen and there are no real peasants, but there is a good representation of the range in between. The highest-ranking pilgrim is the Knight, the lowest the poor Plowman, with a good number from the Church and the newly emergent bourgeoisie in the form of Monk, Prioress, Nun's Priest, Miller, Merchant, Doctor of Physic, and a host of others. There are, as we are promised at the beginning of the work,

'Wel nyne and twenty in a compaignye / Of sondry folk' (*GP* 24–5). They are all described in the *General Prologue* and most, though not all, will go on to tell a tale. Indeed, the exuberant Host has demanded four tales from every pilgrim. Whether or not this was a serious plan, the most we get from anyone is a single tale each. The work consists, therefore, of the *General Prologue* and twenty-four tales, with a story-telling frame in which the pilgrims engage with one another. These link passages help to provide an order for the tales, which have come down to us in various fragments from 55 surviving manuscripts.

The other thing the frame does is draw attention to the process of story-telling, for this is a narrative that is interested in the concept of narrative itself. The whole is presented to us by Chaucer, of course, but not straightforwardly so, for he creates another Chaucer, a pilgrim like the others, described by the Host as rather bashful, staring intently at the ground instead of volunteering to tell the next tale; as being as round in the waist as the bulky Host himself, but who is, nevertheless, a 'popet' [little doll] (*CT* VII.701). This diminutive Chaucer is the vehicle for the tales of all the other pilgrims. What we have here, therefore, is a multi-layered and complex narrative in which Geoffrey Chaucer creates a fictional Chaucer, through whom we hear the stories of his fellow travellers, all of which were already known from ancient or medieval sources, and all of which are undermined or enhanced, both by their relation to their own tellers and by the fact that they exist, not in isolation, but as a collection of tales.

THE *GENERAL PROLOGUE*

The 'popet' Chaucer provides us in the *General Prologue* with admiring portraits of his companions on the way to Canterbury. He is full of enthusiasm for their many talents, whether it is the Miller's ability to heave a door from its hinges by running at it with his head (*GP* 550–1), or the Shipman's tendency to send his enemies 'hoom [home] to every lond' (*GP* 400) via a watery grave. There is scarcely a word of criticism to be found, for the pilgrim narrator is instantly at home in their company and 'of hir [their] felaweshipe anon [at once]' (*GP* 32). This does not mean, of course, that the portraits are uncritical, for there is a lot that is likely to be wrong, even with the pilgrims who are not swashbuckling murderers or human battering rams, but the manner of cheerfully presenting the case and leaving the reader to infer other possibilities is what the critics refer to as Chaucerian irony, and we find its supreme exposition in the *General Prologue*.

THE KNIGHT

The Knight is the first of the pilgrims in terms both of his rank and his position in the *General Prologue*. For a long time, his portrait was widely regarded as unproblematically positive, and it is certainly true that its opening lines can be viewed as straightforward praise:

> A Knight ther was, and that a worthy man,
> That fro the tyme that he first bigan
> To riden out, he loved chivalrie,
> <u>Trouthe</u> and honour, <u>fredom</u> and curteisie.   fidelity; generosity
> (*GP* 43–6)

The virtues here are entirely what we would hope for in a good knight, or 'worthy man' as the narrator would have it. The next line, however, might introduce a disconcerting element, for we are told that, 'Ful worthy was he in his lordes werre' (*GP* 47). He is again 'worthy', and then yet again praised for 'worthynesse' (*GP* 50) a few lines later. Perhaps this would not matter if the reader had not also paused over 'lordes', an interesting word in that it is impossible to tell in medieval English whether it is singular or plural in form. The Knight would, of course, have a lord, but the possibility of more than one changes his situation. We are informed that,

> This <u>ilke</u> worthy knyght hadde been also   same
> Somtyme with the lord of <u>Palatye</u>   Balat (modern Turkey)
> <u>Agayn</u> another hethen in Turkye;   against
> And everemoore he hadde a <u>sovereyn prys</u>.   outstanding reputation
> (*GP* 64–7)

The fact that he is fighting for one Turkish lord against another makes him seem more like a sword for hire than a traditional English knight, and this, coupled with the fourth appearance of 'worthy', might finally lead the reader to assume that what is at stake is really monetary worth. Certainly, 'sovereyn prys' might mean that his reputation was outstanding, but it might also mean that he demanded a high price.

Similarly, the detail that his tunic was stained with rust from his coat of mail (*GP* 75–6) has been variously regarded as a sign of his commendable haste in rushing straight to pilgrimage by some, and by others as a possible indication that he has dispensed with a heavy armoured layer in order to move with the swiftness of a mercenary. He has fought in a remarkable number of places, as far as Russia and Morocco (*GP* 51–63). Again, it is not clear whether or not this indicates his presence at some of the great blood baths of the Middle Ages, or whether it is simply an impressive professional catalogue. What is crucial in the portrait is the possibility of doubt: a delicate balance in which the representative of war and chivalry is placed under gentle scrutiny.

THE PARDONER

Less subtle is the portrait of the Pardoner. While it is not entirely clear what the Knight has been doing across the Mediterranean, the Pardoner's trade is wholly clear. The Church in the late Middle Ages permitted the sale of indulgences, designed to bring about the pardon of sins. The idea behind this was that large donations were an act of charity, itself a virtuous act, and that such virtue goes some way in counterbalancing sin and vice. Instead of repentant sinners atoning for their actions with prayers or fasting, for example, they might measure their penance in terms of money instead. The practice was encouraged by the issuing of formal documents which, in their turn, became pardons. It is easy to see how a complicated exchange becomes a simple one, and soon it was common for money to cancel out sin – even sin yet to be committed – as pardoners traded in easy absolution. What is not clear is whether our Pardoner is even carrying the genuine article with him. He has a pouch full of pardons, which have 'comen from Rome al hoot [hot]' (*GP* 687), but it is evident from his portrait that nothing about him is to be trusted, and the sense of the ink not being dry on these suggests an origin a little closer to home.

Certainly, everything else that he carries is blatantly fraudulent. He has a pillow case that he passes off as the veil of the Virgin Mary, and a piece of sailcloth that he claims came from the fishing boat of St Peter himself. Add to this a brass cross and a jar of pigs' bones, and the Pardoner is ready to fleece the gullible:

But with thise <u>relikes</u>, whan that he <u>fond</u>	relics; encountered
A <u>povre person</u> dwellynge upon lond,	poor parson
Upon a day he <u>gat hym</u> moore moneye	got himself
Than that the person gat in monthes <u>tweye</u>;	two
And thus, with <u>feyned</u> flaterye and <u>japes</u>,	deceitful; tricks
He made the <u>person</u> and the peple his apes.	parson

(GP 701–6)

Much of medieval religion is centred on the body, whether it is the idea of the eventual resurrection of all bodies, or the transformation of bread and wine into Christ's flesh and blood in the mass. By extension, physical objects associated with holy bodies were venerated. There was, therefore, a thriving medieval trade in purported relics, such as bones, and other physical artefacts claimed to be associated with holy persons or places. The Canterbury pilgrims are, after all, on their way to the shrine of St Thomas à Beckett, in order to derive the benefit of proximity to his remains. However, a sense of the possible sanctity of physical things can easily become a belief in talismans or magic, and the Pardoner crosses this line with his fraudulent bits and pieces. The statement that, 'He made the person [parson] and the peple his apes' is as close to direct condemnation as we get in the *General Prologue*.

The Pardoner's own body, too, crosses some kind of line. The initial impression of the Pardoner is of his unattractiveness. His thin, mousey hair – the colour of candlewax – hangs in strands over his shoulders:

By <u>ounces</u> <u>henge</u> his lokkes that he hadde,	thin strands; hung
And therwith he his shuldres overspradde;	
But thynne it lay, by <u>colpons</u> <u>oon and oon</u>.	small clumps; one by one

(GP 677–9)

In order to make the most of this feature, he dispenses with a hood and instead wears only a cap, resulting in the wry observation that, 'Hym thoughte he rood al of the newe jet [It seemed to him that he rode along in the latest fashion]' (*GP* 682). Intriguingly, he has no beard, 'ne nevere sholde have' (*GP* 689) and what this might mean is compounded by the declaration, 'I trowe [believe] he were a geldyng [castrated horse] or a mare' (*GP* 691). The implications of these statements for the Pardoner are not wholly clear, and critical interpretation runs through a range of sexual options from homo-sexuality, to natural eunuch, to the idea that he might, in fact, be a woman. What matters most, however, is that the narrator himself does not know quite how to define the Pardoner.

THE WIFE OF BATH

Unlike the Pardoner, there is no doubt about the sexuality of the Wife of Bath. Five times married, she is in a position to claim pro-fessional status, if anyone can. Women's worth and position were defined in terms of their sexuality: an easy division into virgins, mar-ried women, and widows. The Church advocated the preservation of virginity, but would settle for faithful marriage or chaste widowhood if need be. However, the Wife of Bath does not fit this contained and controlled version of womanhood. She is a serial wife, 'Withouten oother compaignye in youthe' (*GP* 461), the 'withouten' here is far more likely to mean 'not counting' rather than 'without', but, as always, the text retains a delicate ambiguity at crucial moments.

The Wife herself, on the other hand, is far from delicate. Her head-dress alone weighs a hefty ten pounds (*GP* 454) and she sits, 'esily' on an 'amblere' (*GP* 469), a large pacing horse with a rocking motion like a ship. The type of horse and the fact that she wears spurs (*GP* 473) indicate that she does not ride side-saddle, but rather sits astride the horse, like a man. Her power is further emphasised by the com-parison of her enormous hat to a shield (*GP* 471), and her inde-pendence by the fact that she has travelled the world, making the pilgrimage to Jerusalem a staggering three times. She knows a great deal, we are told, about 'wandrynge by the weye' (*GP* 467), a phrase that manages to encompass her experience as a traveller while imply-ing a more general tendency not to stick to the straight and narrow.

Much of the focus in the Wife of Bath's portrait is below the waist. We hear about her 'hipes large' (*GP* 472) and are directed towards her legs, ankles, and suggestive footwear:

Hir <u>hosen</u> weren of fyn scarlet reed,	stockings
<u>Ful streite yteyd</u>, and shoes ful <u>moyste</u> and newe.	stretched tightly over the leg; supple

(*GP* 456–7)

Add to this the fact that, 'Boold was hir face, and fair, and reed of hewe [ruddy of complexion]' (*GP* 458), and the effect is of an overall scarlet woman, with the extra detail that she is 'gat-tothed' (*GP* 468), a space between the teeth being regarded in the Middle Ages as a sure sign of wantonness.

The Wife retains, however, a touching vulnerability. She is slightly deaf, which is described by the narrator as a pity (*GP* 446), though we do not fully understand the true pity of it until we read the Prologue to her tale and discover that it was a blow to the head from her fifth husband that caused her deafness. She remains, however, good company, keen to joke and chat. The final lines of her prologue, in which we hear that, 'Of remedies of love she knew <u>per chaunce</u> [as it happens],/ For she <u>koude [knew]</u> of that art the <u>olde daunce</u>' (*GP* 475–6), link her to a tradition of old women in classical and medieval literature who give advice about love to the young. None of them, however, have the exuberance or joyful vitality of the Wife of Bath. The phrase, 'the olde daunce' is sometimes translated as 'tricks of the trade', but such base trickery and trade is for these other literary figures; for the Wife, love remains a dance, albeit one with many partners.

There are twenty-one other pilgrims described in the *General Prologue*, some very briefly and others at length. The Knight, the Pardoner, and the Wife of Bath, however, serve to illustrate the three basic groups of Chaucer's London society: the gentry, the Church, and the new merchant class.

THE KNIGHT'S PROLOGUE AND TALE

The Host calls for lots to be drawn in order to establish who will tell the first tale and, 'by aventure, or sort, or cas [by chance, or luck, or destiny]' (*CT* I 844), the draw falls to the Knight. Whether or not it really was chance is debatable. The Knight is the highest-ranking pilgrim, addressed by the Host as 'my mayster and my lord' (*CT* I 837), and invited to draw first. It is, therefore, either exceptionally lucky that he will then tell the first tale, or else the process has somehow been given a helping hand. It is a brief but significant prelude to the *Knight's Tale*, which will take questions of chance, destiny, and human free will as its key themes.

PALAMON AND ARCITE

Readers of the *Knight's Tale* frequently find it difficult to distinguish between the two main protagonists, Palamon and Arcite. Indeed, Chaucer takes pains to eradicate most of the differences between the pair of young knights who had existed in his source material. They are cousins, sworn brothers, and are found together, half-dead on the battlefield:

> Two yonge knyghtes <u>liggynge by and by</u>,   lying side by side
> Bothe in <u>oon armes</u>, <u>wroght</u> ful richely,   the same coat of arms;
>   made
> Of whiche two Arcita <u>highte</u> that <u>oon</u>,   was called; one
> And that oother knyght highte Palamon.
>   (*CT* I 1011–14)

The repetition in these lines of 'one', and 'two', and 'by', and 'highte' increases the effect of the knights being indistinguishable, dressed, as they are, in the same heraldic device, and taken off to prison together. In what follows, the fact that we can scarcely tell them apart is going to matter, for Chaucer is setting up an experiment. The question is whether our lives are governed by our own actions or by forces beyond our control, and in order to explore this, we are presented with two knights who are so alike that we cannot at first distinguish between them. They will fall in love at almost exactly the same moment with the same woman, and they will fight for her with equally matched forces. Their lives, however, will have very different endings, for one will die a horrible death and the other will get the girl. How they arrive at this point, and why, is the focus of the first of the *Canterbury Tales*.

PRISONS

At the same time as writing the *Knight's Tale*, Chaucer was translating a work about another life in prison, that of the scholar and defender of democracy, Boethius (ca. 480–524 AD). Having served Rome under Theodoric, king of the Ostrogoths, Boethius was sentenced to be bludgeoned to death. The work he wrote in prison, the *Consolation of Philosophy*, is a dialogue between Boethius and a wise female figure called Lady Philosophy, in which he gradually learns to separate transient good from what is truly good, understand the suffering of the innocent, and the part that his own decisions have played in his imprisonment. It was one of the most popular and influential works of the Middle Ages, to the extent that the appearance of a prison in any work of literature is likely to have prompted thoughts of Boethius. When Palamon and Arcite are locked away in their tower, we are told that it will be 'for everemoore' (*CT* I 1032). Prison will be their state of being for their whole life in a way that goes well beyond the rules of medieval warfare. The prison is, of course, real, but is also a metaphor for the human condition and the tendency of mankind to see itself as hemmed in by forces beyond its control. This is the state of mind that Chaucer will examine in the *Knight's Tale*, using quotations from Boethius at key points in the narrative.

THE STARS

The first speech Arcite makes in the tale is about being controlled by the planets from the moment of our birth:

'Som wikke aspect or disposicioun	evil; disposition
Of Saturne, by som constellacioun,	arrangement of the planets
Hath yeven us this, although we hadde it sworn;	given; sworn otherwise
So stood the hevene whan that we were born.	
We moste endure it; this is the short and playn.'	must; plain
(*CT* I 1087–91)	

In the source, the two knights are born within minutes of each other, and their horoscope is the same, with heavy influence from Saturn, the most malign of the planets. In the eyes of Arcite, there is simply nothing that can be done: they are imprisoned by the stars at birth and must accept the fate that is handed to them. Later, with the same fatalistic resignation, Palamon, too, claims that we are at the mercy of forces beyond our control, like a 'sheep that rouketh [cowers] in the folde' (*CT* I 1308): mere lambs to the slaughter. Inevitably, given that he believes that the universe is in some way controlled, even if only by the planets, he arrives at the key problem of innocent suffering:

> 'What governance is in this <u>prescience</u>,   foreknowledge
> That <u>giltelees tormenteth</u> innocence?'   torments guiltless
> (*CT* I 1314)

It is the same question that Boethius asks as he considers his own suffering while wrongdoers thrive in the world: if there is really a guiding force in the universe, how can tormenting the innocent be part of any kind of reasonable plan (*B* I m.5)?

We have not, however, reached the end of the torment that Palamon and Arcite suffer, for there is one more element to be added to this experiment: the two knights must fall in love at almost the same moment with the same woman. The Middle Ages might claim a belief in the freedom of the will, no matter what we come to face, but what Chaucer is doing here is constructing the ultimate test of human freedom: take one prison, add cosmic forces, throw in over-powering desire. For that, though, love needs to find an object, and both knights find that in Emelye.

EMELYE

Early on a May morning, Palamon is roaming his prison cell when he spots Emelye in the garden below his tower:

> And so bifel, by <u>aventure or cas</u>,   chance or accident
> That <u>thurgh</u> a wyndow, <u>thikke of</u> many a barre   through; thick set with
> Of <u>iren greet</u> and square as any <u>sparre</u>,   solid iron; beam
> He cast his eye upon Emelya,
> And therwithal he <u>bleynte</u> and cride, 'A!'   turned pale
> (*CT* I 1074–8)

The first thing to note is the repetition of the same phrase that we encountered in the *Knight's Prologue*: 'by aventure or cas'. In the Italian source tale, Emilia goes knowingly to the window of the prison and sings in order to attract attention. There is no indication here of anything so contrived. It appears, instead, to be truly an accidental encounter, although the emphasis is still on Palamon's actions. He might later claim to Arcite that, 'I was hurt right now thurghout myn ye [eye] / Into myn herte' (*CT* I 1096–7) in a way that assigns him-self a passive role, but the description of his first glimpse of Emelye is wholly active. The window of his prison cell is heavily barred with iron, each one as thick as a beam, so it can be no casual glance that finds Emelye. It is instead the look of a man intent on seeing the world outside. Further, his tower is so high that he can see the whole city and the garden below, 'ful of braunches grene' (*CT* I 1067). He is above the tree line, a long way from anyone in the garden, held behind stout walls and with one thickly barred window. His falling in love is, therefore, not so much chance as achievement, especially when we consider the very shadowy description of Emelye herself.

We first see Emelye on a May morning as she rises early to perform the rites of spring:

... Emelye, that fairer was to <u>sene</u>	look upon
Than is the <u>lylie</u> upon his stalke grene,	lily
And <u>fressher</u> than the May with floures newe –	more blooming
For with the rose colour <u>stroof hire hewe</u>,	her complexion competed
I <u>noot</u> which was the fyner of hem two –	do not know
<u>Er</u> it were day, as was hir <u>wone</u> to do,	before; custom
She was arisen and al redy <u>dight</u> ...	prepared
<u>Yclothed</u> was she <u>fressh</u>, for to <u>devyse</u>:	dressed; gaily; tell
Hir yellow <u>heer</u> was <u>broyded in a tresse</u>	hair; arranged in a braid
Bihynde hir bak, a <u>yerde</u> long, I gesse.	yard (almost a metre)
(*CT* I 1035–50)	

It feels more like looking at a bouquet of flowers than a woman: more blooming than May, a lily, a rose, a host of Spring blossoms. The only non-floral detail is her hair, blonde, like that of any ideal lady of medieval romance, and falling in a long braid down her back. With this, however, we realise that we are viewing Emelye from behind. She is the epitome of blooming loveliness, and she is facing away from us; not a real woman with a face and expressions, and thoughts and views, but an ideal with which to fall in love at a distance. That this is true will become even clearer as the protagonists align themselves with their gods, but for that, Palamon and Arcite must first escape from prison.

FREEDOM

Although he had contemplated an entire life in a prison from which there was no escape, Arcite is unexpectedly released without ransom a few lines later at the request of an old friend. Even more surprisingly, Palamon, 'dampned [condemned] to prisoun,/ In cheynes and in fettres to been deed [until death]' (CT I 1342–3), decides one night that he has had enough of prison, drugs his gaoler, and escapes. It becomes clear that there was more that could be done about this prison than the knights originally believed, and that their fettered state had at least partly to do with their own state of mind. Certainly, freedom seems to come far more easily than they at first had presented it to themselves. However, they do not embrace this freedom. Arcite does not stray far from his tower, choosing to stay near Emelye and serve her in disguise, as bound by his love for her as he was by his prison chains. As for Palamon, he gets no further with his new-found freedom than fighting with Arcite in the bushes. They both want the same woman and are willing to give up real freedom in order to fight to the death for her.

Their plan to duel, however, is thwarted by the arrival of Duke Theseus, the man who had imprisoned them in the first place, and who now sentences them to death. At the shrieks of the accompanying women he is persuaded otherwise and instead decrees that there will be a tournament to which Palamon and Arcite will each bring a hundred knights, the winner to be granted Emelye as his prize. The language used by Theseus assumes a faith in the will of the gods. His intention is that each knight 'shal have his destynee / As hym is shape [as it has been shaped for him' (CT I 1842–3). 'Destiny' is a strong word, for it implies a foregone conclusion and ignores the choices that the knights will make before they reach the tournament.

CHOICE

The contest is set for a year's time, giving Theseus the opportunity to construct a grand amphitheatre in which to hold it, complete with temples sacred to Venus, Mars, and Diana. Both the date and time of the tournament and the design of the circular amphitheatre are very specific (CT I 1887–1913; 2209–11), leading some critics to argue that the building mirrors the cosmos and the position of the planets on a particular date. In effect, the amphitheatre becomes a microcosm and Palamon, Arcite, and Emelye will each align themselves not just with specific gods, but with the planetary influences of those gods. What is crucial, however, is that each chooses their deity, and that each will ultimately get what they ask for.

In the case of Palamon, he chooses to pray to Venus. Given that his first reaction to Emelye was that he thought he had seen Venus herself walking in the garden (*CT* I 1102), his choice is in keeping with what little we know of him, as is his prayer for what he wants most: to 'have fully possessioun' of Emelye (*CT* I 2242). Arcite, who, at the first sight of Emelye had abandoned his vows of brotherhood and declared that it was 'ech man for hymself' (*CT* I.1182), unsurprisingly goes to the temple of Mars, god of war, and prays for victory. By implication he, too, wants Emelye, but it is his nature to focus on winning. Finally, Emelye herself, described by Arcite as the bone over which the dogs fight (*CT* I 1177), goes to the temple of Diana and pledges herself to the goddess of chastity. She makes it clear that she does not want either of the knights, and that she would prefer never to be a wife or a mother. However, Emelye is used to being disregarded. She is not asked what she wants by Theseus, nor is she asked by Palamon or Arcite. Indeed, her usual position in the text is to be tacked on at the end of sentences, rather as an afterthought ('... and so dide Emelye' *CT* I 1749). She does not, therefore, stop speaking once she has stated her own desire. She assumes that she must aim lower and expect that other forces will take precedence over her own wishes:

> And if so be thou <u>wolt nat do me grace</u>,   will not grant my wish
> Or if my destynee be shapen so
> That I <u>shal nedes</u> have oon of hem two,   must
> <u>As</u> sende me hym <u>that moost desireth me</u>. then; who desires me most
>   (*CT* I 2322–5)

It may not be what she wants, but it is what she asks for: that she should be given to whichever of the two knights desires her more.

This, then, is the tangle of the last stages of the tale, and it leads to strife in the heavens. Venus and Mars each take the side of their own knight, and it is left to Saturn to intervene, which he does by sending a 'furie infernal' into the arena (*CT* I 2684). Arcite wins the battle, but then, captivated by the sight of his prize in Emelye, his helmet cast aside, he fails to control his horse as it rears at the sight of the hellish fury. Arcite dies and his death then means that Palamon is able to marry Emelye. In this way, both Mars and Venus are satisfied, and it would seem that the case for a universe controlled by the gods is very strong. However, at the crucial moment, Chaucer reminds us that we are dealing not with Olympian gods, but with planets. Even as Saturn boasts of his power to Venus, he defines himself as the outermost planet, his power being derived from orbiting the others: 'My cours [orbit], that hath so wyde for to turne, / Hath moore power than woot [knows] any man' (*CT* I 2454–5). We are dealing, therefore, not with the irresistible whim of the gods, but with planetary influence, and it is crucial to remember that each of the protagonists gets what they asked for.

That Arcite wins the battle is not surprising given his more martial inclinations. He desired victory and, having achieved it, fails to pay attention to anything else. His death, however, means that Palamon then gets what he asked for: he will marry Emelye. As for Emelye herself, her compromise prayer that she be sent whichever knight desires her more is also granted, for it was Palamon who thought of her from the first moment as a goddess, and Palamon who thought only of her in his prayers before the contest: a less warlike motivation that explains his failure to defeat Arcite in the first place. Insofar as these characters are individualised, the outcome is true to their natures. The less cautious temperament of Arcite does not look out for last minute snags once he has the victory; the more romantic Palamon is at the sidelines when danger appears; the undemanding Emelye will settle for whatever comes her way. What we have here, therefore, can be seen not as the will of any gods, but as the natural response of individuals to the slings, arrows, and infernal furies of fortune. Such responses remain, however, like groping in the dark.

THE DRUNK MOUSE AND THE PILGRIMAGE OF WOE

Earlier, when Arcite was released from prison and was lamenting the fact that he would no longer be able to glimpse Emelye from the window, he had compared the human condition to a man

'that <u>dronke</u> is as a <u>mous</u>.	drunk; mouse
A dronke man <u>woot</u> wel he hath an hous,	knows
But he <u>noot</u> which the righte wey is <u>thider</u>,	does not know; to get there

> And to a dronke man the wey is <u>slider</u>. slippery
> And <u>certes</u>, in this world so <u>faren we</u>; certainly; do we proceed
> We <u>seken</u> faste after <u>felicitee</u>, seek; happiness
> But we <u>goon</u> wrong ful often, trewely.' go
> $\qquad$ (CT I 1261–7)

We stagger around in the dark, like a mouse that has been in the beer, unable to find our way. Arcite uses the image to refer to his own useless desires: he had prayed for freedom, but when it came, he realised it was not what he wanted. His victory, too, brings not what he had expected, but instead brings his death. Human striving and human choice lead only to suffering.

Much the same view is put forward by the elderly Egeus, who enters the text only to declare that the inevitable outcome of life is death, and that the route from one to the other is full of torment:

> 'This world <u>nys</u> but a <u>thurghfare</u> ful of wo, is nothing; thoroughfare
> And we been pilgrymes, passynge to and fro.
> <u>Deeth</u> is an ende of every worldy <u>soore</u>.' death; misery
> $\qquad$ (CT I 2847–9)

He is no Lady Philosophy, and the consolation he offers is only that we will finally be put out of our misery.

THESEUS

It is Duke Theseus who takes these views and attempts to establish belief in a universe constructed by love. Theseus was often thought of as the great civiliser, the man who conquered the Amazons and restored order to the classical world. The *Knight's Tale* begins with Theseus encountering on the road the dispossessed widows of Thebes and responding to their grief by attacking the new leader of the city and his people. However, this, of course, creates more widows and produces more casualties, two of whom are the knights Palamon and Arcite. The same pattern is followed when Theseus later finds the young knights fighting in the grove. In order to put right the wrong that he encounters here, he calls for a tournament instead, but it is this act that leads to the death of Arcite. Good intentions, as we saw in Palamon's story of the drunk man, lead only to suffering.

In spite of this, Theseus promotes a view of an ordered universe shaped and protected by the love of a 'First Mover' who brought it all into being:

> 'The Firste Moevere of the cause above,
> Whan he first made the faire <u>cheyne</u> of love,   chain
> Greet was th'effect, and <u>heigh</u> was his <u>entente</u>.   exalted; intention
> Wel <u>wiste</u> he why, and what <u>thereof</u> he mente,   knew; concerning it
> For with that faire cheyne of love he <u>bond</u>   bound together
> The <u>fyr</u>, the <u>eyr</u>, the water, and the lond   fire; air
> In certeyn boundes, that they may nat <u>flee</u>.'   escape
>   (*CT* I 2987–93)

There are echoes here of one of the best-known passages from Boethius (B 2 m.8), and many critics have responded positively to the image of a world created and contained by a benign being that knew what it was doing. However, there remains a sense of forces only barely kept in check, their natural inclination being to 'flee'. As for the rest of Theseus' speech, it concerns itself only with death. It contains many promising words, such as 'stable', 'eterne', 'purveiaunce [foresight]', 'ordinaunce' (*CT* I 3004–12), that can distract from the fact that there is nothing being offered here except the wisdom of accepting the inevitable. We must learn, 'to maken vertu of necessitee' (*CT* I 3042), a famous phrase, recorded here in English for the first time. However, it is not much. Ultimately, the only consolation that Theseus can offer is that all things must pass away: the mighty oak, the greatest of rivers, even the rock that seems impervious beneath our feet. Each one will eventually cease to be, and men and women are no different, no matter what their situation in life might be (*CT* I 3017–34). Since death, then, is inevitable, it might be best to accept it at the height of one's fame – 'to dyen whan that he is best of name [reputation]' (*CT* I 3056) – rather than in the forgotten depths of old age. It is a lengthy speech, that takes us only to the grave.

DEATH

The death of Arcite is protracted and horrible. In a surprising passage we are taken inside the body of the dying man in order to see him slowly drown in his own blood:

The <u>clothered</u> blood, <u>for any lechecraft</u>,	clotted; in spite of all medicine
<u>Corrupteth</u>, and is in his <u>bouk</u> <u>ylaft</u>,	decays; trunk; left
That neither <u>veyne-blood</u>, ne <u>ventusynge</u>,	blood-letting; cupping
Ne drynke of herbes may ben his helpynge.	

(*CT* I 2745–8).

Such technical descriptions are very rare in medieval literature. The glorious exploits of knights might lead to death, but such death is not traditionally dwelt upon. Here, however, there is nothing glorious. The focus on the body as a biological entity makes it clear that we are no different from the beasts. As for belief in an immortal soul, we are given no consolation there either. In the source tale, the soul of Arcita ascended into the spheres (the ending that Chaucer would later give to Troilus). However, Chaucer grants no such celestial journey to Arcite. The voice of the Knight as narrator is heard clearly at this point as he refuses to make any guesses about a life to come:

His spirit chaunged hous and wente <u>ther</u>,	to a place
<u>As</u> I cam nevere, I kan nat tellen wher.	to which
Therfore I <u>stynte</u>; I <u>nam</u> no <u>divinistre</u>;	stop; am not; theologian

(*CT* I 2809–11)

The finality of it all is emphasised by the heavy pause after 'stynte'. There is no solace as we view the body of the young knight and contemplate the road that brought him here, and while a case can be made that his own decisions led him to this point, the death of Arcite is nevertheless cruel. That cruelty is expressed in Arcite's own dying words:

'What is this world? What asketh men to have?	
Now with his love, now in his colde grave	
Allone, withouten any <u>compaignye</u>.'	company

(*CT* I 2777–9)

The tone is one of simple bewilderment. Our circumstances change so suddenly, and what is here one moment is gone the next. Both the companionship of love and the solitariness of the grave are brought together in a single line. They are both 'now', the time between them being nothing at all. Perhaps this is why the eventual marriage of Emelye to Palamon brings no consolation. We are told that, 'For now is Palamon in alle wele [complete happiness]' (*CT* I 3101), but we know the value of that 'now'. What lingers instead is the image of the grave and our isolation, the fact that we will ultimately be 'alone, without any company'.

THE MILLER'S PROLOGUE AND TALE

The first tale having been told by the Knight, the Host looks around for another high-ranking pilgrim and decides upon the Monk. However, the Miller, so drunk that he can scarcely stay on his horse, decides that he wants to be the next one to tell a story. He interrupts the Host, quarrels with the Reeve, and declares that he will be the one to 'quite [repay] the Knyghtes tale' (*CT* I 3127); and he 'pays back' the tale in more ways than one, for the *Miller's Tale* is a distorted image of the story told by the Knight. With its 'love-triangle' and cosmic machinery it resembles the earlier tale, but this is a fabliau: a comic adventure in which normal rules of morality are suspended, and where quick-wit and brazen cheek are rewarded. Sex replaces love; wily cunning replaces nobility; and a carpenter's house in Oxford replaces the landscape of ancient Greece.

NICHOLAS

Towards the end of the *Knight's Tale*, a dying young knight had expressed the ultimate isolation of the grave in the line, 'Allone, withouten any compaignye' (*CT* I 2779). The same line appears right at the beginning of the *Miller's Tale*, but in a very different context, for it describes the room of Nicholas, a student lodger in the home of a carpenter:

> A chambre hadde he in that hostelrye   room; boarding-house
> Allone, withouten any compaignye,
>   (*CT* I 3203–4)

What had been a statement of solitary anguish in the previous tale is here transformed into an opportunity, as Nicholas revels in that rare medieval possession: a room of his own. As for the stars that had dominated the lives of the young knights, Nicholas has all the paraphernalia of the student of astronomy, 'couched' (*CT* I 3211) on shelves at the head of his bed, in a manner more suggestive of tools for seduction than of serious study. For Nicholas is 'hende' (*CT* I 3199), a word with a wealth of meanings that encompasses 'courteous', 'gracious', 'clever', 'handy', and 'nice'. Perhaps the last of these, with its modern lack of enthusiasm, describes Nicholas best, for he is 'nice' in a way that allows for a self-serving charm, a charm that he will happily direct towards the carpenter's young wife, Alison.

ALISON

Descriptions of ladies in medieval romance tend to focus upon the beautiful grey of their eyes, the gleaming gold of their hair, with perhaps a reference to the slenderness of their arms as a token mention of the body. They are compared to flowers, usually lilies or roses, with a few reaching ethereal heights as 'angels'. Alison is not that kind of woman. She is full of animal vitality, and the description of her focusses immediately on her waist and works its way down:

Fair was this yonge wyf, and <u>therwithal</u>	in addition
As any <u>wezele</u> hir body <u>gent</u> and <u>smal</u>.	weasel; lithe; slender
A <u>ceynt</u> she <u>werede</u>, <u>barred</u> al of silk,	belt; wore; striped
A <u>barmclooth</u> as whit as <u>morne</u> milk	apron; morning
Upon hir <u>lendes</u>, ful of many a <u>goore</u>.	thighs; slash
(*CT* I 3233–7)	

Her skin is not lily white, but she has instead an apron that is on the creamy side and is also fashionably 'slashed' to reveal the lining within. She has a waist. She has thighs. In fact, she has the lithe and slender body of a weasel, a simile that manages to make her both desirable and slightly dangerous. A host of country and farmyard comparisons follow: she is as pretty as a tree of early-ripening pears; as soft to the touch as the wool on a ram; as tuneful as a swallow; as playful as a calf; and as sweet to the taste as a hoard of apples lying in the straw. Of course, none of these similes are particularly complimentary, but what is significant is that the description engages all our senses: we know what it is like to touch Alison and even to taste her. She is not an ethereal beauty to be viewed from a distance; she is not even blonde. Her eyebrows are as richly dark as sloe berries and plucked (probably for the first time in English literature) so that they are very thin and arched (*CT* I 3245–6). She has a complexion like a newly minted coin, the posture of a cross-bow bolt, and a brooch like a shield, all of which suggest a woman capable of looking after herself in more ways than one.

NOT-SO-COURTLY LOVE

Certainly, Alison is able to deal with Nicholas. As soon as the carpenter has gone off for the day, Nicholas makes all the usual protestations of the noble courtly lover (see p. 95), claiming that he will die of his secret love, while at the same time groping between her legs (*CT* I 3276–8). Alison, too, knows how to play the game, responding with mock outrage:

"Why, <u>lat be</u>!" quod she. "Lat be, Nicholas,	stop it
Or I wol crie '<u>out, harrow</u>' and 'allas'!	help
<u>Do wey youre handes</u>, for youre curteisye!"	take your hands off me
(*CT* I 3285–7)	

The hands are currently gripping her tight by the 'haunchebones [thighs]' (*CT* I 3279), but Nicholas begs for mercy and offers his service like any courtly lover should and is rewarded by Alison granting him her love 'atte laste' (*CT* I 3290). In a typical romance this 'atte laste' might take anything up to a decade, but Alison is willing to refine the process to a few minutes.

The same cannot be said of the third member of the love triangle, the local parish clerk, Absolon. While his ultimate aim might not be so far different from that of Nicholas, Absolon takes himself very seriously as a practitioner of the art of courtly love. His elaborate 'curteisie' and 'love-longynge' (*CT* I 3349–51) makes him unwilling to accept the money brought to the church as offerings by the women of the parish, and it is Absolon who has the golden hair and grey eyes that usually mark out the courtly lady. His eyes, however, are comically 'greye as goos' and his hair, of which he is inordinately proud, protrudes from his head like a fan (*CT* I 3315–17). He dresses himself in the latest fashion and goes from tavern to tavern visiting the barmaids. He is rather prim in his speech, however, and 'somdeel squaymous [somewhat squeamish] / Of fartyng' (*CT* I 3337–8), an aversion that will play its part in the tale that follows.

THE NOAH PLOT

Alison and Nicholas have plenty of opportunity to do as they please while the carpenter is out, but this way of proceeding is not clever enough for Nicholas. His epithet is, after all, 'hende' and he decides to come up with a plan that will allow him to seduce Alison, fool the carpenter, and display his own cleverness in the process. In the *Knight's Tale* there had been the constant worry that we are at the mercy of the stars, but the *Miller's Tale* turns this around and shows astronomy being manipulated instead. In fact, Nicholas harnesses not just the planets, but the Bible to his purposes and declares that he has seen the Second Flood predicted in the stars. The only way to save themselves, he tells the carpenter, is to suspend three wooden tubs from the rafters – one for himself, one for Alison, and one for Nicholas. Of course, the plan is that Nicholas and Alison will sneak away in the night, leaving the carpenter suspended from the ceiling while they go to bed together.

JOHN THE CARPENTER

The surprise aspect of all of this is John the Carpenter himself. He is described at the outset as a 'riche gnof' (*CT* I 3188), a lout, who keeps his young wife 'narwe in cage [closely confined]' (*CT* I 3224). However, John turns out to be very unlike the typical old and jealous husbands of fabliaux. He cares about Nicholas, feeding him ale and attempting a home-made exorcism when he thinks that his lodger has turned his mind with too much studying (*CT* I 3449–67); and his response to Absolon singing to Alison outside the bedroom window is more bewildered than jealous:

"What! Alison! <u>Herestow nat</u> Absolon,	can you not hear
That <u>chaunteth</u> thus under oure <u>boures</u> wal?"	sings; bedroom
And she answerde hir housbonde <u>therwithal</u>,	immediately
"Yis, God <u>woot</u>, John, I heere <u>it every deel</u>."	knows; every bit of it
<div align="center">(*CT* I 3366–9)</div>	

Certainly, he is greeted with sublime wifely indifference, an indifference he does not feel for her. His response to the news of an imminent Flood is to think not of himself, but wholly of Alison: "Allas, my wyf! / And shal she drenche [drown]? Allas, myn Alisoun!" (*CT* I 3522–3). The rules of the fabliau genre dictate that it is every man and woman for themselves, but John does not abide by such rules. He is generous in his dealings, though wholly gullible, and yet pleased with what he regards as his own good sense. The science of astrology, so revered in the *Knight's Tale*, becomes for John a cautionary tale about a student who went looking for the future in the stars and fell into a clay pit: 'He saugh [saw] nat that' (*CT* I 3461). He declares, instead, a simple faith in the Church's creed, and proceeds to swallow the story that Nicholas feeds him, preparing in earnest for the Second Flood.

THE JOKE AT THE WINDOW

While John sleeps in his tub suspended from the ceiling, Nicholas and Alison sneak out of their own tubs and go to bed together. Sometime before daybreak, however, Absolon arrives and calls for Alison at the bedroom window. In response to his pompously courtly language and insistence upon a kiss, Alison decides to play a trick on him. In the pitch darkness, she sits on the window ledge and offers another part of her anatomy to be kissed:

Derk was the nyght as pich, or as the cole,	dark; pitch; coal
And at the wyndow out she putte hir hole,	anus
And Absolon, hym fil no bet ne wers,	no better or worse befell him
But with his mouth he kiste hir naked ers	
Ful savourly, er he were war of this.	with relish; before; aware
Abak he stirte, and thought it was amys,	jumped
For wel he wiste a womman hath no berd.	knew; beard
He felte a thyng al rough and long yherd,	haired
And seyde, "Fy! allas! what have I do?"	done
"Tehee!" quod she, and clapte the wyndow to	slammed
(*CT* I 3731–40)	

Alison's 'Tehee!' is a glorious expression of mischievous freedom and triumphant fun. As for Absolon, his slow-dawning realisation about what he has kissed gives way to rage. He fetches a red-hot shaft of iron from the nearby blacksmith and takes up his place once more at the window.

This time, however, it is Nicholas who responds when Absolon begs for a kiss. Thinking that he will make the joke even better ('amenden al the jape' *CT* I 3799), Nicholas sticks his own buttocks over the window ledge. In the pitch blackness outside, Absolon calls for his 'sweet bird' to speak to him and tell him where she is:

This Nicholas anon <u>leet fle</u> a fart	let fly
As greet as it had been a <u>thonder-dent</u>,	clap of thunder
That with the strook he was almoost <u>yblent</u>;	blinded
And he was redy with his iren hoot,	
And Nicholas amydde the ers he <u>smoot</u>.	struck

(CT I 3806–10)

It is a parody of the window scenes in medieval romance, including the one in the *Knight's Tale*, where a beautiful form is glimpsed in the distance, or an angelic voice heard. At this point the knight is frequently struck by the metaphorical darts of love and feels that he might die. There is nothing metaphorical, however, about the injuries sustained by Nicholas. Branded in the 'toute [rump]' (*CT* I 3812), his screams of pain echo around the house and reach the ears of John the Carpenter. We had forgotten about John the Carpenter. However, Nicholas's cries of 'Help! Water! Water! Help' (*CT* I 3815) rouse the older man from his slumbers and clearly signal to him that the Flood has arrived. He cuts the ropes to 'launch' his tub from the ceiling, and crashes to the ground in an unconscious heap.

In the *Knight's Tale*, the protagonists had claimed to be assailed by forces beyond their control: stumbling in the dark like drunks who cannot find their way home (see p. 38). In the *Miller's Tale*, however, everything is reassuringly literal. The Miller confides to the company that he is, indeed, very drunk ('I knowe it by my soun [sound]' *CT* I 3138), and the darkness in his tale is not that of the benighted human condition, but of night time in medieval Oxford. Moreover, we understand exactly why and how things happen. The link between a thunderous fart and Noah's Flood is unexpected, but this is a world in which there is a beautiful sense of cause and effect between one outrageous incident and the next. Nothing is exactly under control, but the part each individual plays in the eventual out-come is very clear.

THE MORAL

Fabliaux are not moral tales and we should not expect a moral end-ing: they simply operate by a different code. Cleverness and daring are what win out; and pretentiousness and foolishness are always punished. John the Carpenter, an old man thinking that he can happily marry an 18-year-old wife, pays for this foolishness, and for his gullibility and complacency, too. Absolon, with his vanity and pretensions, will no longer have any desire to pester the women of Oxford. As for Nicholas, his cleverness is rewarded in that he gets to spend the night with Alison, but his mistake is to repeat Alison's joke. The fabliau world demands quick wits and inventiveness, and repeating a joke is simply not good enough. As for Alison, centuries of literature pull women back into line and punish them for any sexual impropriety; but not here. Alison emerges unscathed because she is funnier, quicker, more daring, and more clear-sighted than all the men. Of course, she faces a future with John the Carpenter, but the townspeople now regard him as mad and will not listen to anything he has to say, and her 'Teehee!' remains one of the most liberated female utterances in the history of English literature.

THE WIFE OF BATH'S PROLOGUE AND TALE

The Wife of Bath ambles into the *Canterbury Tales* straddling a large, comfortable horse, her red stockings on show and a pair of sharp spurs on her feet. She is a 'wife' in the medieval sense of 'woman', but she is also as close to being a professional wife as anyone can get, having already had five husbands and looking forward to the sixth, whenever he might happen to present himself. She has her own business as a cloth-maker (*GP* 447), which makes her the pro-fessional equal of many of the men on the pilgrimage, but hers is also a symbolic role, because spinning was the task that the Middle Ages envisaged for Eve after she was cast out of the Garden of Eden. The Wife of Bath therefore represents womankind, but in a form not often encountered in medieval literature. She is not one of the many virgin martyrs whose virtues were extolled in the legends of the saints, nor is she one of the bitter, scheming old women who appear in literature from classical times onwards, advising the young on how to lie and cheat their way through love affairs. She is sexual, loud, occasionally vulnerable, and determined to tell both a tale and the story of her life. She has the longest prologue in the *Canterbury Tales* by a considerable margin, longer than her tale itself. In it we find many of the things traditionally said against women in medieval writing, but turned around and changed by a female voice.

EXPERIENCE AND AUTHORITY

The very first word we hear from the Wife of Bath is 'experience' (*CT* III 1). Having had so many husbands already, she is ideally placed to speak about marriage, and is determined to measure her first-hand experience against the writings of the celibate men who represent the views of the Church on the subject. In a system in which virginity was prized, chaste widowhood encouraged, and marriage often seen as no more than a necessary evil, the Wife finds herself in opposition to Church authority. She declares her intention from the outset, 'To speke of wo that is in mariage' (*CT* III 3), which was a subject dear to the hearts of many medieval clerics, but she almost instantly digresses in order to consider whether or not she can claim to have been married so many times at all. The male writers of the Church tell her that she cannot have been, and they use the ultimate authority of the Bible to substantiate their claim.

THE BIBLE

Very few men and even fewer women in the Middle Ages were able to read and write. The number who could read Latin was even smaller, so the whole population relied upon the Church to translate the Latin of the Bible. However, the Bible is a vast work, and all translation inevitably involves interpretation, so what was conveyed to the people was often a partial truth, or a simplified part of a complicated whole. The Wife is only a few lines into her prologue when she begins to take issue with this, starting with the claim that since Christ attended only one wedding in the gospels, then only one marriage was permitted in a lifetime (*CT* III 10–13). The difficulty of basing real life on a symbolic reading is not lost on the Wife and she counters with another piece of the Bible. It is the story of the

Samaritan woman who had had five husbands and was criticised by Christ:

> 'Thou hast yhad fyve housbondes,' quod he,
> 'And that <u>ilke</u> man that now hath thee   very
> Is noght thyn housbonde,' thus seyde he <u>certeyn</u>.   without doubt
> What that he mente therby, I kan nat seyn;
> But that I <u>axe</u>, why that the fifthe man   ask
> Was noon housbonde to the Samaritan?
> How manye myghte she have in marriage?
> Yet herde I nevere tellen <u>in myn age</u>   I have never in all
>   my life heard
> <u>Upon this nombre diffinicioun</u>.'   an exact number
>   specified

(CT III 17–25)

There is a sense here of daringly challenging Christ on a technicality: if the fifth husband was not acceptable, does that mean that the fourth was? Where in the Bible is the number stated? It is overly literal as interpretations go, but no worse than the reading of wedding attendance at Cana as a metaphorical marriage quota, and the Wife follows up with examples of the holy men of the Old Testament who married more than once, including Solomon, with his seven hundred wives and three hundred concubines.

In the face of symbolic interpretation, she invokes the literal; when presented with one biblical example she presents a counterexample; and when she encounters the idealistic teaching of the Church, she resorts to a logical debunking of what this idealism would mean in practice. Where exactly would all the much-praised virgins come from, she asks, 'if ther were no seed ysowe [sown]' (*CT* III 71). As for the design of the human body, it is difficult to argue that sexual organs have no sexual purpose:

> <u>Glose</u> whoso wole, and seye <u>bothe up and doun</u>   interpret; in all
>   respects
> That they were maked for purgacioun
> Of uryne, and oure bothe thynges smale
> Were <u>eek</u> to knowe a femele from a male,   also
> And for noon other cause – say ye no?
> The experience <u>woot</u> wel it is noght so.   shows

(CT III. 119–24)

We can hear the lofty terms of the theologians in the phrase 'pur-gacioun of urine' and the disbelieving attitude of the Wife as she mimics them. There is a gentle mockery in her dismissal of the waste disposal argument and the notion that genitals are simply to tell the sexes apart, and just for good measure there is a little joke in the otherwise redundant phrase 'bothe up and doun'. It is all, as far as the Wife of Bath is concerned, an exercise in 'glossing': interpreting the Bible – and sometimes interpreting even basic biological facts – in the way that best suits the agenda of the Church. She will go so far as to countenance more than one use for the 'sely instrument [innocent tool]' (*CT* III. 132), but one of those uses must be – and at this point she heightens her language to match that of the clerks – 'engendrure [procreation]' (*CT* III. 134). In fact, she is so pleased with this word that she employs it three times in quick succession, alighting on the body of Christ himself, who was 'shapen as a man' (*CT* III. 139), but wisely concluding that, in spite of such 'harneys' (*CT* III.136), no one is explicitly required to use it 'in engendrure' (*CT* III.137). The clerics have gone too far towards a world of total celibacy and, for a moment, the Wife is in danger of swinging too far in the other direction. Their sins are her sins, she is simply the other side of the coin.

THE HUSBANDS

We see this particularly in the Wife's account of her life with her various husbands. The first three were old men, and she cheerfully claims that she led them a merry dance. She gives a lengthy account of all the things they said to her, shaping it essentially into 150 lines of vitriole:

'Thou <u>liknest</u> eek wommenes love to helle,	compare
To <u>bareyne</u> lond, <u>ther</u> water may nat dwelle.	barren; where
Thou liknest it also to <u>wilde fyr</u>;	Greek fire
The moore it <u>brenneth</u>, the moore it hath desir	burns
To consume every thyng that <u>brent wole be</u>.'	can be burned

(CT III.371–5)

It is strong stuff: women are destructive, insatiable, and hellish. However, the catch comes in the next lines as she gleefully addresses her audience:

Lordynges, right thus, as ye have
  understonde,
Baar I stifly myne olde housbondes on honde   I vehemently swore to
That thus they seyden in hir dronkenesse;   they said these things
And al was fals,

(CT III. 379–82)

The old husbands did not, in fact, ever speak to her in this way: it is merely a ploy of the Wife's to put them at her mercy. But it is a complicated ploy, because the Wife did not invent these words: they are well-known pieces of anti-feminist literature, mostly written by the theologians in order to subjugate wives. The Wife of Bath, however, takes them and uses them as a weapon to subjugate her husbands. What we have therefore is the author, Chaucer, creating a pilgrim Chaucer, who recounts the words of the Wife of Bath, which are taken from the clerics, and put in the mouths of men who, in fact, never uttered them. It is a fascinating exercise in reflection and refraction, summed up in the Wife's later demand, 'Who peynt-ede [painted] the leon, tel me who?' (CT III.692). It is the medieval equivalent of the modern observation that history is written by the winners, for while men might paint pictures of lions being killed, the lions themselves, given the opportunity, would produce very different pictures:

By God, if wommen hadde writen stories,
As clerkes han withinne hire oratories,   have; chapels
They wolde han writen of men moore   about
  wikkednesse
Than al the mark of Adam may redresse.   than all the male sex
                                               could ever put right

(CT III. 693–6)

THE BOOK OF WICKED WIVES

The supreme example of the story being told by those with power comes in the form of the tales of wicked women that were popular in the Middle Ages. The Wife's fifth husband, Jankyn, had possessed such a book and had read it aloud every evening until the Wife could take no more. It contained all the usual tales from the classical world and from the Bible, tales of women who harmed their husbands because they hated them or harmed them because they loved them too much; of women who gave bad advice, or whose words otherwise betrayed their men. Some were murderers, some were lecherous, and some managed to combine both qualities:

Of latter date, of wyves hath he <u>red</u>	read
That somme han slayn hir housbondes in hir bed,	
And <u>lete</u> hir lecchour <u>dighte</u> hire al the nyght,	allowed; copulate with
Whan that the corps lay in the floor <u>upright</u>.	face up
(*CT* III. 765–8)	

Most collections begin their history of the faults of womankind with the creation of the very first woman: Eve. She features prominently wherever there are stories of wicked women, and Jankyn's book is no exception:

Of Eva first, that <u>for</u> hir wikkednesse	on account of
Was al mankynde broght to wrecchednesse,	
For which that Jhesu Crist hymself was slayn,	
That <u>boghte</u> us with his herte blood agayn.	redeemed
Lo, heere <u>expres</u> of womman may ye fynde	explicitly
That womman was the <u>los</u> of al mankynde.	perdition
(*CT* III. 715–20)	

The biblical account of Eve's fall from Paradise is more evenhanded and does not attribute all the calamities of existence to her. The fault is shared between Adam and Eve and there is no condemnation in the text itself of the woman over the man. However, the Eve of the Middle Ages is a popular villain in a very straightforward story of a good man deceived by his evil spouse. The blame that might have been given to the serpent was instead apportioned to Eve, the story becoming in the process a straight division between bad women and good men, for 'womman', not the Devil, 'was the los of al mankynde'.

One evening, the Wife, unable to bear any more of this, lunges for the book, tearing three pages from it and knocking Jankyn into the fire. The mystery of the Wife's deafness, mentioned in the *General Prologue* ('But she was somdel deef, and that was scathe [a pity]' *GP*

446) is solved, as Jankyn gets to his feet and hits her on the head with his fist (*CT* III. 795). For a moment there is silence and it seems that the Wife might be dead. Her recovery, however, is closely followed by her demand for a kiss, and Jankyn's capitulation in terms of the control of all their affairs. It is a fairy tale ending. The Wife's words, however, reveal perhaps a less pretty reality:

God helpe me so, I was to hym as <u>kynde</u>	kind
As any wyf from Denmark unto <u>Ynde</u>,	India
And also <u>trewe</u>, and so was he to me.	True
(*CT* III. 823–5)	

It is possible that it is indeed a happy ending, but there is some ambiguity in the Wife of Bath's words. 'Kynde' can mean 'kind', but it can also mean being true to one's nature, an idea followed up in the 'trewe' of the third line. It is not clear, therefore, whether there is mutual kindness and fidelity, or whether the Wife acted like any other wife anywhere in the world, with all that that might imply. Whether or not it is a threat or a promise depends on what one is inclined to think about wives. It is, therefore, a trick that relies on the reader's point of view, and one that will be repeated in the tale the Wife goes on to tell.

THE TALE

The tale of the Wife of Bath is a romance, a story of adventure set in King Arthur's court. It is, however, an unusual romance, not simply because it begins with a rape, but because something is done about the crime. The rapist knight is sentenced to death but, even more unusually, the queen and her attendant ladies intervene and ask for the knight's fate to be handed over to them. Instead of execution, they want to set the knight a task, and if he is successful, he will be permitted to live. His task is to answer a question: What is it that women most desire? (*CT* III 905). He has 12 months in which to find the answer, but with his year almost expired he begins to despair of reaching any conclusion. His last hope is an old woman he encounters in a forest, 'A fouler wight [creature] ther may no man devyse [imagine]' (*CT* III 999). This 'loathly lady' is willing to solve the puzzle for him, but in return he must promise to grant whatever request she later makes. The deal is done, and the knight returns to the queen's court ready to give his answer:

> This knyght ne stood nat stille as doth a <u>best</u>,   beast
> But to his questioun anon answerde
> With manly voys, that al the court it herde:
> 'My <u>lige</u> lady, generally,' quod he,   liege
> 'Wommen desiren to have <u>sovereynetee</u>   sovereignty
> As wel over <u>hir</u> housbond as hir love,   their
> And for to <u>been in maistrie hym above</u>.'   have the upper hand
>
> (*CT* III 1034–40)

As he stands uncowed ('nat stille as doth a best') before the court of women, addressing them with his confident 'manly' voice, it is clear that the knight might have returned with the right answer, but that he has learned nothing about what 'sovereynetee' for women really means, or how it should be a part of his own life. However, his education is not yet at an end, for the loathly lady interrupts the general murmur of agreement in order to remind the knight of the promise he had made to her: he had agreed to grant whatever request she would later make, and she asks that he should now take her as his wife.

THE CHOICE

The knight, whose crime had been sexual force against a woman, now finds himself compelled to go to bed with his aged wife, expressing outrage and horror as he goes. Her response is a beautiful speech about true 'gentillesse', the virtue that transcends lineage, wealth, age, and beauty (*CT* III. 1109–212), but, suspecting that this is a man who is swayed more by 'worldly appetit' (*CT* III. 1218) than words, she then offers him a choice: would he like her to be old, foul, and faithful, or would he prefer her to be young, fair, and possibly unfaithful. In the source for the story the choice had been fair by day or fair by night, but the Wife has introduced an element of misogyny, for the standard medieval line was that beautiful women would inevitably betray their men. It is exactly the kind of thing that the old husbands were accused of saying (*CT* III.253–6) and it now becomes a final test for the knight.

His response is very telling, for he becomes, for the first time in the tale, both thoughtful and resigned, arriving at the right answer this time not because he has made a deal with a faerie in the forest, but because he has given the question painful consideration:

This knyght <u>avyseth hym</u> and sore <u>siketh</u>,	deliberates; sighs
But atte laste he seyde in this manere:	
'My lady and my love, and wyf so deere,	
I <u>put me in</u> youre wise governance;	submit myself to
Cheseth <u>youreself</u> which may be moost <u>plesance</u>	for yourself; pleasure
And moost honour to yow and me also.	
I do no <u>fors</u> <u>the wheither</u> of the two,	force; which
For as yow liketh, it <u>suffiseth me</u>.'	is enough for me

(*CT* III 1228–35)

It is a polite speech that puts her needs and desires before his own, and his willingness to leave the choice to his new wife is expressed in a significant way, for he declares that he will 'do no fors the wheither of the two'. This is frequently translated as 'I don't care' in a manner that leads some critics to condemn his reply as sulky dismissal. However, it is a key moment in his rehabilitation, for his original crime had been one of force against a woman: 'By verray force, he rafte hire mayden-hed [took her virginity]' (*CT* III 888). The fact, therefore, that his submission is phrased in terms of absence of force is a promising sign. Certainly, the loathly lady is willing to take it as such. Having refused to make the misogynistic choice and having surrendered 'maistrie' (*CT* III. 1236) to his wife, the knight has passed the test. The no-longer loathly lady now emerges from behind the curtain:

'Kys me,' quod she, 'we be no lenger <u>wrothe</u>,	angry
For, <u>by my trouthe</u>, I wol be to yow bothe –	upon my word
This is to <u>seyn</u>, ye, bothe fair and good.	say
I prey to God that I <u>moote sterven wood</u>,	should die insane
<u>But</u> I to yow be <u>also</u> good and trewe	unless; as
As evere was <u>wyf</u>, <u>syn</u> that the world was newe.	woman; since

(*CT* III 1239–44)

It is a happy ending, with a wife who will be both beautiful and good. However, the knight would do well to read the small print, for his wife declares that she will be as good and true as any woman ever has been since the world was new. The wife when the world was new was, of course, Eve, the frontrunner in the 'Book of Wicked Wives', but, as the Wife of Bath has argued throughout, the interpretation of events depends on the teller. If the knight has truly learned his lesson about women, then there is no threat in the promise that his wife will be as good a woman as Eve. If, on the other hand, his attitude towards women has remained fundamentally the same, then it becomes a promise of a very different kind. In the end, he will get the life he deserves to have, depending on what he chooses to see around him. The final words of his lady make this clear: 'Cast up the curtyn, looke how that it is' (*CT* III 1249).

THE CLERK'S PROLOGUE AND TALE

The story of 'Patient Griselda' was well-known throughout Europe in the Middle Ages. It is a tale of female virtue, which the Clerk of Oxford, a scholar learned in the kinds of stories that have infuriated the Wife of Bath, chooses to offer his fellow pilgrims. The Host twice implores him to tell a 'myrie [merry] tale' (*CT* IV 9, 15), but this tale is very far from merry. It is a relentless account of almost unbearable suffering and almost inhuman endurance in which a woman is tested in the most extreme way.

In the beginning, it appears that we might be about to encounter some kind of medieval romance or fairy tale. A young marquis is urged by his people to marry, and he decides that his wife will be a poor girl from the village. In such stories it is common for the girl to be tested and to triumph in each test, at which point she is revealed to be of noble birth, and she and her husband live happily ever after. But this is not the turn that the *Clerk's Tale* takes, and from the first moment there is something disquieting about this husband and this marriage:

Therwith he was, to speke as of lynage,	lineage
The gentilleste yborn of Lumbardye,	most noble; Lombardy
A fair persone, and strong, and yong of age,	handsome
And ful of honour and of curteisye;	
Discreet ynogh his contree for to gye,	with sufficient prudence; govern

> Save in somme thynges that he was to blame;
> And Walter was this yonge lordes name.
> (*CT* IV 71–7)

Walter has no shortage of pedigree, and he has all the traditional attributes, but doubt creeps in towards the end of the stanza. 'Ynogh' is an interesting word in Middle English because it can mean both 'enough' and 'an abundance'. We might have expected a ruler like Walter to have a great deal of prudence, but the vague, disconcerting reference to the 'some things in which he was to blame' casts its shadow back over the rest of the description and provides a sense of foreboding about what is to come.

GRISELDA

What comes is Griselda, in her turn described as 'fair ynogh' (*CT* IV 209), but her real attraction for Walter is her virtue:

> But for to speke of vertuous beautee,
> Thanne was she <u>oon the faireste</u> under sonne;   the fairest of all
> (*CT* IV 211–12)

The initial 'but' and 'thanne' construction here appears to indicate that her beauty was of the 'sufficient' rather than 'abundant' kind, it being the case that it is her virtue that is her most attractive attribute. She is not, however, a bland female paragon. Chaucer greatly expands his source to linger over his account of Griselda hurrying over her numerous chores, keen to stand in the doorway like her friends and catch a glimpse of the new bride of the marquis going past. Griselda is a humble girl, with innocent desires, though the reference to God's grace being sent into the 'oxes stalle' (*CT* IV 207) would have triggered thoughts of the humility of the Virgin Mary in a medieval audience. The same echoes are heard when Walter arrives and summons Griselda:

> And as she wolde over hir <u>thresshfold gon</u>,   threshold; go
> The <u>markys</u> cam and <u>gan</u> hire for to calle;   marquis; began
> And she set doun hir water pot <u>anon</u>,   at once
> Biside the thresshfold, in an oxes stalle,

And doun upon hir knes she gan to falle,
And with <u>sad contenance</u> kneleth <u>stille</u>,   solemn expression;
                                                     quietly

Til she had herd what was the lordes wille.
              (CT IV 288–94)

The kneeling, the obedience to the will of the 'lord', the ox's stall, are all evocative of Mary, and even the water pot is nicely biblical. Her 'sad' expression does not mean what it does in Modern English, for 'sad' is one of those words that has changed in meaning over time. In the Middle Ages it means something closer to 'steadfast' than 'sorrowful'. Griselda waits in calm solemnity while Walter states his desires.

WALTER AND GOD

By logical extension, if we see the humility of Mary in Griselda's response, then Walter could be an amalgamation of the Angel Gabriel and God, and it is certainly true that in the testing of Griselda that follows, some critics have seen in him the demanding deity of the Old Testament, trying the patience of a Job or a Jonah. However, Griselda's patience, powerful as it is, does not turn Walter into God. There is a great deal of difference between the kind of biblical testing that allowed its recipients to display the virtues that God already knew they would display and the kind of demand for proof of obedience that motivates Walter. God's foreknowledge and Walter's neediness are not at all the same thing, in spite of the power over life and death that Walter wields. Nowhere in the tale is there any admiration for Walter's actions, or any sympathy. He is, instead, roundly condemned by the narrator for wanting to put Griselda to the test:

He hadde <u>assayed</u> hire ynogh bifore,   tested
And <u>foond</u> hire evere good; what neded it   found
Hire for to <u>tempte</u>, and alwey moore and moore,   test
Though som men preise it for a <u>subtil wit</u>?   clever mind
              (CT IV 456–9)

Indeed, the use of the word 'tempte' and the use of the word 'subtil' are associated in most medieval works not with God, but with the demonic serpent who beguiled Eve. This is not, therefore, a symbolic story in which Walter stands in for divinity. While it may be read at various levels, in none of them is Walter God.

THE PEOPLE

Walter exerts his authority initially on his people, demanding that they unquestioningly accept his choice of bride, and proceeding to inflict upon them the daughter of the poorest man in an already poor village. The ladies in waiting are not happy about handling Griselda's rags, but the girl herself is quickly transformed and is declared 'so deere' (*CT* IV 400) to the people. It is the same kind of emotional response that they had given when Walter had made his demand, and they had unanimously assented with 'hertely wyl [cordially]' (*CT* IV 176). They need an heir and will agree to anything to secure one; and, later, when Walter prepares to take a new bride, they forget Griselda and place their hopes for the succession in the younger model. Their readiness to change their minds as it suits them is condemned within the text itself:

'O <u>stormy</u> peple! <u>Unsad</u> and evere untrewe!	turbulent; inconstant
Ay <u>undiscreet</u> and chaungynge as a <u>fane</u>!	undiscerning; weathervane
Delitynge evere in <u>rumbul</u> that is newe,	upheaval
For lyk the moone ay wexe ye and wane!'	
(*CT* IV 995–8)	

The repetition of the prefix 'un-' emphasises that the people are being measured against a standard which they fail to achieve. The lines are full of movement: the weathervane in the wind, the waxing and waning moon, and the evocative 'rumbul', sometimes translated as 'rumour', but really a term that embraces all kinds of shifting movement. They are not calm, constant, steadfast. They are not, in short, Griselda. They are a reminder, when Griselda's steadfast endurance becomes almost too much to bear for the audience, that we do not like inconstancy either.

OBEDIENCE

For Griselda, the price of marriage to Walter is her complete obedience to his will. Such obedience was, for the woman, part of any marriage vow, but Walter does not hide the reality of what such a promise would mean. He asserts the primacy of his will and demands not just unquestioning obedience, but wholehearted acceptance of whatever he chooses to inflict upon his wife:

'I seye this : be ye redy with good herte
To al my lust, and that I frely may,   desire
As me best thynketh, do yow laughe or smerte,   as seems best to
                                                        me; make;
                                                        suffer

And nevere ye to grucche it, nyght ne day?   complain about
And eek whan I sey "ye", ne sey nat "nay,"
Neither by word ne frowning contenance?   face
Swere this, and heere I swere oure alliance.'
                              (CT IV 351–7)

It is not a matter of obeying only until obedience becomes unpleasant, or only while the demands are reasonable. As for Griselda's answer, it shows that she understands this, for she takes the hypothetical 'smerte' of his demand and raises the bar considerably: 'In werk [action] ne thoght, I nyl [will not] yow disobeye, / For to be deed [even to the point of death], though me were looth to deye.' (CT IV 363–4). Her life is precious to her, but she will give it up for Walter, if that is what he requires of her.

What Walter requires of her, however, is more than her own life. He will ask, first of all, for the life of their newborn daughter, and then for the life of their infant son. It is a ruse, aimed to test Griselda's obedience, but Griselda is unaware of this. When she surrenders her children, she does so believing that they are going to die. Nevertheless, 'she noght ameved [changed] / Neither in word, or chiere [expression], or contenaunce' (CT IV 498–9). Unlike the inconstant and adaptable populace, Griselda shows not a flicker of change in her demeanour. She does, however, meekly ask the henchman to allow her to kiss her child before it is taken from her. She lays the baby in her lap, blessing it and kissing it, with 'ful sad face' (CT IV 552), before commending it to Christ, for the child, she says, is dying for her sake. Once again, there are echoes of Mary, and the medieval tradition of lullaby lyrics in which Mary soothed the baby who would die on the cross. It is a moment of great stillness and of total sacrifice.

PATIENCE

However, while Griselda can bear her loss, many of the critics cannot. The kind of virtue that can permit the deaths of innocent children is not easily viewed as a virtue. Active virtues, such as courage, are more easily appreciated than the passive kinds of goodness, and, even among these, patience is perhaps the least attractive. It is a virtue for those who find themselves at the bottom of life's heap, because those who are winning have no need of patience. It is a virtue for the losing and the lost, and it offers not a way out, but a way of accepting the loss. What Chaucer does in the *Clerk's Tale* is force us to take a look at patience, not in action, because patience does not act, but in submission, and there can be no greater submission for a mother than to surrender her children to what she imagines will be their death.

Having tested Griselda in this way twice, Walter is still not satisfied. He has thrown love in front of patience and Griselda has not yielded; he now decides to test patience with humiliation and declares that their marriage is at an end and that Griselda must prepare for the arrival of a new bride. Still Griselda's resolve does not break. She accepts this news as calmly as she had accepted Walter's previous tests, only warning him that he should not 'prikke with no tormentynge' his new bride, as he 'han doon mo [others]' (*CT* IV 1038–9). For a moment, it might look like a direct accusation, but 'mo' does not mean 'me'. It is, instead, a reference to unspecified 'others', an acknowledgement of the torment she has undergone, without acknowledging the pain, for Griselda remains, 'ay sad and constant as a wal' (*CT* IV 1047). The simile is Walter's own. He has assailed Griselda, and she has withstood the tests. It is not, however, that she is simply 'made of stone'. A wall exists to defend something more vulnerable, and while we have seen Griselda submit to all of Walter's plans, the cost of that submission is finally revealed. The children are not dead, and the bride is not a bride, but the couple's own daughter. The news causes Griselda to faint clean away as her children are restored to her:

And in hire <u>swough</u> so <u>sadly</u> holdeth she	swoon; tightly
Hire children two, whan she <u>gan hem t'embrace</u>,	embraced them
That with greet <u>sleighte</u> and greet difficultee	ingenuity
The children from hire arm they <u>gonne arace</u>.	tore away

(*CT* IV 1100–3)

We see past the wall of steadfast resolve as the unconscious Griselda clasps her children to her and will not let them go. The word 'sadly' that had described her steadfast lack of emotion during all her tribulations is now used in a different context, to describe the tightness of her grip as her unconscious self refuses to relinquish the children.

THE MEANING OF PATIENCE

The shift in meaning of 'sadly' at the end of the tale is only one of the words that has been subtly displaced in the course of the narrative. The Clerk, being a scholar, has more of a professional connection to words than the other pilgrims, and it is appropriate, therefore, that questions about 'meaning' should somehow lie at the heart of his tale. Fundamentally, it is a perplexing story, the response to which cannot simply be that patience is a virtue and that all women should be as patient as Griselda. Nor can the response be as straightforward as that found in the final 'Lenvoy de Chaucer' in which 'archewyves [quintessential women]' (*CT* IV 1195) are urged to stand against, argue with, and torment their husbands. These stalwart matronly 'camels' and ferocious female 'tigers' (*CT* IV 1196, 1199) are certainly easier to deal with than Griselda, which is why the narrative turns towards them in the end, in the hope that women can be pushed back into familiar roles. Griselda, however, cannot be pigeon-holed.

The Clerk explicitly says that his story is told,

... nat for that wyves sholde	not so that; women
Folwen Grisilde as in humylitee	follow
For it were inportable, though they wolde	unbearable; even if
(*CT* IV 1143–5)	

However, what does this mean? Certainly, the suffering of Griselda has been almost unbearable to watch and would be almost unbearable for anyone to endure, but the Clerk may have something else in mind too, for Griselda is an 'inportable' problem for the Clerk as well. She is beyond doubt not a 'bad' wife, nor does she fit into the easy category of what it means to be a 'good' one. Walter stops testing her in the end, not because she has managed to live up to what is required by his tests, but because she constantly surpasses them in ways he can neither understand nor control. His cry of, 'This is ynogh, Grisilde myn' (*CT* IV 1051) signals this: her patience has not been 'enough' in our modern sense, but rather far too much for him to bear any longer. The clerks, the controllers of words, write the texts and define what it is to be good or bad as a woman, as the Wife of Bath argues (see p. 52) but Griselda, a woman of very few words, cannot be contained or fitted into any kind of box.

When Walter had demanded her unquestioning obedience to his will, Griselda had responded, 'as ye wole youreself, right so wol I' (*CT* IV 361). What might have seemed initially like simple agreement is now discovered to be so much more, for this goes beyond a simple 'yes'. It refuses the dichotomy of dictating husband and obedient wife, insisting instead on only one will, changing the fundamental roles even as she appears to agree to adopt them in a way that makes her equal to her husband. This is Griselda's achievement. She does not 'win' in the way that the final envoy urges, because, in reality, neither woman nor man 'win' that way. Instead, resolved on her course, difficult as it might have been for the reader to accept, she slowly emerges from her tribulations with her children unharmed. There has been too much suffering and too much loss for this to feel like a triumph, but they have all survived. If, in the end, the reader is not sure quite where to place Griselda among the available categories of 'womanhood', then that is no bad thing. Real patience, as we have seen, does not involve sitting prettily like a monument. It requires a willingness to accept not fully understanding, and it requires accepting that matters will not be as we would choose them to be. In the end, this applies to the reader as much as to anyone else.

THE FRANKLIN'S PROLOGUE AND TALE

Medieval franklins were country gentlemen, often reasonably rich and with responsibilities that included overseeing the law courts, ensuring the collection of taxes, and even acting as member of Parliament. Chaucer's Franklin, as we see him in the *General Prologue*, has done all these things, but they take up only a few lines of a description that otherwise focusses on his love of fine living. The table always stands ready in his hall, laden with the best foods in season, not just for himself, but for the many people he wishes to entertain, for, 'It snewed [snowed] in his hous of mete and drynke' (*GP* 345). With his ruddy face and snow-white hair, he looks benignly like a daisy (*GP* 332–3). For some critics, there is too much conspicuous consumption in his portrait, while for others the Franklin is the embodiment of hospitable country life. What he is not, however, is a nobleman, and the *Franklin's Prologue and Tale* reveals a speaker not so much at ease in the world as the portrait of the Franklin might initially suggest. He interrupts the more aristocratic Squire in order to praise his gentility and becomes focussed on 'gentillesse' and the desirability, especially for his son, of spending his time with those of 'gentil' rank (*CTV* 674, 688–94). His tale, when he gets around to telling it, will concern itself with the true nature of 'noble' behaviour. It is also very much the tale of someone caught in the 'in-between', aristocratic desires and everyday life vying in its telling.

THE VOICE OF THE FRANKLIN

The Franklin is a self-conscious speaker. We first hear his voice when he interrupts the Squire and he then comments on his own style of speaking in the prologue to his tale. What is said, or, more precisely, how it is said, is a matter of great concern to the Franklin, and he announces himself here as 'a burel [unlearned] man' (*CTV* 716). However, what appears at first to be a modest beginning might in fact be a more complicated device. In spite of his protests that he is not a man who engages with rhetoric, he uses a surprising number of rhetorical devices. The very act of claiming that he does not know 'colours [rhetorical ornaments]' (*CTV* 723) and referring us instead to the 'colours' of the flowers in the field, is a rhetorical device in itself. He refers to Mount Parnassus, the home of the muses, and gives the great Roman orator, Cicero, his full name (*CTV* 721–2) while in the very act of claiming never to have read him.

However, the effect is not of a natural public speaker, but rather of a man who is trying hard to impress. There is no need to refer to Cicero as 'Marcus Tullius' and the dismissal of 'colours' would have been more powerful had he stopped after referring to the flowers, rather than pursuing his theme all the way to the men who 'dye or peynte' (*CTV* 725). He is like a man who thinks that, 'Unaccustomed as I am to public speaking' is a good way to begin a speech, and what he would really like is to be admired for his untutored skill. His tale contains similar moments of overdone rhetoric that he feels the need to flag for an audience less 'learned' than himself. He might tell us that, 'th'orisonte [horizon] hath reft [robbed] the sonne hys lyght', but he will follow up immediately with, 'This is as muche to seye [say] as it was nyght' (*CT* V 1017–18). He stands, therefore, on the cusp between two different worlds: an aristocratic world of nobility, knights, and ladies, and the workaday world of men and women, coming to terms with what nobility of behaviour means for them.

COURTLY MARRIAGE

The very first words of the Franklin's tale display the same tension between the lofty and the prosaic as his prologue had done: 'In Armorik, that called is Britayne' (*CT* V 729). 'Armorica' is the ancient name for the northern coast of France and would have been entirely in keeping with a romance narrative, but we are no sooner there than we are transported to plain old Brittany. The Franklin has already told us that he will tell a Breton lay (*CT* V 709–15) – an old-style romance of love and adventure, with usually a little bit of magic thrown in for good measure – and he is as good as his word, at least for the first 14 lines. In the space of those lines, a knight falls in love with a beautiful, high-born lady, accomplishes many chivalric exploits in her name, suffers for her love, earns her pity for his noble distress, and is finally rewarded by her acceptance of him in marriage. It is a medieval romance in miniature, but there is a vast quantity of tale still to come. In fact, the Franklin has chosen to give us a romance that begins where most other medieval romances stop. He has passed over the accounts of knightly adventure and will give us instead an account of the marriage that follows. It is a brave undertaking, for one of the difficulties of medieval courtly love (see p. 95) was the shift in power from lady to knight upon marriage. While the pair remained unmarried, the power was, in theory at least, wholly in the hands of the lady, who could command her knight as she chose; as a wife, however, the lady would be at the command of her husband, and her rights would be only those she derived from being, in legal terms, his property.

The lady, whose name, we will later learn, is Dorigen, having decided to accept the knight as her lord, surrenders power to him. As for the knight, he instantly makes a radical decision, and vows that

... nevere in al his lyf he, day ne nyght,	
Ne sholde upon hym take no <u>maistrie</u>	dominance
<u>Agayn</u> hir wyl, ne <u>kithe</u> hire jalousie,	against; show
But hire obeye, and folwe hir wyl in al,	
As any lovere to his lady <u>shal</u>,	ought

(CT V 746–50)

It is an unexpected turn in what has been, until now, a wholly conventional (if very compressed) romance. The part of the story that is normally briskly passed over, or omitted completely, as the romance comes to a halt, will be the focus of the Franklin's tale. Even more strikingly, the 'maistrie' that had been the Wife of Bath's fantasy possession in marriage, is here offered as a matter of shared responsibility between husband and wife. It is a most promising start. The only fly in the ointment is the knight's residual insistence that he must keep 'the name of soveraynetee, / That wolde he have for shame of his degree [status as a knight].' (CT V 751–2). That the world should still think of him as sovereign in this marriage perhaps does not seem like a great deal to ask, given that he has otherwise surrendered so much. However, it introduces a niggling doubt in that it bases their marriage upon an illusion, and illusion will become a very real danger in this tale.

However, the Franklin is not concerned with such matters at this point. He has a few things he wants to say about marriage, many of them sensible. Unlike the Wife of Bath, he does not wrest 'mastery' from one partner to the other. Instead he speaks of the desire on both sides, 'nat to been constreyned as a thral [slave]' (CT V 769). He emphasises the need for patience rather than rigour, and for understanding in the face of the many mistakes that either partner might make. However, he runs into difficulties at the point at which he attempts to define these brave new roles:

Heere may men seen an humble, wys <u>accord</u>;	agreement
Thus hath she take hir servant and hir lord –	
Servant in love, and lord in mariage.	
Thanne was he bothe in lordshipe and <u>servage</u>.	servitude
Servage? Nay, but in lordshipe above,	
<u>Sith</u> he hath bothe his lady and his love;	since
His lady, <u>certes</u>, and his wyf also,	certainly
The which that lawe of love <u>acordeth to</u>.	consents

(CT V 791–8)

The term 'servant' has come to him from the courtly love tradition in which the man must serve his lady; the term lord, with all that it implies about dominion, is the language of marriage. He wants, of course, to break free of this master–slave terminology, but the language he has inherited is not allowing him to do so and instead he shifts the terms backwards and forwards as if they might somehow transform into something else. He realises himself that he is going nowhere and questions his own use of the terms ('Servage? Nay') before switching his attention to the female roles and discovering the same unhelpful division in 'lady' and 'wyf'. His attempt at describing this 'humble, wise agreement' collapses under its own weight as it becomes clear that he does not possess even the basic terminology to take it forward and seeks refuge instead in a vague reference to 'the law of love'. The ground-breaking 'accord' dwindles into 'acordeth' as the revolutionary noun becomes a law-abiding verb and the Franklin abandons his attempt at describing this experiment in marriage. For the couple, however, it is the life they choose to lead, whether anyone can describe it or not.

ROCKS

In spite of the lexical difficulties of their union, Dorigen and her husband, whom we now discover is named Arveragus, live blissfully together for more than a year until new adventures take the knight across the channel to England. Dorigen's reaction to his absence is extreme and she, 'moorneth [mourns], waketh, wayleth, fasteth, pleyneth [complains]' (*CTV* 819). In fact, she embarks on a whole-hearted grief-stricken lament of several years' duration. It is no easy task to console Dorigen, but little by little the efforts of her friends take effect, in the same way, the narrator tells us, that a stone will eventually bear the imprint of repeated engraving (*CTV* 830–1). It is the first connection between Dorigen and stone in the tale, and it signals a rigidity of mind that will define her, most notably in connection with another mass of stone: the dangerous rocks beneath the sea that separates her from her husband.

The rocks become Dorigen's obsession. Standing on top of the cliff, she watches the ships and fixates on the 'grisly rokkes blake [black]' (*CTV* 859). Her terror is without bounds and she is led to question the God who would create a universe so full of dangers. The rocks, to her,

'... semen rather a foul confusion	seem
Of werk than any fair creacion	
Of swich a parfit wys God and a stable,	perfect; wise
Why han ye wroght this werk unresonable?'	have; made; contrary to reason

(*CT* V 869–72)

It is the age-old problem of the existence of evil and suffering in a world that is said to be created by an all-powerful and benign deity. If there is an order to things, and a divine plan, then how, Dorigen wonders, can the rocks be part of such a plan? It is a question that interests Chaucer in his other works, too, specifically in his translation of Boethius. There, the answer provided by Lady Philosophy is that we are too close to the things of this world and, therefore, incapable of seeing the plan that structures the universe. In fact, prone to focussing on details when we cannot see the whole, we have a tendency to misconstrue the importance or relevance of things. Certainly, Arveragus will not founder on the rocks and die, but Dorigen's obsession with the rocks is, instead, a very real danger. She thinks that she knows what the plan ought to be, and that she has identified life's perils. However, the tale will show how little she understands, and that danger is as likely to arrive in a pretty garden as in a storm-tossed sea.

AURELIUS

In an attempt to quieten Dorigen's troubled mind, her friends encourage her to leave the cliffs and venture into a beautiful garden nearby. Among those gathered to sing and dance is Aurelius, a handsome squire, 'fressher ... and jolyer' (*CT* V 927) than the month of May, and capable of composing songs and poems, all of which he dedicates to Dorigen, for it emerges that he has loved her from afar for more than two years. Unable to declare his love, he has suffered in silence as courtly convention demands. Now, however, he seizes his moment and begs for her merciful love. Dorigen's reaction is slightly strange, at least in the way it appears to consist of contradictory elements. Her initial disbelief is palpably hostile, the 'she saids' introducing a slightly menacing pause between each phrase that she directs at her would-be lover:

'Is this youre wyl,' quod she, 'and sey ye thus?   what you want
Nevere erst,' quod she, 'ne wiste I what ye mente.   before; did I know
But now, Aurelie, I knowe youre entente,   intention
By thilke God that yaf me soule and lyf,   that; gave
Ne shal I nevere been untrewe wyf ...   unfaithful
Taak this for fynal answere as of me.'

(CT V 980–7)

The repeated use of 'never', the accumulated negatives, and the scathing use of 'Aurelie', all make for an answer that is nothing if not clear. It is not, however, 'final' as she claims, for she immediately supplies an addendum, 'in pley' (CTV 988). She will, she says, agree to be his love (CTV 990), providing that he removes all the rocks, 'stoon by stoon' (CTV 993) from the coast of Brittany, pledging her 'trouthe' to love him best of any man if he completes the task (CTV 997–8). She then launches into another tirade, similar to her initial response, in which she commands Aurelius to forget his folly, demanding to know what business he thinks he has in loving another man's wife, a man moreover who can have her body whenever he pleases (CTV 1000–5).

It is a hard-hitting response, or, at least, a hard-hitting response for two-thirds of the time. The middle section, 'in pley', has, however, caused great critical difficulty. As Dorigen has scarcely stopped weeping in the years that her husband has been abroad, it seems unlikely that there is any attempt at humour here. Flirtation also seems unlikely given that the task is sandwiched between two brutal rejections; but the fact that it is a task is key. Having been a courtly lady for so long, and now inhabiting a role so new that even describing it has proved difficult, it seems that Dorigen has lapsed back into what she knows. Squires on their knees must be given tasks, and so she 'plays' the courtly lady once again. In the source for this tale, the lady had asked that a garden be made to bloom in January. For Dorigen, however, the task is all about the safety of her husband, and it is wholly her belief that what she asks should be, as Aurelius himself acknowledges, 'an inpossible [impossibility]' (CTV 1009).

A 'MAGIC' TRICK

Aurelius's brother, meanwhile, studying the sciences and inspired by a book on 'magyk natureel [natural science]' (CTV 1125) remembers the tales he has heard of 'tregetours [magicians]' (*CT* 1143), capable of making whole castles and ships appear and disappear. Such a person, he decides, is what his brother needs, and Aurelius soon finds himself in the house of a 'magicien' (*CT* V 1184) watching a vision of himself and Dorigen dancing. The two men reach a very precise agreement: that the magician will remove all the rocks not just from the coast of Brittany, but also from the rivers Gironde and Seine, an added detail that leads to the magician raising difficulties and his prices (*CT* V 1221–5). The exchange has all the hallmarks of a legal contract and a business deal rather than employment of the mystical arts, and the magician some-how becomes a 'clerk' along the way. Armorica is becoming Brittany once again as the clerk arrives at the coast equipped not with a wand, but with all the paraphernalia of a medieval astronomer:

His <u>tables Tolletanes</u> forth he brought,	astrological tables
Ful wel corrected, ne ther lakked nought,	
Neither his <u>collect ne his expans yeeris</u>,	tables for single years and twenty
Ne his <u>rootes</u>, ne his othere <u>geeris</u>,	root values; equipment
<u>As been</u> his <u>centris</u> and his <u>argumentz</u>	such as; centres; angles
And his <u>proporcioneles convenientz</u>	tables of proportions
For his equacions in every thyng.	

(*CT* V 1273–9)

This is highly technical astronomical terminology and very clearly maths, rather than magic. The focus in the lines that follow is on the moon, and therefore the tides, so that it emerges that the clerk has somehow calculated the moment when the rocks would naturally be covered by high water. At any rate, we are told, 'It semed that alle the rokkes were aweye' (*CT* V 1296). The important word here is 'seemed'. Whatever has been accomplished, and regardless of how it has been accomplished, the rocks have not been removed stone by stone as Dorigen had demanded, nor have they been removed as stipulated in Aurelius's contract with the clerk. No one dwells on this, however, as Aurelius races to tell Dorigen the news that the rocks are 'gone'.

DORIGEN

It takes Aurelius 26 lines of insidious dodging and weaving to get to the point. He reminds Dorigen of his suffering, claims he has only done as he was commanded, reminds her of her promise, and claims that he is thinking only of her honour. Interestingly, he does not restate her promise, but refers to it in such a way that its content is taken as given: 'ye woot [know] what ye han hight [promised]', 'Ye woot right wel what ye bihighten [have promised] me' (*CTV* 1323, 1327). But what has Dorigen promised? Reverting to her role as courtly lady, she had issued Aurelius a task for which he would be rewarded with her love. But as a courtly promise in a courtly context, 'love' does not naturally equate to sex. However, Dorigen does not challenge the assumption; nor does she go to the coast to look. Faced with the news, the rock-obsessed Dorigen is simply 'astoned' (*CT* V 1339), and, in her astonishment, she once again looks for some time-honoured model of female behaviour. At the outset of her marriage she had been granted equality, which she had interpreted as 'so large a reyne [rein]' (*CTV* 755). But a long rein is not equality, and it gradually becomes clear that Dorigen is not perhaps the ideal candidate for this brave new kind of marriage. It is possible that even her name embodies the inflexible force of rock, the Droguen being a prominent rock off the coast of Brittany.

At any rate, Dorigen's response to unexpected threat is to retreat to something she thinks she knows. Distraught for the safety of her husband, she had, when Aurelius first appeared, added an interlude of courtly ladydom to her refusal. Faced with Aurelius again, she retreats further back, seeking a role model among the threatened women of antiquity. In her own mind the choice is simple – 'deeth or elles dishonour' (*CTV* 1358) – and she mentally scours the ancient tales for female suicides. There is, of course, Lucrece (see p. 171), and she considers, too, the various women of the ancient world who jumped from cliffs or into wells to escape male force (*CTV* 1368–413). There are more than enough of these, but still not enough for the three-day lament that Dorigen has in mind. Her list, therefore, continues with an account of those women who preferred to die along with their husbands, or killed themselves rather than remarry (*CTV* 1414–50). Soon, however, she has drifted to those who simply built their husbands fine tombs, like Artemisia, or even the innocent Bilia, who was able to tolerate her husband's famously bad breath, on the assumption that all men must smell that way (*CTV* 1451–6). It is a long list, but even antiquity notably runs out of stories that advocate suicide, and the tragic becomes comic as the tale dwindles in its customary fashion from death to halitosis.

TROUTHE

The response of Dorigen's husband is similarly ambiguous. Faced with his distraught wife, Arveragus's initial reaction is a very human: 'Is ther oght [anything] elles, Dorigen, but this?' (*CTV* 1469). There is almost palpable relief as he realises that no one has, in fact, died, and that all this trauma is simply related to a promise. However, the tale's characteristic movement from Armorica to Brittany now swings the other way as Arveragus begins to think about the keeping of promises. Knights in romance narratives are bound by their oaths, and his declaration in the face of Dorigen's predicament is a very noble assertion of such behaviour: 'Trouthe is the hyeste [highest] thyng that man may kepe' (*CTV* 1479). But 'trouthe' is such a big word. For the Middle Ages it encompasses all kinds of 'truth' – everything from universal principles to the simple plighting of troth – and while 'man' can simply be shorthand for all of humanity, the feeling in this line is that Arveragus is clinging, like Dorigen earlier in the tale, to a romance-genre life that he understands. Keeping promises, no matter what, is what knights in romances do. It does not matter that 'truth' here is immensely complicated. The rocks are not really gone, the wording of Dorigen's promise was ambiguous, and there is a marriage vow that, in reality, would supersede all other promises, but for Arveragus the way through the whole mess is a rigid adherence to the keeping of one's word at the most basic level. The result is that a still weeping Dorigen is dispatched to the arms of Aurelius, commanded by her husband not to make a fuss, 'up [upon] peyne of deeth' (*CTV* 1481).

GENTILLESSE

Aurelius has been watching the home of Dorigen, which is no longer the 'castel faste by the see' (*CTV* 847) of the early tale and has dwindled instead to a 'hous' in the busiest street in town (*CTV* 1502–7). The fact that she has been sent to him by a husband intent on her keeping her 'trouthe' strikes him as an act of 'franchise [generosity]

and alle gentillesse' (*CT* V 1524), and he is moved to declare that
a squire can 'doon a gentil dede / As wel as kan a knyght' (*CT* V
1543–4). He sends Dorigen home unharmed and goes to face the
clerk, whom, it now occurs to him, he has not paid and has no way
of paying. But the clerk is inspired by the actions of the other two
men and chooses to release Aurelius from his debt:

'Everich of yow <u>dide gentilly</u> til oother.	each; behaved nobly to
Thou art a squire, and he is a knyght;	
But God forbede, for his blisful myght,	
<u>But if a clerk koude doon</u> a gentil dede	if a clerk could not do
As wel as any of yow, <u>it is no drede</u>!'	there is no doubt
(*CT* V 1608–12)	

The words, 'gentilly', 'gentil', 'gentillesse' are liberally applied by
the men to themselves and to one another in their final speeches as
the vie to be equals in virtue. But is this really noble conduct? The
clerk has not removed the rocks, Aurelius knows what he was really
promised, and Arveragus has surrendered the traumatised Dorigen
to harm; and yet it seems that the way out of the great mess that
has been created by a few ill-chosen words is to keep a promise, no
matter how badly phrased or wrongly interpreted it might be. Such
oath-keeping can only be 'trouthe' in its most debased form, and the
'gentillesse' that arises from it is equally debased, but it is enough for
them all to muddle their way back to positions of safety. Dorigen,
whom we had last seen on her knees thanking Aurelius, has been
demoted from wifely equal, and will now instead be cherished, 'as
though she were a queene' (*CT* V 1554), a far more conventional and,
notably, passive role.

It is all presented by the Franklin as a great success as he brings his
tale to an end with the question, 'Which was the mooste fre [gener-
ous], as thynketh yow?' (*CT* V 1622). Such a *demande* is a traditional
way of ending a courtly narrative and in Chaucer's source for this tale
the question is followed by a debate that eventually finds in favour
of the husband. However, the question of 'generosity' in the circumstances here is not easy to apply, or easy to answer. It is notable that
the Franklin provides no answer as he shuts down his narrative with
a firm, 'I kan [know] namoore [no more]; my tale is at an ende' (*CT*
V 1624). The failed marriage-experiment of Dorigen and Arveragus

has been similarly dispatched with a terse, 'Of thise two folk ye gete of me namoore' (*CT*V 1556). The tale that had initially promised so much *more* – a narrative that began where others had ended; a whole new way of men and women living together – has dwindled, like so much else within it, to something more ordinary. We had been promised a brave new world, but it appears that our choice is Armorica or Brittany after all.

THE PARDONER'S PROLOGUE AND TALE

The Pardoner and his wares are described in detail in the *General Prologue* (see p. 28). He is a trader in 'holy' objects and in the material manifestations of what he would like us to believe is forgiveness. Indeed, this juxtaposition of the spiritual and the material is central to his prologue and his tale. He will tell us a story about three young men who go hunting for Death, and who find him. It is almost a sermon, but not quite, for nothing that he delivers to his audience is entirely what it seems to be.

THE ART OF MAKING MONEY

The Pardoner is essentially a salesman, and while his prologue does not rival that of the Wife of Bath for length, he has a similar need to tell his audience about the ways in which he does business. The Host, endearingly claiming that the sad tale the Physician has just told has almost given him a 'cardynacle [heart attack]' (*CT*VI 313), calls upon the Pardoner to tell them all something funny. This, however, is greeted with disapproval by the more refined pilgrims, who cry out *en masse* that they do not want any 'ribaudye [coarse jesting]' and instead want to hear a 'moral thyng' (*CT*VI 324–5). There have been such squabbles before in the link passages, but no one deals with matters as skilfully as the Pardoner. Like a salesman with his foot in the door, he reassures everyone that he must think about some 'honest thyng' to tell them while he has a drink (*CT*VI 328). In the meantime, he simply keeps talking.

His approach is at once honest and dishonest. His whole life is based upon trickery, and he proceeds to tell his fellow pilgrims all about the kinds of tricks that he practices on the world at large. He gathers his fellow travellers to him, addressing them as 'lordynges' (*CT* VI 329) and making it clear that they are not the 'lewed [ignorant] peple' (*CT* VI 392) whom he exploits for money; but that they are special, not likely to be susceptible in the way that other people are. It is, of course, an old trick in itself, but the Pardoner goes further than most, giving details of how he dupes his clientele. He has, for example, mounted in brass, the shoulder bone of 'an hooly Jewes sheep' (*CT* VI 351) that he uses to heal snake-bitten livestock and which, incidentally, will also cure jealous rages in husbands if used in the making of their soup. A subtler ploy is his assertion that only women who have *not* made cuckolds of their husbands will be able to make offerings to him, a trick that like the others has brought him a good living. At no point does he attempt to hide his crimes. It is all, as he tells us, about, 'wynne [profit], / And nothing for correccioun of synne' (*CT* VI 403–4). Moreover, he does not care if the souls of those he has duped end up 'goon a-blakeberyed [blackberry picking]' in hell (*CT* VI 405). It is perhaps the picnic phrasing of this that prevents it from being truly shocking. He claims he is a 'vicious' man (*CT* VI 459), which he is in the sense that he is full of vice, but his honest proclamation of villainy, his sense of performance, and the fact that his victims are taken in so readily, keeps him on the right side of his fellow travellers, at least until the end of his tale.

UNHOLY BODIES

Cranking up the level of his performance, the Pardoner begins his tale proper with an account of the so-called 'tavern vices'. The sins of drunkenness, gluttony, gambling, blasphemy, and lechery are all condemned in the opening lines as doing 'the devel sacrifise' within the 'develes temple' as the Pardoner plays with full force to the gallery (*CT* VI 469–70). He paints a vivid picture of tavern life with its

... <u>tombesteres</u>,	dancing girls
<u>Fetys</u> and <u>smale</u>, and yonge <u>frutesteres</u>,	elegant; slim; fruit-sellers
Syngeres with harpes, <u>baudes</u>, <u>wafereres</u>,	brothel keepers; wafer-sellers
Whiche been the verray <u>develes officeres</u>	servants of the devil
To kyndle and <u>blowe</u> the fyr of lecherye,	fan
That is <u>annexed</u> unto glotonye.	linked

(CT VI 477–82)

Not since the Garden of Eden has fruit seemed so alluringly dangerous. Lechery and gluttony find themselves partners in crime. In fact, in the mind of the Pardoner, the Fall of Adam and Eve was due to nothing more than an act of base greed (*CT* VI 505–11). For him, everything is physical. He trades in the tangible objects of a religion in which the body is situated at the centre of belief (see p. 29), but instead of using the physical to reach the spiritual, he cannot see past it to anything higher. Even the Eucharist – the bread and wine in the mass that becomes the body and blood of Christ – finds itself deployed in a metaphor about cookery (*CT* VI 538–9). The human form is not praised as something made in the image of God, but is rather reviled as a farting, snoring bag of dung:

O <u>wombe</u>! O bely! O stynkyng <u>cod</u>,	stomach; bag
<u>Fulfilled of</u> <u>dong</u> and of corrupcioun!	filled with; dung
At either ende of thee foul is the <u>soun</u>.	sound
(*CT* VI 534–6)	

In fact, the Pardoner is so delighted with the onomatopoeic 'Sampsoun, Sampsoun!' of the drunken snorer that he uses it not once but twice (*CT* VI 554, 572). There are many bodies in the *Canterbury Tales*, but nowhere are their noises, effluvia, and waste more apparent than in the *Pardoner's Tale*. Everything is debased. Even the great mystery that is death will be tackled head-on in the tale in a misguided attempt to kill him. Death, however, will prove to be more than a match for anyone.

THE OLD MAN

Three young revellers are drinking in a tavern, sometime around six o'clock in the morning, when they hear the bell that signals the carrying of a corpse to its grave. It emerges that it is a friend of theirs, slain by 'a privee [sneaky] theef men clepeth [call] Deeth' (*CT* VI 675). Death, it seems, has been very busy during the plague, slaying thousands, even wiping out whole villages, and the young men resolve to do something about it. The servant of one of them reports what his mother had told him about 'Death', which is that one should always be ready to meet him (*CT* VI 680–4), but this pious advice is taken by the literal-minded bunch as a call to arms, and they pile out of the tavern in a drunken rage in search of their adversary. Their rallying cry, 'Deeth shal be deed' (*CT* VI 710) is biblical, profound, illogical, and a favourite of medieval authors contemplating Christ's redemption of mankind through his own death. All this, however, is lost on the revellers, who see it as a simple statement of intent.

Not long afterwards they encounter an old man, whom they challenge at once:

> '... What, <u>carl</u>, <u>with sory grace!</u>   fellow; bad luck to you
> Why <u>artow</u> al <u>forwrapped save</u> thy face? are you; wrapped up except for
> Why <u>lyvestow</u> so longe in so greet age? do you live
> (*CT* VI 717–19)

His great age and the fact that he is 'wrapped' with only his face showing, makes him seem corpse-like, and he tells the revellers that he spends his days trying to return to the earth. It is this that makes some critics think that he is, in fact, Death, and yet he tells us that death is what he is seeking for himself. For others, therefore, he is an embodiment of wisdom, and it is true that he points the young men in the direction of Death and that death is exactly what they find. His quoting from the Bible, his initial greeting that 'God yow see! [May God watch over you]' (*CT* VI 715), and his references to redemption, lead others to think of him as a Christ figure; while for still others he is simply the embodiment of weary old age. What is clear is that we are not told exactly who or what he is. There is something mysterious about him that makes it seem that he must be a symbol and that the metaphors of his speech ought to be unpacked for us, but this is a tale told by the Pardoner who, in spite of his profession, seems singularly unable to deal with anything other than literal meaning. His wares should be important not for what they are, but for what they symbolise, or even what they embody in a spiritual sense beyond symbol, but this is not how the Pardoner understands them, and it should be no surprise that the potential meanings of the Old Man should be left unexplored. Chaucer, however, has deepened what he has found in his sources. Only in his version of the tale is it 'Death' that the young men seek, and we know that we have encountered something profound here, without having been helped towards understanding what it is. This is the Pardoner's failing and it is perhaps the point.

SPIRITUAL TREASURE

The young revellers are, however, of the Pardoner's frame of mind and they are not inclined to ponder the old man any longer than is required for a bit of hostile mockery. They do not tend towards introspection and their tale races along partly because it consists mostly of nouns and verbs. However, the pace slows as the men discover, not Death, but treasure lying beneath a tree:

> ... and ther they founde,
> Of floryns fyne of gold <u>ycoyned rounde</u>   made into round coins
> <u>Wel ny</u> an eighte <u>busshels</u>, as hem thoughte. almost; sackfuls
> (*CT* VI 769–71)

The sudden insertion of these strangely redundant adjectives – because florins are already expected to be gold and coins are already expected to be round – conveys the way in which their eyes linger on the treasure, all thought of their hunt for Death being replaced by a stupefied gazing upon the hoard. Once again, everything has been reduced to material fact.

It is a huge fortune, but within a few lines, two of the revellers are plotting to kill the third, who has gone off to find them all some food. The third, meantime, is also intent upon murder and there is a vivid account of him buying poison from the local apothecary, his criminal intent being revealed by the far too numerous justifications for his purchase. He claims that he wants

> Som poyson, that he myghte his rattes <u>quelle</u>; kill
> And eek ther was a <u>polcat</u> in his <u>hawe</u>, weasel; yard
> That, as he seyde, his <u>capouns</u> hadde <u>yslawe</u>, capons (chickens);
>   butchered
> And <u>fayn</u> he wolde <u>wreke hym</u>, if he myghte, gladly; avenge himself
> On vermyn that destroyed hym by nyghte.
> (*CT* VI 854–8)

Detail, as we have seen throughout the *Pardoner's Prologue and Tale*, most frequently accompanies lies. The remainder of the sparse tale is given over to the plotting and planning of the three murders. The two men kill their fellow when he returns and then die in their turn by drinking the poisoned wine he had brought with him. The ease with which the revellers end the life of another human being is shown in the matter-of-fact delivery of the Pardoner:

> What nedeth it to <u>sermone</u> of it moore?   speak
> For <u>right</u> as they hadde <u>cast</u> his deeth bifoore,   just; planned
> Right so they han hym slayn, and that <u>anon</u>.   at once
>   (*CT* VI 879–81)

The 'right as … right so' construction has the feel of a job well done, and it is interesting that the Pardoner, in the middle of what can broadly be called a sermon, feels no need to 'sermone' more on this act of murder. The great mystery of death that had been so apparent in the words of the Old Man is not evident here, nor is it seen in the deaths of the other men who are dispatched equally jauntily by the narrative: 'For which anon they storven [died] bothe two' (*CT* VI 888). The narrator deigns to 'suppose' that their deaths by poison might have surpassed the horrors described in the best medical textbooks (*CT* VI 889–92), but he does not describe them himself. The demise of the three revellers is reported as sparely as that of their friend at the beginning of the tale and we are none the wiser about death.

THE END-GAME

His tale finished, the Pardoner treats his audience to a display of rhetoric:

> O cursed synne of alle cursednesse!
> O <u>traytours</u> homycide, O wikkednesse!   treacherous
> O glotonye, <u>luxurie</u>, and <u>hasardrye</u>!   lechery; gambling
>   (*CT* VI 895–7)

'O' indeed. The Pardoner likes to flex his verbal muscles, and this is possibly the earliest appearance of the word 'homicidal' in English, but it is nevertheless a wholly empty display. It condemns all sin, murder, and wickedness in two lines, before disposing of the usual trio of gluttony, lechery, and gambling in the next. From there, there is a slight detour to blasphemy, but the sin the Pardoner really wants to get to is avarice, for greed is where the money is. There is, therefore, no part of this sermon that dwells on what might be morally profitable for his makeshift congregation; he focusses instead on what he hopes will be just plain profitable for himself.

Having earlier revealed all his tricks to his fellow pilgrims, it is not clear what the Pardoner expects as he presents his wares to all and sundry in the last few lines. He possibly thinks that his skills as a salesman are up to the ultimate challenge of telling his customers that he is lying and convincing them to buy anyway; or perhaps he feels that fear and superstition will guarantee his clientele, no matter what. Certainly, he offers himself as some kind of medieval travel insurance for those who might suffer 'aventures' on their journey (*CT* VI 932–6). His choice of the Host as his first victim is, however, unwise. Having been marked out by the Pardoner as someone mired in sin, the Host erupts in fury, refusing to kiss the 'relics' offered to him:

'Thou <u>woldest</u> make me kisse thyn olde <u>breech</u>,	want to; pants
And swere it were a relyk of a seint,	
Though it were with thy <u>fundement</u> <u>depeint</u>!'	anus; stained
(*CT* VI 948–50)	

He follows this up with a very personal reference to the 'coillons [testicles]' of the Pardoner and a plan to enshrine them in a hog's turd (*CT* VI 952–5). It is an outraged response to an outrageous display and there is a sense in which it has all gone simply too far. The Host declares that he will no longer 'pleye' with the Pardoner, the sense being that the easy live and let live attitude of the pilgrimage has been breached. The Pardoner professionally depends on such tolerance, for it is clear to everyone that his crop-multiplying mitten is a hoax without them having to be told, but that there is nevertheless something genuine in the principle behind relics and pardons. The pilgrims are, after all, on their way to Canterbury, the aim being to visit the shrine of St Thomas whose body is venerated as a relic. The Pardoner's potential justification for his sin – that it can somehow be permitted if his own avarice cures the same sin in others – is a cleverer hoax than the mitten, and even as he lies to us, he tells us it is a lie (*CT* VI 427–34), but the final lines do not manifest his earlier honest dishonesty. In the end, it is perhaps this loss of self-awareness that is his downfall. Fortunately, however, the Knight is there to make peace, calling for everyone to kiss and make up, and return to 'laughe and pleye' (*CT* VI 967).

THE NUN'S PRIEST'S PROLOGUE AND TALE

The Monk is one of the tale-tellers who tries the patience of the rest of the pilgrims, not knowing when to stop and having to be interrupted by the Knight. His tale has been a catalogue of tragedies, starting with Lucifer, the rebel angel who rose up against God himself and was cast down into Hell to become Satan. It is not an obvious modern topic for tragedy, but the medieval sense of the genre focusses very much on the turning of Fortune's wheel and the way in which those who find themselves placed at the very top, in terms of power and status, can easily be cast down as the wheel turns once more. The Monk himself gives us this definition:

'Tragedie is to seyn a certeyn storie,	means; a certain kind of
As olde bookes maken us memorie,	remind us
Of hym that stood in greet prosperitee,	he
And is yfallen out of heigh degree	status
Into myserie, and endeth wrecchedly.'	
(*CT* VII 1973–7)	

The extent to which any individual is responsible for their fall, or merely subject to forces beyond their control, is a key question. With it comes a desire for meaning, because history – even prehistory if we begin, like the Monk, with the rebel angels – delivers example after example of greatness brought low. In the hands of the Monk, however, no questions are answered: lives are reduced to a steady tumble in a never-ending list of tragic reversal. The Monk does not stop, because the Wheel of Fortune does not stop, and there is always another tragic tale to tell. To bring an end the Knight must intervene, and the Host selects the Nun's Priest to tell a tale that will gladden their hearts (VII 2811). The Nun's Priest does indeed gladden everyone's hearts. His tale takes up the central theme of the *Monk's Tale*, the inevitability of tragic reversal, and adds prophecy, predestination, theories of rhetoric – and chickens.

THE ORDINARY (AND NOT-SO-ORDINARY) FABLE OF THE COCK AND THE FOX

The Nun's Priest (a priest, that is, whose job it was to be the confessor and protector of the nuns on the pilgrimage) chooses to tell a beast-fable. Animal fables exist in almost all cultures and tend to be simple, homely tales with a basic moral: country mice learn that they are better off living in cosy poverty than amidst the fearful plenty of the towns; proud lions learn that what goes around comes around. As for the Cock and the Fox, they are a classic pairing, and the story that the Nun's Priest tells was known in its basic form throughout Europe: the vain Cock, flattered into singing by the Fox, closes his eyes in tuneless ecstasy, and is seized by the throat; the Fox, in turn, goaded by the Cock, opens his mouth to shout at his pursuers and allows the Cock to escape. It is, in essence, a fable about pride, and about the need to keep one's eyes open and one's mouth shut.

HEROIC STYLE

It soon becomes clear, however, that this is no ordinary beast-fable. While the creatures are the traditional farmyard variety, Chauntecleer the Cock is evidently a bird of distinction:

His coomb was redder than the fyn coral,	comb
And batailled as it were a castel wal;	had crenellations like a castle wall
His byle was blak, and as the jeet it shoon;	bill; jet; shone
Lyk asure were his legges and his toon;	azure; toes
His nayles whitter than the lylye flour,	whiter; lily flower
And lyk the burned gold was his colour.	burnished
(*CT* VII 2859–64)	

The lily-complexions, coral lips, and golden hair of medieval romance heroines are transferred to the claws, coxcomb, and feathers of the bird, with precious stones and castles now metaphors for shiny beaks and coxcombs. The Cock is even compared to a clock (*CT* VII 2854), a word only just recorded in English to describe the wondrous new timepieces appearing in the cities. In all, the effect is mock-heroic, and applied throughout the narrative, from the description of Chauntecleer's favourite mate, 'faire damoysele [damsel] Pertelote' (*CT* VII 2870), to the lurking Fox as part of a legion of 'homycides' (*CT* VII 3224), to the very unlikely reference to 'bour [bower] and ... halle' (*CT* VII 2832) in the widow's sooty hovel.

At every turn, the lofty heights of medieval literature, learning and rhetoric are applied to the world of the farmyard. The lowly chicken yard, the 'clos' shares a rhyming couplet with 'Eneydos' (the great Latin epic poem, the *Aeneid*), as the hens lament the fate of Chauntecleer in the manner of the widows of ancient Troy (*CT* VII 3359–60). But why stop at Troy? The destruction of Carthage and Rome are then heaped on top of one another as the narrator attempts to convey the full extent of the tragedy unfolding in the hen house.

The Nun's Priest has read his medieval poetry manuals and reaches for a device known as apostrophe ('O destinee ... O Venus ... O Gaufred' *CT* VII 3338–47) as he aims for the rhetorical heights. 'Gaufred' is none other than Geoffrey de Vinsauf, the author of the best-known medieval textbook on rhetoric, famed for its lamentation on the death of Richard the Lionheart. The Nun's Priest, however, laments not the death of a king, nor even the almost-death of a rooster, but rather his own inability to lament the existence of Friday, an unlucky day for both Lionheart and chicken-heart:

O Gaufred, deere maister soverayn,	Geoffrey; most excellent
That whan thy worthy king Richard was slayn	
With shot, compleynedest his deeth so soore,	by an arrow; lamented; bitterly
Why ne hadde I now thy sentence and thy loore,	meaning; learning
The Friday for to chide, as diden ye?	reproach
(*CT* VII 3347–51)	

It is, of course, a piece of faux-modesty in the middle of a piece of mock-epic, the narrator's very lament that he cannot lament being a rhetorical device in itself. It is not that he cannot approach the achievement of the master, but rather that he intends to surpass him. What he imagines to be a virtuoso performance is, however, simply too much. Indeed, the whole tale is 'too much'. Only about one-tenth of the narrative is given over to the capture and pursuit of

Cock and Fox. The rest consists of verbal excess, rhetorical inter-ruptions, anecdote, and digressions, one of which – the section on dreams – is Chaucer's most sustained treatment of a theme that per-vades his work, albeit taking place in the chicken coop.

DREAMS

Almost half the narrative is given over to the discussion of dreams conducted by Chauntecleer and Pertelote. The rooster, never hav-ing seen a fox, nevertheless dreams of a terrifying dog-like crea-ture of a yellowish-red colour and cries out in his sleep. This does not endear him to Pertelote, who invokes her husband's wattle, and utters the scathing, 'Have ye no mannes herte, and han a berd?' (*CT* VII 2920). Her stance is that of the natural scientist, convinced that dreams are 'all nonsense' ('but vanitee' *CT* VII 2922) and must arise from biological causes, whether as a result of an imbalance in the body's humours, or as a reaction to overeating. A profoundly orderly chicken, she favours the theory that each of the four humours will cause dreams about objects of different colours, and that visions of red beasts are the simple result of too much red choler in the system. As a result, she urges that he should, 'For Goddes love, as taak som laxatyf' (*CT* VII 2943) and proceeds to issue a prescription for plants and herbs of which any medieval apothecary would have been proud, and all of which Chauntecleer can easily pick up as he pecks his way round the farmyard.

Chauntecleer is less impressed than the reader by his wife's knowl-edge, his dignity having been impugned, and he maintains instead that his was an oracular dream, signifying future events. With as much knowledge, and greater politeness than Pertelote, he proceeds to argue the case for dream prophecy. It is a lengthy and mostly eloquent discourse in which he provides not one but two 'real-life' examples, and cites a whole range of authorities, including the Bible. With measured assurance, he even graciously acknowledges that not all dreams are oracular in nature: 'Wher dremes be som-tyme – I sey nat alle [always] – / Warnynge of thynges that shul after falle' (*CT* VII 3131–2). He has the same vices as his narrator in that he piles in too many references to classical literature and occa-sionally becomes distracted by moral conclusions ('Mordre wol out' *CT* VII 3052), but it is a speech that would have found favour with medieval authorities on dreams. Furthermore, the tale is about to present him with a creature exactly like the one in his vision. The difficulty is that he fails to listen to his own advice and proceeds instead like the bird-brain he is. Arguments and authorities are swept aside as he gazes upon the face of Pertelote and decides that, because of his pleasure in her, he will 'diffye [defy]' (VII 3171) his dream. Instead,

> He <u>fethered</u> Pertelote twenty tyme,   ruffled the feathers of
> And <u>trad hire</u> eke as ofte, er it was <u>pryme</u>.   copulated with her; 6 am
>   (*CT* VII 3177–8)

TRUTH AND WORDS

His words have not led Chauntecleer towards truth; they have simply enabled him to reassert his authority as rooster. He immediately calls his hens together with 'a chuk … For he hadde founde a corn, lay in the yerd' (*CT* VII 3174–5). It is an exultant cluck that shows that natural order has been restored to the farmyard. The same chicken noises assert fundamental truth a moment later as the appearance of the Fox is greeted with an instinctive, 'Cok! cok!' (*CT* VII 3277) by a frightened Chauntecleer. He is moved not by scholarly learning or by dreams, but by the deep truth of natural antipathy:

> For natureelly a beest desireth flee
> Fro his <u>contrarie</u>, if he may it see,   natural adversary
> Though he never <u>erst</u> hadde seyn it with his <u>ye</u>.   before; eye
>   (*CT* VII 3279–81)

Instinct is, however, subdued by words as the Fox launches into a torrent of flattery designed to make the Cock close his eyes and sing. Immediately, the Fox seizes him by the 'gargat [throat]' (*CT* VII 3335), the choice of the native word for what the Fox had previously described as an almost divine instrument showing us the nature of the lie; but, as we had seen in his loquacious encounter with Pertelote, the Cock, too, can use words to his own ends. He goads his captor into mocking their pursuers and, as soon as the Fox's jaws unclench, escapes into the nearest tree. All the Fox's coaxing will not bring him down again. The power of words to overcome has been seen several times in the tale, but ultimately the tongue is less power-ful than the teeth.

A MORAL (OR TWO)

The tale ends, therefore, with yet another turn of Fortune's wheel. The Cock, who had been turned upside down in the chase, is restored to the heights and can crow at his assailant. It is a parody of tragedy in which a great chicken has been brought low but has been saved. The narrative style, too, has gone up and down, moving from the teetering towers of rhetoric to the noises of the barnyard. The narrator does not wait for the end of the tale to deliver his message but, instead, peppers the narrative with bits of proverbial wisdom. We learn, among other things, that 'all good things must come to an end' (VII 3205), and that 'women's advice is deadly' (*CT* VII 3256). The Cock gets to deliver his own piece of wisdom on the need to keep one's eyes open. The Fox delivers a completely different mes-sage: that loose lips cost lives. But none of this is quite enough for the Nun's Priest, who warns against recklessness, negligence, and flattery in a great catch-all, invoking St Paul and the notion that absolutely everything that is written is there to instruct us (*CT* VII 3441–2). For some critics, that instruction extends to a full-scale allegorical reading in which the Cock and Fox are to be interpreted in some way, perhaps as representatives of different parts of the Church (e.g., preachers and friars), or, in other readings, Chauntecleer becomes a second Adam, whose Fall is brought about by a devilish Fox. It is pos-sible to apply such interpretations, but only because it is possible to apply almost anything to the great shifting toyshop that is the *Nun's Priest's Tale*. The narrator ends by telling us to gather up the fruit, ignore the chaff, and take 'the moralite' (*CT* VII 3440) – whatever that might be. It is a fitting final moral for this fable: like the chickens in the yard we can sift through whatever we find and pick up what-ever we choose.

FURTHER READING

There are informative annotated editions in *The Canterbury Tales: Fifteen Tales and the General Prologue* (2005). Ed. V. A. Kolve and Glending Olson. 2nd edn. New York: Norton.

There is a comprehensive collection of original texts and translations of Chaucer's sources and analogues in *Sources and Analogues of the Canterbury Tales*, 2 vols. (2002, 2005). Ed. Robert M. Correale and Mary Hamel. Cambridge: D. S. Brewer. For useful backgrounds and contexts, see *Chaucer: Sources and Backgrounds* (1977). Ed. Robert P. Miller. New York: Oxford University Press.

See also *The Literary Context of Chaucer's Fabliaux* (1997). Ed. Larry D. Benson and Theodore M. Andersson. Indianapolis: Bobbs Merrill.

For succinct and lucid overviews of the critical questions relating to each tale, see Helen Cooper (1996). *The Canterbury Tales*. 2nd edn. *Oxford Guides to Chaucer*. Oxford University Press.

For a fundamental contextualisation of the General Prologue, see Jill Mann (1973). *Chaucer and Medieval Estates Satire*. Cambridge: Cambridge University Press, now supplemented by the highly informative *Historians on Chaucer: The General Prologue to the Canterbury Tales* (2014). Ed. Stephen H. Rigby with the assistance of A. J. Minnis. Oxford: Oxford University Press.

On the order of the Tales and many questions relating to genre, see Helen Cooper (1984). *The Structure of the Canterbury Tales*. London: Duckworth. In *The Cambridge Companion to Chaucer* (2003). Ed. Jill Mann and Piero Boitani.

2nd edn. Cambridge: Cambridge University Press, there are lucid introductions by J. A. Burrow on 'Romance', Derek Pearsall on 'Comedy' and by A. C. Spearing on 'Exemplum and Fable'. Tison Pugh (2013). *An Introduction to Geoffrey Chaucer*. Gainesville: University Press of Florida also addresses Chaucer's works in terms of genre theory, and John Hines (1993). *The Fabliau in English*. Harlow: Longman provides contexts for the comic tales.

For a shrewd analysis of the whole collection of tales, see Derek Pearsall (1985). *The Canterbury Tales*. London: Allen and Unwin, and Winthrop Wetherbee (1990). *The Canterbury Tales*. Cambridge: Cambridge University Press, together with Helen Phillips (2000). *An Introduction to the Canterbury Tales*. Basingstoke: Macmillan, while for insights into Chaucer's compositional techniques, see Peter Brown (1994). *Chaucer at Work: The Making of the Canterbury Tales*. Harlow: Longman, and for analysis of the narratorial dimension of Chaucer's works generally, see David Lawton (1985). *Chaucer's Narrators*. Cambridge: D. S. Brewer. For analysis and contexts for two particular tale-tellers, see A. J. Minnis (2008). *Fallible Authors: Chaucer's Pardoner and Wife of Bath*. Philadelphia: University of Pennsylvania Press, together with the chapters on the Knight's, Millers', and Wife's Tales in Lee Patterson (1991). *Chaucer and the Subject of History*. London: Routledge. Still valuable is the discussion of individual tales in Charles Muscatine (1957). *Chaucer and the French Tradition.* Berkeley: University of California Press, chapter 6. For interpretations that helped form the mainstream of current readings, see Elizabeth Salter (1962). *The Knight's Tale and the Clerk's Tale.* London: Edward Arnold, together with A. C. Spearing (1972). *Criticism and Medieval Poetry.* 2nd edn. London: Edward Arnold, chapter 4 ('The Clerk's Tale as a Medieval Poem').

For richly illustrated and illuminating explorations of relations between Chaucer's narratives and the visual culture of his times, see V. A. Kolve (1984). *Chaucer and the Imagery of Narrative: The First Five Canterbury Tales.* London: Edward Arnold, more recently supplemented by V. A. Kolve (2009). *Telling Images: Chaucer and the Imagery of Narrative II.* Stanford: Stanford University Press.

Serious discussion of gender questions in Chaucer's works really begins with such pioneering studies as Carolyn Dinshaw (1989). *Chaucer's Sexual Poetics.* Madison: University of Wisconsin Press, and also Priscilla Martin (1990, 1996). *Chaucer's Women: Nuns, Wives and Amazons.* Basingstoke: Macmillan. These were closely followed by Jill Mann (1991). *Geoffrey Chaucer.* London: Harvester Wheatsheaf (revised as (2002). *Feminizing Chaucer.* Cambridge: D. S. Brewer), along with Elaine Tuttle Hansen (1992). *Chaucer and the Fictions of Gender.* Berkeley: University of California Press, as well as Susan Crane (1994). *Gender and Romance in Chaucer's Canterbury Tales.* Princeton: Princeton University Press, and Catherine S. Cox (1997). *Gender and Language in Chaucer.* Gainesville: University Press of Florida. On how moral analysis was not gender-neutral but presupposed certain virtues and failings were gender-specific, see Alcuin Blamires (2006). *Chaucer, Ethics, and Gender.* Oxford: Oxford University Press.

See also the classic intervention: Mary Carruthers, 'The Wife of Bath and the Painting of Lions', in *Feminist Readings in Middle English Literature: The Wife of Bath and All Her Sect* (1994). Ed. Ruth Evans and Lesley Johnson. London: Routledge, 22–53.

On Chaucer's Pardoner in his context, see Alastair Minnis, (2007). *Fallible Authors: Chaucer's Pardoner and Wife of Bath.* Philadelphia: University of Pennsylvania Press. On the question of the Pardoner's sexuality, see Robert S. Sturges (2000). *Chaucer's Pardoner and Gender Theory: Bodies of Discourse.* New York: Palgrave Macmillan along with Glenn Burger (2003). *Chaucer's Queer Nation.* Minneapolis: University of Minnesota Press. More particularly, see Monica McAlpine, 'The Pardoner's Homosexuality and How It Matters', *PMLA*, 95 (1980), 8–22; together with Steven Kruger, 'Claiming the Pardoner: Toward a Gay Reading of Chaucer's Pardoner's Tale', *Exemplaria*, 6 (1994), 115–39, and also

Alastair Minnis, 'Chaucer and the Queering Eunuch', *New Medieval Literatures*, 6 (2003), 107–28.

On Chaucer and the animal world, see particularly Carolynn van Dyke (2012). Ed. *Rethinking Chaucerian Beasts*. New York: Palgrave, and more generally Susan Crane (2013). *Animal Encounters: Contacts and Concepts in Medieval Britain*. Philadelphia: University of Pennsylvania Press, together with Jill Mann (2009). *From Aesop to Reynard: Beast Literature in Medieval Britain*. Oxford: Oxford University Press.

4

TROILUS AND CRISEYDE

Troilus and Criseyde is a love story set during the Trojan War. It is the account of how two people fall in love, and the eventual betrayal of that love. To say this is not to spoil the story, for it was the thing about Troilus and Criseyde that everyone knew. But in case anyone in the audience had forgotten, Chaucer makes it clear in the opening lines, as he declares the purpose of his poem:

> The double sorwe of Troilus to tellen,
> That was the <u>kyng Priamus sone</u> of Troye,   the son of King Priam
> In lovynge, how his aventures fellen
> Fro <u>wo to wele</u>, and after out of joie,   sorrow to happiness
> $\qquad\qquad$ (*TC* I 1–4)

Troilus will suffer. Not only that, but he will suffer at the hands of a very bad woman, for the other thing that a medieval audience knew was that Troilus was a true and trusty prince, and that he was wickedly and undeservedly betrayed by Criseyde. It is not, therefore, a 'will they? won't they?' kind of love story; it is a, 'they will, and it will all go disastrously wrong' kind of story. However, in the process, Chaucer takes the harsh divisions of his sources – the basic pattern of an honest man and a duplicitous woman – and shows that love is not so plain and simple.

Troilus and Criseyde are both medieval inventions. They are not present in the classical sources, but came into being early in the Middle Ages and captured the literary imagination right through to the time of Shakespeare. There were, of course, love stories available in the ancient texts. After all, the whole of the Trojan War was said to have come about because of the passion of Paris for Helen of Troy, but this is not a love that much inspires medieval writers. The couple's extreme beauty is perhaps too much like staring into the sun, for what, the Middle Ages seems to think, might be learned from that couple's semi-divine passion? Instead, the Middle Ages turned to Paris's younger brother and the woman who was not Helen of Troy. Here, in Troilus and Criseyde, they found a more human love, a love that might be scrutinised and explored.

BOOK I

The first book of *Troilus and Criseyde* belongs, essentially, to Troilus. In this book, Troilus sees Criseyde for the first time, falls in love, and confides in his friend, Pandarus, who, it emerges, is also the uncle of Criseyde.

There is a lovely moment towards the end of Book I, where Pandarus reminds Troilus of how judgmental he used to be when it came to matters of the heart:

How often <u>hastow</u> maad thi <u>nyce japes</u>	have you; foolish jokes
And seyd that Loves servantz <u>everichone</u>	every one
Of <u>nycete</u> ben <u>verray</u> Goddes apes ...	folly; truly
And som, thow seydest, hadde a <u>blaunche fevere</u>,	lovesickness
And preydest God he sholde nevere <u>kevere</u>.	recover
And som of hem took on hym, for the cold,	
More than ynough, so <u>seydestow</u> ful ofte.	you said
And som <u>han feyned</u> ofte tyme, and told	have pretended
How that they <u>waken</u>, whan thei slepen <u>softe</u>;	lie awake; deeply
And thus they wolde han <u>brought</u> himself <u>alofte</u>,	kept; aloof
And natheles were under at the laste.	
Thus seydestow, and <u>japedest</u> ful faste.	joked

(*TC* I 911–24)

The accumulation of 'ands' reveals the glee of Pandarus as he lists Troilus's previous misdemeanours and general lack of sympathy towards lovers. Pandarus, as we will discover, has a tendency to be long-winded but, nevertheless, what he says about Troilus here is true. Before we know much else about Troilus, we know that he is dismissive of love. We see him for the very first time in the poem as he steers the men at his command into the temple, his attention divided between coolly assessing the women (*TC* I 189) and watching the men for any signs of amorous attachment. It is at this moment that we are granted a glimpse into his mind, as he smiles to himself and ridicules the 'veray fooles' (*TC* I 202) who fall in love. These are Troilus's first thoughts in the poem, and he is rather pleased with himself for thinking them:

> And with that word he gan caste up the <u>browe</u>,   eyebrow
> <u>Ascaunces</u>, "Loo! is this naught wisely spoken?"   as if to say
> (*TC* I 204–5)

A lift of the eyebrow in salute to his own good sense is, of course, a direct invitation to Cupid's dart, and the arrival of Criseyde. Troilus is a man who has protested too much. The reason that he is on the lookout for those in the grip of passionate feelings, and the reason that he is so keen to criticise those who succumb is because he has love very much on his mind. He is clearly very ready to fall in love himself, but his approach has all the hallmarks of immaturity. This will be, after all, first love, and Troilus is entitled to make all the traditional mistakes, beginning with vehement denial.

THE NARRATIVE VOICE

The narrator, on the other hand, is entirely ready for a traditional love story. He might have begun the poem by reminding everyone that this is not going to end well, but he is full of romantic enthusiasm, nevertheless. Troilus has no sooner finished congratulating himself than the narrator lines up Cupid and nine stanzas on the irresistibility of love against him. What is key, however, is that Cupid is not a character within this poem. He is only one of the narrator's metaphors in a speech that demands obedience to the laws of love. The narrator also compares Troilus to Bayard, a medieval Dobbin the Horse, taught to obey the whip:

As proude Bayard <u>gynneth</u> for to skippe	begins
Out of the weye, so <u>pryketh</u> hym his corn,	incites
Til he a lasshe have of the longe whippe –	
Than thynketh he, 'Though I praunce <u>al byforn</u>	in front of the others
First in the <u>trays</u>, ful fat and newe shorn,	Cart
Yet am I but an hors, and horses lawe	
I <u>moot</u> endure, and <u>with my feres drawe</u>'	must; pull with my companions

(TC I 218–24)

The narrator has managed to endow Troilus with all the nobility of a talking cart horse, but he is as clear about Troilus's subjection to love as he is that Criseyde is a most worthy object of that love. He waxes lyrical about her at the first opportunity, praising her as an ethereal being,

So aungelik was hir <u>natif</u> beaute,	natural
That lik a thing inmortal semed she,	
As doth an hevenyssh <u>perfit</u> creature,	perfect
That down were sent in scornynge of nature.	

(TC I 102–5)

Criseyde fares much better than Troilus, but the narrator seems to get stuck somewhere within his own comparison: she is angelic, which makes her like a thing immortal, which is like a perfect heavenly creature and, therefore, we assume, like the angel with which he began. The narrative voice shifts and changes in the course of the poem and is capable of finer moments than these, but it is clear that the narrator is not necessarily a reliable guide. Certainly, the two beliefs he holds most dear in Book I – that Criseyde is a veritable goddess and that Troilus is a slave to love – are the very ideas that Chaucer seems to be seeking to challenge.

LOVE AT FIRST SIGHT?

As he makes his way through the crowd in the temple, Troilus's eye falls upon Criseyde. More precisely, he has been scanning all the women, until

... upon cas bifel that thorugh a route	by chance; crowd
His eye percede, and so depe it wente,	pierced
Til on Criseyde it smot, and ther it stente.	struck; stopped

(TC I 271–3)

The narrator had prepared us, of course, for Cupid's arrows to afflict Troilus, but the difficulty here is that the dart has gone the wrong way. It is the eye of Troilus that has pierced a dense crowd and only stopped when it strikes Criseyde like a target. His response is a mixture of astonishment and control. On the one hand, he is brought to a sudden halt and takes a closer look; but, on the other hand, it is a look 'in thrifty wise' (*TC* I 275), in other words, a 'prudent' look. Prudence at such a moment is not what we expect and, while Troilus then utters the medieval equivalent of 'Where have you been all my life?' ('wher hastow woned?'), he manages to sigh quietly and go back to acting as he had done before (*TC* I 274–80). Indeed, when he leaves the temple, he is described as 'nat fullich al awhaped' (*TC* I 316), a surprising phrase in that one might expect to be stunned or not stunned, but 'not entirely fully stunned', is simply comically reductive. It reveals a gap between where Troilus is and where the narrative voice would like him to be. It is not a passionate collapse, but Troilus has found an object for his desires, and he clearly wants to be in love, so he goes home, sits down at the bottom of his bed, and thinks about Criseyde, remembering exactly how she looked in the temple. He starts off sighing about her and works his way up to groans (*TC* I 358–64), until finally, 'took he purpos loves craft to suwe [follow]' (*TC* I 379). Like his earlier prudence, this might come as a surprise, for it means that, 'he decided to pursue the craft of love'. He makes the decision, and he makes it not because he is shot by Cupid, or blinded by desire, but because love is a game that he has decided he would like to play.

COURTLY LOVE

The term 'courtly love' is one that is found throughout critical works on medieval literature, though it is a modern expression. The Middle Ages called it *fin' amors* or, to use Chaucer's own term, 'fyn lovynge'

(*LGW* F.544). In *Troilus and Criseyde*, it is simply 'love's craft', a signal that love requires skill and thought, a certain refinement, and a willingness to follow a certain pattern of behaviour. The young man (it almost always has to be a man of noble birth) falls in love with a young woman, either having encountered her, or having heard of her, for it was possible, the poets felt, to have a passionate love based on reputation alone. Having found his object, the man would then serve her devotedly for several years, composing songs and verses in her honour, performing deeds of heroism on her behalf, and generally offering up his life to her, though not necessarily informing her of any of this. Worship from afar was encouraged for a lengthy period, during which the unrequited lover would grow pale, tremble at the very sight of his lady, suffer sleepless nights, and be engaged at all times in a constant process of self-mortifying doubt about his own worthiness. This, in turn, would lead him towards ever more noble behaviour (*gentilesse*), his suffering spurring him towards greater honour, courage, refinement, and understanding, all of which are contained in the medieval word *curteisie*. Finally, he will call upon the lady to show *pite* (pity) and grant him the *grace* that he desires. Both are terms that are also found in a religious context, because the lady has essentially become an object of worship. The power is hers, and she can choose whether or not to bestow her favours, sexually or otherwise.

Chaucer is obviously completely familiar with this kind of love literature, and it pervades his work. Troilus shapes himself as exactly this kind of courtly lover, trying everything on for size, and deciding that he will surrender himself to Criseyde:

> And over al this, yet muchel more he thoughte
> What for to speke, and what to holden inne;
> And what to <u>arten</u> hire to love he soughte,   urge
> And on a song anon-right to bygynne,
> And gan loude on his sorwe for to <u>wynne</u>.   win
> (I, 386–90)

It might seem strange to find the word 'win' in the context of 'sorrow', but this is the paradox of courtly love: a pain that is sweet and desired, an illness that is wondrous. The noble youth will lament his sorrow, but he will, like Troilus, have worked hard to get there.

CRISEYDE

What, then, of the object of this love? There are two points in the text when we take a sustained look at Criseyde. The first is in Book I when Troilus sees her in the temple. The second comes towards the end of the poem, when we view her through the eyes of the narrator. Both descriptions are vague, though there is a little more detail in the second of the two:

Criseyde <u>mene</u> was of hire <u>stature</u>,	average; height
Therto of shap, of face, and <u>ek</u> of <u>cheere</u>,	also; demeanour
Ther myghte ben no fairer creature;	
And ofte tymes this was hire manere,	
To gon <u>ytressed with hire heres clere</u>	with her shining hair arranged
Doun by hire <u>coler</u> at <u>hire bak byhynde</u>,	collar; down her back
Which with a thred of gold she wolde bynde.	
And <u>save</u> hire <u>browes joyneden yfeere</u>,	except for; eyebrows joined together
Ther nas no <u>lak</u>, in aught I kan <u>espien</u>;	flaw; see
But for to speken of hire <u>eyen cleere</u>,	bright eyes
Lo, trewely, they writen <u>that hire syen</u>,	who saw her
That Paradis stood formed in hire <u>yën</u>;	eyes
And with hire riche beaute evere more	
<u>Strof</u> love in hire ay, <u>which of hem was more.</u>	vied; to see which of them was greater

(*TC* V 806–19).

It is a shadowy description that will end with the narrator's famous disclaimer that he does not know her age (*TC* V 826). In the Italian source text she had been tall, but Chaucer makes her only 'average' in height, with a general claim for her complete fairness that fails to make her distinctive. Indeed, in the middle of the first stanza, the focus shifts to the back of Criseyde's head, and the way in which she styled her hair. We might have expected at least to learn its colour, with golden hair being traditional for medieval heroines, but the gold mentioned here refers only to the hair ribbon that adorns it. Her eyebrows, often a focus of attention in medieval accounts of female beauty, are joined together, a flaw ('lak') that the narrator acknowledges. As for her eyes, they are, just like her hair, a slightly underwhelming 'cleere'. The narrator mentions 'Paradis' within them, but distances himself from the claim by attributing it to those who had actually seen Criseyde. This is disconcerting. It is not something the narrative does with anyone else in the poem. Indeed, it is a very unusual manoeuvre in the middle of a formal description, suddenly to remind the reader that they are not viewing a person at all, but rather an account by a poet who has gleaned what he knows about the protagonist from the works of other authors. We suddenly feel a long way from Criseyde. It is this sense of distance, of not really knowing Criseyde at all, that is key to her role in the poem.

With this in mind, we can see that a certain obscurity and a sense of distance are also crucial in Book I's sustained description of Criseyde, when Troilus encounters her for the first time. In the Italian text, Criseida had made a space for herself in the crowd and had removed her veil. By contrast, Chaucer's Criseyde is hidden away 'under cloude blak' (*TC* I 175) in her enveloping widow's cloak, somewhere at the back of the crowd. Troilus must, therefore, work hard to find her; and, having done so, he proceeds to project his own thoughts onto this obscured, shadowy, creature:

She nas nat with the <u>leste</u> of hire stature,	shortest
But alle hire <u>lymes</u> so wel <u>answerynge</u>	limbs; corresponding
Weren to wommanhod, that creature	
Was nevere <u>lasse</u> mannyssh in semynge;	less
And ek the pure <u>wise</u> of hire <u>mevynge</u>	manner; moving
Shewed wel that men myght in hire <u>gesse</u>	guess
Honour, <u>estat</u>, and wommanly noblesse.	class
(*TC* I 281–7)	

As a description, it amounts to very little: she was not the shortest of women. The double negative of 'nas nat' emphasises what she was not, but without revealing what she was; and yet, this is the closest we come to a firm statement about Criseyde. Everything else here must be conjecture, given that she is engulfed in her widow's cloak and hard pressed by the throng of people. The limbs that cannot be seen and the movements that she can scarcely perform are, nevertheless, enough for a whole host of attributes to be claimed for her as things that 'men myght in hire gesse'. The final word is telling, for there is a lot of guesswork going on about Criseyde here. In essence, it is an exercise in imaginative projection, even to the point that Troilus puts words in her mouth:

To Troilus right wonder wel with alle	
Gan for to like hire mevynge and hire <u>chere</u>,	expression
Which <u>somdel deignous</u> was, for she let falle	slightly haughty
Hire look a <u>lite</u> aside in swich manere	a little
<u>Ascaunces</u>, 'What, may I nat <u>stonden</u> here?'	as if to say; stand

(TC I 288–92)

His gaze upon her is so powerful that he gives her a voice; but, in fact, Criseyde does not consciously look at him, and this voice is not her own. The whole first encounter is an imaginative exercise that allows Troilus to engage with the idea of love, and to direct it towards an image of his own construction.

BOOK II

Book II of the poem belongs essentially to Pandarus and Criseyde. Having learned that the object of Troilus's love is his own niece, Pandarus sets about winning her over for him. The book focuses on his attempts at persuasion and on the thoughts and responses of Criseyde.

PANDARUS

Pandarus is one of those distinctive characters whose name has become a mode of behaviour. To pander is to be a procurer, a go-between in a love affair, named after the literary Pandarus, who gives himself over so completely to the role. In the Italian source text, Pandaro had been the young friend of Troiolo, but Chaucer makes his Pandarus older, and also makes him the uncle of Criseyde. The result is a shift in the balance of power, with Pandarus still being a friend and confidante of Troilus, but with wider experience and greater control.

Pandarus is not, however, an old man. When Book II opens he, too, is languishing in bed on a May morning on account of his own sorrows in love and, in the course of the poem, Criseyde makes a few pointed references to his 'mistress'. But the many hundreds of lines that Troilus spends thinking about love are matched by a mere seven in Pandarus: his subjection, his grief, and his sleeplessness are all dealt with in a single stanza (*TC* II 57–63), leaving him free to run off and involve himself instead in the affairs of Troilus. It is a role that appeals to him much more than being the suffering lover himself, for Pandarus likes activity. He rushes from one place to another, absorbing himself fully in the lives of those around him, and calling for dancing and games and merriment as he goes.

He is a wonderful combination of grand hyperbole and pragmatism. He declares that his secret news about Troilus is 'five times better' than Criseyde's guess that the siege of Troy is over (*TC* II126); and his sentences tend to be crammed with superlatives. But alongside this habit of exaggeration, he likes to be in charge of everything. His speech tends towards proverb and aphorism, for he likes to tie everything up neatly. Faced with a weeping Troilus, he launches a barrage of homely wisdom along the lines that, 'A friend in need is a friend indeed' (*TC* I 694–5) and that 'Misery loves company' (*TC* I 708–9), until even Troilus tells him that his 'proverbes may... naught availle' (*TC* I 756). Most of all, he is the master builder and the arch manipulator. The metaphors surrounding him are often associated with construction or directing, as he checks his plans with a mental builder's line (*TC* I 1068).

Much of Book II sees Pandarus throwing himself wholeheartedly into his scheme to unite Troilus with Criseyde. It is a project that brings together his liking for control and taste for the dramatic, and he expends considerable thought and energy on it. When he arrives at Criseyde's house, he does not rush to tell her about Troilus, and instead hints at wonderful news and simply drops the name of the prince into the conversation six or seven times (*TC* II 157–98). He moves the topic towards love and moves away; he tells her that all talking has a purpose, and moves away again. Finally, we glimpse the workings of his own mind as he assesses Criseyde and decides on his plan of attack:

Than thought he thus : "If I my tale endite	compose
Aught harde, or make a proces any whyle,	at all; elaborate story
She shal no savour have therin but lite,	enjoyment; little
And trowe I wolde hire in my wil bigyle;	think; want to deceive
For tender wittes wenen al be wyle	believe; all is trickery
Theras thei kan nought pleynly understonde;	whenever
Forthi hire wit to serven wol I fonde" –	therefore; try
	(*TC* II 267–73)

It is a slightly convoluted stanza that assesses Criseyde's likely response, her propensity for paranoia, and his best method of success, ending with the shrewd observation that he must try to adapt his methods to her frame of mind. Accordingly, he studies her 'in a bysi wyse [busy fashion]' (*TC* II 274), with the kind of intensity that she cannot fail to notice, referring repeatedly to the news he has for her until Criseyde herself can stand it no longer and exclaims, 'come of, and telle me what it is!' (*TC* II 310). At long last, he reveals the feelings of Troilus in a strange juxtaposition of emotional styles that brings together his trademark pragmatism and hyperbole:

'The noble Troilus, so loveth <u>the</u>,	you
That, <u>but</u> ye helpe, it wol his <u>bane</u> be.	unless; destruction
Lo, here is al! What sholde I moore seye?	
Doth what yow <u>lest</u> to make hym lyve or deye.	please
But if ye <u>late</u> hym deyen, I wol <u>sterve</u> –	let; die
Have here my <u>trouthe</u>, nece, I nyl nat lyen –	promise
<u>Al sholde I</u> with this knyf my throte <u>kerve</u>.'	even if I had to; cut
With that the teris <u>breste</u> out of his yën,	burst; eyes
And seide, 'If that ye <u>don</u> us bothe dyen	cause
Thus gilteles, than have ye <u>fisshed fayre</u>!	made a fine catch
<u>What mende ye, though that we booth appaire?</u>'	what good will it do you, even if we both die?
	(*TC* II 319–29)

The matter-of-fact statement of the case lasts only as long as the stanza break before Pandarus pitches himself headlong into a tearful declaration of suicidal devotion in support of Troilus's endeavour. Indeed, it has ceased to be strictly Troilus's endeavour as the two men become inseparably hooked together in Pandarus's fishing metaphor. While the intervention of the best friend is often crucial in medieval love plots, none of the others has quite Pandarus's enthusiasm, dedication, or sense of drama. He is happily putting on a show that will not reach its finest moments until Book III, but in the meantime, he will spend the rest of Book II concocting ingenious and unnecessarily complex plans to bring Troilus and Criseyde together.

The plot involving a fake lawsuit is a case in point. In an attempt to get Troilus and Criseyde into the same room, Pandarus invents a lawsuit against Criseyde; he implicates Helen and the princes of Troy;

he involves them all in a tale of Criseyde's distress; he has Troilus pretend to be taken ill; he choreographs exits and entrances from the sickroom; he has a decoy letter ready to distract the chaperones; and he finally manages both to invite and exclude Criseyde's companion in a move worthy of the best salesmen:

> 'Rys, take with yow youre nece Antigone,
> Or whom yow <u>list</u>; or <u>no fors</u>; <u>hardyly</u>   please; no matter;
>   certainly
> The <u>lesse prees, the bet</u>; com forth with me.'   fewer the better
>   (*TC* II 1716–18)

It is deftly done, at least in this final moment. There would have been easier ways to get the couple together, of course, but Pandarus is not looking for simple or subtle. He wants results, and he is not willing to see Troilus languish for years (*TC* II 1298), but he also enjoys the artistic effect. He thinks of himself as someone with an eye for how things ought to be done, explaining how a love letter should be smudged with tears; the choice word used only for emphasis; the metaphors never mixed (*TC* II 1027–43).

FALLING IN LOVE AGAIN

In spite of all of Pandarus's schemes, the first glimpse that Criseyde has of Troilus is entirely unplanned. Glancing from her window, she catches sight of him as he returns from the battlefield. His armour bears the scars of fierce conflict, and the people are cheering for him as a returning hero. He is, as the narrator makes clear, an impressive sight:

> So lik a man of armes and a knyght
> He was to seen, fulfilled of <u>heigh prowesse</u>,   great bravery
> For bothe he hadde a body and a <u>myght</u>   power
> To <u>don</u> that thing, as wel as <u>hardynesse</u>;   do; boldness
> And <u>ek</u> to seen hym in his <u>gere</u> hym dresse,   also; armour
> So <u>fressh</u>, so yong, so <u>weldy</u> semed he,   vigorous; powerful
> It was an heven upon hym for to see.
>   (*TC* II 631–7)

Troilus never looks better than this. The metaphorical darts of Cupid have been replaced by real arrows, and his earlier self-engrossed gaze is supplanted by the open admiration of the crowd. Criseyde, in turn, looks upon the Trojan prince and claims to feel giddy at the sight of him:

Criseÿda gan al his <u>chere</u> aspien,	appearance
And <u>leet</u> it so softe in hire herte synke,	let
That to hireself she seyde, 'Who <u>yaf</u> me drynke?'	gave
(*TC* II 649–51)	

Her claim that she feels drunk – 'Who gave me drink?' – is such a strong statement that it is easy to believe that Criseyde falls headlong in love with Troilus at this moment. However, such a view overlooks the little word, 'leet' in the preceding line. Criseyde *lets* the image of Troilus sink softly into her heart, carefully manoeuvring it into position, before telling *herself* that she is intoxicated with love. It is a very controlled and careful response, both in terms of her reaction to Troilus and in terms of the way in which she wants to represent her reaction to herself. Her claim is that she is out of control, but the surrounding lines reveal a woman making a very careful choice, no matter how she wants to represent it to herself, and no matter what the narrative voice then has to say.

After Criseyde has finished listing the excellences of Troilus one by one, the narrator feels the need to have his say and intrudes with the wholly unexpected, 'Now myghte som envious jangle thus: / "This was a sodeyn [sudden] love"' (*TC* II 666–7). It is a surprising intervention. Having watched Criseyde enumerate the prince's virtues, rolling them over in her mind, the reader is not expecting the accusation of 'sodeyn' to be levelled against her. Of course, the narrator is raising the issue in order to defend Criseyde against the charge, but had he not mentioned it, then it would not have occurred to anyone else. This is, after all, an exercise in courtly love, where the convention is to be immediately overwhelmed by desire and, if anything, Criseyde is too controlled, too carefully thoughtful. The narrator, therefore, in a rush to defend his heroine from any criticism, casts doubt where none existed before, giving a vivid and memorable voice to the imaginary detractor and repeatedly using the word he does *not* want us to associate with Criseyde: 'sodeyn' (*TC* II 667); 'sodeynly' (*TC* II 673); 'sodeyn' (*TC* II 679). It is an exercise in how not to be persuasive. Criseyde will continue to move between agonies of decision and doubt for another eighteen stanzas, but her anxieties are not as memorable as the malicious voice invented by the narrator. In the end, vulnerable and cautious as Criseyde is, her love for Troilus is suspended between the two misleading signposts that she and the narrator erect: 'Who gave me drink?' and 'This was a sudden love'.

BOOK III

Book III finds Pandarus busily plotting ways in which he might arrange for Troilus and Criseyde to be alone together. He feigns illnesses, fabricates danger, invents tales of other suitors, and finally brings the two would-be lovers to bed.

COMEDY

Left to his own devices, it is likely that Troilus would have continued to worship Criseyde from afar – possibly very far. The role of male supplicant, begging only for a kind look from his lady in return for complete devotion and loyal servitude, is wholeheartedly embraced by Troilus. His extreme passivity in love is nowhere more evident than in Book III, where by turns he is prostrate in bed, down on his knees, or actually unconscious. He is everything short of dead, though even this he airs as a constant possibility. Within ten lines of first speaking to Criseyde, he offers to kill himself if that would please her (*TC* III 108–9) and finishes off the speech with the declaration that he can now die happy (*TC* III 112). His thoughts throughout turn readily to the notion that he will willingly die rather than offend Criseyde/Panadarus/the God of Love, or else surrender his life should it be demanded by Criseyde/Pandarus/the God of Love; and preferably not just once, but a 'thousand tymes' (*TC* III 389). Rhyming couplets are often very revealing, and for Troilus the notion of what we 'deserve' in love is almost always accompanied by the idea that we must 'serve' and be more than willing to 'sterve' [die]. Such death is not, however, active; it is the kind of death that involves simply ceasing to be. All around, men are dying on the battlefield, but what Troilus fears is not the Greek army, but the displeasure of his lady. His attitude prompts an exclamation from Pandarus:

Quod Pandarus, 'Thow wrecched mouses herte,
Artow agast so that she wol <u>the</u> bite?   are you afraid; you
Wy! <u>Don</u> this furred cloke upon thy sherte,   put
And folwe me, for I wol have the <u>wite</u>.'   blame

(*TC* III 736–9)

The choice of the furry cloak, combined with the metaphor, produces a giant mouse Troilus, scampering after Pandarus through the
'trappe' [trap door]' (*TC* III 741). It sets the tone for the next few
hundred lines, for Troilus is not in control of what happens next.
Indeed, he is not even conscious for all of it.

Having been brought to Criseyde's bedside, Troilus instantly drops
to his knees, while the blushing Criseyde finds herself unable to
speak. The confusion of both Pandarus and the narrator is clear, as
the would-be lovers remain inert. Pandarus throws himself into the
breach with his customary gusto: 'Nece [niece], se how this lord kan
knele!' (*TC* III 962). There is a missing syllable in the line (see p. 21)
so that the weight comes down heavily on the final word, 'knele'. It
emphasises the comedy of the scene, as Pandarus rushes off to fetch
a cushion for Troilus. As for the narrator, he is perplexed by the
fact that Criseyde leaves her knight kneeling on the floor and does
not instantly invite him to get up (*TC* III 967–70), but it is clear
that the couple are operating at a different speed from that of their
audience. Even when Pandarus succeeds in placing a seated Troilus
within the curtains of the four-poster bed, what follows is 11 stanzas
by Criseyde on her unsullied character and the evils of jealousy. The
tone is somewhere between righteous indignation and reprimand
as she insists on dwelling at length on the matter of 'Horaste', the
purely fictitious youth invented by Pandarus as part of his grand
plan. It all proves too much for Troilus. Trapped by Pandarus's lie
and seeing the tears of his lady, he drops to his knees again before
fainting clean away.

There is a moment of shocked silence; then Pandarus springs into
action:

This was no litel sorwe for to se;
But al was <u>hust</u>, and Pandare up as faste;   hushed
'O nece, <u>pes</u>, or we be lost!' quod he ...   quiet

(*TC* III 1093–5)

The unconscious Troilus is hoisted into bed and stripped off by Pandarus as he calls upon a bewildered Criseyde to help. The two of them rub Troilus's hands and bathe his forehead in an attempt to bring him round. That strong emotion might lead to loss of consciousness, even in a knight, was an accepted medieval notion, but here it is taken beyond normal bounds. In Chaucer's Italian source text, the hero also faints, but not until his lady is taken away from him. Troilus alone faints when he is brought to the bedroom; Troilus alone has to be lifted unconscious into his lady's bed. It is a state of affairs that leads to an exasperated cry of, 'is this a mannes herte?' (*TC* III 1098), from Pandarus, and an echoing, 'Is this a mannes game?' (*TC* III 1126), from Criseyde. Love at this moment is not an ennobling state for Troilus. Even when he recovers, he is more scolded child than Trojan prince as Criseyde continues to berate him about his imaginary suspicions, demanding to know if he is going to keep acting like a jealous infant (*TC* III 1168). But it is, in fact, worse than that: he is acting like someone *acting* like a jealous child, as he fabricates stories to cover, not his own tracks, but those of Pandarus. It is a humiliating tangle. His motives and his love are pure, but even pure earthly love, it seems, can leave anyone in a mess.

Troilus is, in comparison with Criseyde or Pandarus, a straightforward character. He scarcely has a thought that we do not get to hear, but crucially our interpretation of his thoughts and actions can go in different directions. In Book III he moves between humility and being ineffectual, idealistic, and naïve. Not knowing how to behave, he makes a pendulum swing from the extreme passivity of the faint to a slightly absurd posture of control as he tells Criseyde that she must 'yield' (*TC* III 1208). Accepting no such nonsense from Troilus, she simply tells him that, had she not already made up her own mind, she would not be in the bed at all (*TC* III 1210–11).

CONSUMMATION

The description of Criseyde's body at 1.1247 is entirely what we would expect it to be. It is the standard body of medieval romance, but it is a rather beautiful description nonetheless:

> Hire armes <u>smale</u>, hire streghte bak and softe,   slender
> Hire sydes longe, <u>flesshly</u>, smothe, and white   shapely

> He gan to stroke, and good thrift bad ful ofte
> Hire <u>snowissh</u> throte, hire brestes rounde and <u>lite</u>.   snowy; small
> <div align="center">(<i>TC</i> III 1247–50)</div>

What is crucial about it, is the acknowledgement that this is physical love, celebrated in solemn terms as 'Benigne Love … holy bond of thynges' (*TC* III 1261). The words are taken from the philosopher Boethius (*B* III m.12) as he explains that what holds the whole universe together, the force that stops planets falling from the sky, and oceans breaking their bounds, is love (see p. 32). The language of feudal service and enslavement that typified the speeches of Troilus gives way to a new love that binds 'withouten bond' (*TC* III 1358), as the lovers rejoice in one another, confessing previous doubts and fears, content now to reassure one another with kisses:

> And evere <u>mo</u>, when that <u>hem fel</u> to speke   more; they happened
> Of any wo <u>of swich a tyme agoon</u>,   in times passed
> With kissyng al that tale sholde <u>breke</u>   interrupt
> And fallen in a newe joye <u>anoon</u>;   at once
> And diden al <u>hire myght</u>, <u>syn</u> they were oon, in their power; since
> For to recoveren blisse and ben at eise,
> And <u>passed</u> wo with joie <u>contrepeise</u>.   previous; to balance
> <div align="center">(<i>TC</i> III 1401–7)</div>

The stanza's focus is upon peace and harmony. The lovers are at last 'at eise' in a couplet paired with 'contrepeise', a word that encompasses both balance and mutuality. The constant references to 'disease' and the sickness of love have been supplanted. They are finally 'oon', at one, their 'oneness' emphasised not just by rhyme, but by the recurrence of the word within other words in the stanza: 'ag*oon*', 'an*oon*'. Their unity is embedded within the verse and they have achieved peace. Indeed, 'peace' is the very word that Criseyde uses to describe Troilus: 'Welcome, my knyght, my pees, my suffisaunce!' (*TC* III 1309). In 'suffisaunce' she is declaring him to be everything she needs, and the word is particularly important because it comes from Boethius. It is the word used when Lady Philosophy is discussing the nature of true happiness. In the midst of the vast whirligig that is their universe, the lovers find a point of stillness and mutual contentment. The exact midpoint of the whole poem, significantly in a stanza about being 'numbered' (*TC* III 1269), sees Troilus 'bistowed in so heigh a place' (*TC* III 1271) by love. It is literally true, because the poem is an arc, taking Troilus from sorrow to the heights of bliss and down again. This is the highest point, and for a brief time there is a hiatus, but it cannot last.

BOOK IV

The war continues and the Greeks and Trojans set about exchanging prisoners. It is agreed that Criseyde will be returned to her father in the Greek camp, a decision that makes both Troilus and Criseyde distraught.

THE WHEEL OF FORTUNE

The first few lines of the poem had promised us a story that would run, 'Fro wo to wele, and after out of joie' (*TC* I 4). It is the great turning movement of the Wheel of Fortune. The Middle Ages knew the story – it knew the ending before the beginning – and so what is established is a cyclical sense of time and change. This is what tragedy is in the Middle Ages: an awareness that everything must pass, and that such movement will inevitably lead eventually to sorrow (see p. 82). In the divine realm there is no time and no change. God is eternal and sees everything simultaneously, existing out with the moment-by-moment progression of human life where the great pattern of the universe can be glimpsed only in fragments. For a little while, at the pinnacle of Book III, the lovers had experienced a sense of the peace and stillness that the Middles Ages thought of as heavenly, but in Book IV love is once again pinned down in the context of time, anchored by words such as 'ever' and 'never' as the minutes move inexorably towards the separation of Troilus and Criseyde.

The Prologue to Book IV gives us the tragedy in miniature:

| But al to litel, weylaway the whyle, | alas, all too short a time |
| Lasteth swich joie, ythonked be Fortune, ... | thanks to |

| From Troilus she gan hire brighte face | |
| Awey to writhe, and tok of hym non heede, | to turn away |

But caste hym clene out of his <u>lady grace</u>,	lady's favour
And on hire <u>whiel</u> she sette up Diomede	wheel

(*TC* IV 1–11)

Fortune is frequently thought of as a fickle woman in the Middle Ages, turning a wheel on which men and women rise and fall as their lives reach a peak of happiness, only for it to pass away. Chaucer uses that image here, though the behaviour of Fortune sounds very much like that of Criseyde, turning her face away from Troilus and choosing Diomede instead. This raises a fundamental question: to what extent are we at the mercy of events, or choose our own path? It is a key question in the remaining books, each of the protagonists having a different view as they negotiate the final stages of the war and of their lives together.

The standard medieval view of fortune is that it is the name we give to the jumble of events that influence our lives. The word 'influence' here is crucial, because the prevailing view of the Middle Ages is that we have the free will necessary to make our own decisions. While God – existing outside time – is aware of the outcomes of those decisions even before they are taken, he is not the cause of those decisions. The Christian view is that the choices are our own, though we of course live in a world where we must respond to the, often difficult, eventualities that come our way, much of it seeming chaotic in spite of the idea that ours is supposed to be a universe ruled over by an all-powerful deity. This is the interaction of free will and fortune. Expressed in this way, it seems simple, but the free-will debate was one of the most complicated philosophical questions of the Middle Ages, being bound up with questions of human suffering and God's goodness. Chaucer explores it in a number of his works, such as the *Knight's Tale* and the *Nun's Priest's Tale* (see pp. 36, 82), and it is central to *Troilus and Criseyde*.

The response of Pandarus to the news that Criseyde is about to be taken away from Troy is the most straightforward of the three. He may be moved to tears by the lovers' plight, but, pragmatic as ever, he quickly moves to the 'plenty more fish in the sea' argument: 'This town is ful of ladys al aboute; … If she be lost, we shal recovere an other.' (*TC* IV 401–6). In Pandarus's view, when one door closes another one opens, and so the way forward is to accept what fortune throws at us and try to turn it all into the next opportunity. Fortune, he argues, favours the brave ('Helpeth hardy man' *TC* IV 601) and a certain capacity to adapt to change is the way to survive.

Criseyde takes a more oppositional stance to fortune than that of her uncle. At first, she is prostrate with grief, but before too long she begins to think of ways in which she might escape the Greek camp. She has not one plan, but a whole list of schemes and counter-schemes. She reasons that she will be only a half-morning's ride away and will be able to make her way back; she imagines that her father will return her to Troy once he realises her situation; she feels that a fast-approaching peace will make everyone free to be wherever they choose; she proposes tricking her father into sending her back to Troy in order to retrieve valuable possessions, and so on (*TC* IV 1296–414).

TROILUS ON FORTUNE

The most sustained speeches on the nature of fortune, however, come from Troilus. The passivity that we had seen in the earlier books as the lover Troilus failed to act is here seen again, this time in the form of a firm belief that we are not only at the mercy of fortune, but that whatever actions we take are not in themselves free and lead only to further suffering. Troilus muses at length on the subject, parts of his speeches being taken from the work of the philosopher Boethius, but never from the parts where Boethius comes to terms with the timelessness of God, and with man's free will. Instead, Troilus's arguments are always those of the unenlightened man, the self-defined victim of destiny:

'For al that <u>comth</u>, comth by necessitee :	comes
Thus to ben <u>lorn</u>, it is my destinee.'	lost
(*TC* IV 958–9)	

It is the nature of Troilus not to act: not in the early books when he thinks he will die for love of Criseyde, and not in Book IV when he thinks he will die at her departure. His brother, Hector, is a lone voice, arguing against the Trojan parliament, rightly declaring that Criseyde is not a prisoner to be exchanged (*TC* IV 179–82), but Troilus does not add his voice to Criseyde's defence and departs 'withouten wordes mo [more]' (*TC* IV 219).

Ironically, we learn that the prisoner for whom Criseyde will be exchanged is Antenor, the very man who will later betray Troy (*TC* IV 203–5). The tragedy here is that inaction, just as much as action, is a choice, and Troilus's submissive acceptance of the will of others is as crucial a part of the downfall of Troy as are the voluble demands of the parliament. The narrator's ominous insistence on the vices of Antenor allows us to see the larger picture and to realise this. We have acquired an almost God-like view, able to see how individual acts of free will can end in tragedy. It is a smaller version of the foreknowledge we have possessed from the beginning: knowing how the story of Troilus and Criseyde will end even before we meet them, and yet wondering if the outcome might somehow be different this time. The complex medieval questions of free will, of preordained fate, and of foreknowledge are, therefore, not only played out in the lives of the protagonists, but in our experience as readers and listeners.

BOOK V

Criseyde leaves Troy and is escorted to the Greek camp. Time passes and Troilus continues to expect her return, until one day he catches sight of a brooch he had given Criseyde on the tunic of the Greek warrior, Diomede. He assumes that Criseyde has given it to Diomede as a love token and hopes to kill him in battle. However, Troilus is himself killed by Achilles. His soul ascends into the heavens where he is able to look down upon the world.

THE LADY VANISHES

Criseyde becomes an increasingly distant figure, both literally and metaphorically, as Book V progresses. As she is led off to the Greek camp by Diomede, we hear nothing from her except the single word, 'Allas!' (*TC* V 58), but the narrator's account of her response to Diomede's words of love is disconcerting:

Criseyde unto that purpos lite answerde,	little
As she that was with sorwe oppressed so	
That, in effect, she naught his tales herde	not at all
But here and ther, now here a word or two.	
(*TC* V 176–9)	

In fact, all is well until the final line. She is preoccupied in her grief and hears almost nothing that Diomede says. Except for a word or two. Except for a word or two more than that. It is the addition of the second 'here' that does the damage, implying as it does that Criseyde listened to a little more of Diomede's wooing than was strictly necessary. She almost falls from her horse at the sight of her father, but still remembers to act with the greatest courtesy to her escort:

> But natheles she thonketh Diomede
> Of al his travaile and his goode cheere,   for; trouble; company
> And that hym list his frendshipe hire to bede;   he wanted; offer
> And she accepteth it in good manere,
> And wol do fayn that is hym lief and dere,   gladly; pleasing to him
> And tristen hym she wolde, and wel she myghte,   trust
> As seyde she; and from hire hors sh'alighte.   she dismounted
> (*TC* V 183–9)

Partly what is at issue here is the overly effusive declaration that she 'would gladly do whatever was pleasing and dear to him', but, more than this, the repetitive accumulation of 'and' turns what had been the hasty departure of a woman almost falling from her horse into a protracted and profuse speech. We do not actually get to hear it, of course, but it is nevertheless somehow too much.

When Criseyde later accepts Diomede, the narrator attempts to distance us from the betrayal by repeated references to his source: 'And after this the storie telleth us' (*TC* V 1037); 'But trewely, the storie telleth us' (*TC* V 1051). He then turns the tables and declares that no one can say how soon Crisyede betrayed Troilus because they will not find it in the sources (*TC* V 1086–92). However, Criseyde's own voice is heard for the final time at this point. We will hear from her later in a letter to Troilus, but this is the last unfiltered moment of Criseyde, and it is a disappointment from start to finish. The poignancy of her earlier grief as she had wondered what Troilus was doing, and whether or not he was thinking of her (*TC* V 734–5) has disappeared. Instead, she is concerned about what posterity will think of her (*TC* V 1054–64) and attempts to make amends by stating that, 'To Diomede algate [at least] I wol be trewe' (*TC* V 1070). All the sadness of love's failures and compromises is contained in that little word 'algate'.

Her final stanza, such as it is, she addresses to Troilus:

> 'And certes <u>yow ne haten shal I nevere</u>;   I shall never hate you
> And <u>frendes</u> love, that shal ye <u>han of</u> me,   a friend's; have from
> And my good word, <u>al sholde I lyven evere</u>.   even if I live forever
> And trewely I wolde sory be
> For to seen yow in adversitee;
> And <u>gilteles</u>, I <u>woot</u> wel, I yow leve.   without guilt; know
> But al shal passe; and thus take I my leve'.
>   (*TC* V 1079–85)

She vows that she will remain his friend; that she will never think ill or speak ill of him; that she would not like to see him in trouble; that she knows he is innocent of any wrongdoing. It does not amount to much after what we had imagined was a great love; but, meagre and unadorned, it appears at least to be honest. The repetition of 'leve' in the couplet is worth noting, managing to be both poetically unsatisfying (for mere repetition does not really count as rhyme) and emotionally satisfying. The forsaking of Troilus for Diomede is an ordinary act of calculated self-interest that neither deserves to reach, nor can reach, any poetic heights; and at the same time, we feel the tug of a little reluctant delay in the repetition that does not quite 'leave'. It is the final word that we see Criseyde utter. Later, there is a letter that Troilus regards as 'straunge' (*TC* V 1632), in which she claims the need for secrecy and accuses him of impatience and of possibly deceiving her. However, this is the last we hear from her. Criseyde's fate is not recorded by Chaucer. She simply disappears from the narrative, with the words of Pandarus left in her place: 'I hate, ywis [truly], Cryseyde' (*TC* V 1732).

As for Troilus, he responds to Criseyde's initial absence with enthusiasm, addressing her empty palace ('O paleys desolat,/O hous of houses' *TC* V 540–1) and wishing that he could kiss its doors; visiting all the places in which he had formerly seen her (*TC* V 561–81), imagining that every farm cart he glimpses on the horizon might be her coming back to him (*TC* V 1158–62). He returns to the earlier state of love-longing in which he had spent the first two books of the poem, thinking and speaking only of her. His initial willingness to die for his lady's love is replaced, however, in Book V by a very real engagement with death. Realising what the sight of his own love token on Diomede's tunic must mean, he seeks Diomede on the battlefield. He slays the Greeks in their thousands, but without being able to murder his rival. Troilus finally dies at the hands of Achilles, an act that is dismissed in a single line at the end of the stanza: 'Despitously [without pity] hym slough the fierse Achille' (*TC* V 1806). The reader is caught for a moment in the confusion of battle, for this sparse sentence might be read either way in Middle English (see section Word Order, Chapter 2). It is, however, Troilus who is dead, and his soul that immediately ascends into the heavens.

For us, there is simply no time for grief as Troilus looks down from the spheres, 'and fully gan despise/ This wrecched world' (*TC* V 1816–17). His rejection of his entire previous existence is immediate and absolute, but in particular,

... in hymself he <u>lough</u> right at the wo	laughed
Of hem that <u>wepten</u> for his deth so <u>faste</u>,	wept; much
And <u>dampned</u> al oure <u>werk</u> that foloweth so	condemned; actions
The blynde lust, the which that may nat laste,	
(*TC* V 1821–4)	

The inward laughter is reminiscent of the early Troilus, who had mocked the love affairs of his friends in Book I. Now, in Book V he is laughing at love again: at those who mourn his loss, and at transient lust. There is no explicit mention of Criseyde. There could well be a good moral lesson here – that what is all-consuming on earth is simply of no importance in the life to come – but the laughter is as joyless as it was in Book I, and as critical. Heaven, we might have thought, would bring peace and understanding, but what we encounter here instead is condemnation and a dismissal of human love and loss. For the reader who has followed Troilus and Criseyde for over eight thousand lines, it is this sense of loss that dominates the end of Book V, as Troilus rejects the world and everything in it from his heavenly vantage point:

And down from thennes <u>faste he gan avyse</u>	he fully contemplated
This litel spot of erthe that with the <u>se</u>	sea
Embraced is, and fully gan despise	
This wrecched world, and <u>held</u> al vanite	considered
<u>To respect of</u> the pleyn <u>felicite</u>	in comparison to; joy
That is in hevene above;	
(*TC* V 1814–19)	

The earth might be a mere 'spot', but the image of it 'embraced' by the sea is a beautiful one, and the only sign of love in the stanza. Heaven's joy, by comparison, is 'pleyn', which no doubt means 'unalloyed' and 'complete', and yet still manages to be uninspiringly 'plain' and unsatisfying when compared to the image of worldly affection that has been left behind. Perhaps this is because we are not where Troilus is and, earth bound as we are, cannot yet understand his heavenly perspective; or perhaps, it is because the view of Troilus is not yet heavenly.

Not much is made of Troilus and Criseyde as pagans in the course of the poem, but this is, of course, what they are. Their gods are the classical gods, and it is significant here that Troilus is finally taken wherever 'Mercurye sorted [allotted] hym to dwelle.' (*TC* V 1827). Without baptism, so the Christian Middle Ages believed, his eternity would be spent on the margins, not in heaven itself, and so we last see him in the eighth sphere (*TC* V 1809) on the edge of the heavenly realm. From here, he can understand some things, but not all. Earthly loss and finality are presented by the narrator in a tour de force of *repetitio*, the same words beginning six successive clauses:

<u>Swich fyn</u> hath, lo, this Troilus for love!	such an end
Swich fyn hath al his grete worthynesse!	
Swich fyn hath his <u>estat real</u> above!	royal status
Swich fyn his <u>lust</u>, swich fyn hath his <u>noblesse</u>!	desire; nobility
Swich fyn hath false worldes <u>brotelnesse</u>!	fickleness
And thus bigan his lovyng of Criseyde,	
As I have told, and in this wise he deyde.	

(TC V 1828–34)

We hear the celestial doors slamming closed as, one after the other, worldly goods and concerns meet their end. Criseyde's name appears for the final time in the poem, in a couplet with 'deyde'. The death of Troilus, which he had offered Criseyde so many times in the course of the poem, is finally linked to her name. Loving her has, in a real sense, led to his death. But as the repetition in the stanza shows, an ending to that love was inevitable, one way or another.

The final stanzas, however, offer an alternative love, one not open to the pagan Troilus, but central to medieval Christian life. The reader is instead directed towards salvific love in the form of Christ who died on the cross and rose again, 'oure soules for to beye [buy]' (*TC* V 1843). Rather than bringing death, this is the love that redeemed mankind; death was overcome, and eternal life granted. There is no longer any ending, for this is a love that will enfold (circumscrive) us, while being itself 'uncircumscript [boundless]' (CT V 1865). The transition from the love of Troilus and Criseyde that has occupied us through five books and eight thousand lines, to these few final stanzas and its different kind of love, is a difficult one. But what is key is that it is not, essentially, a different kind of love. The Christ who died on the cross was wholly God, but also wholly man, and what interested the Middle Ages was not the divinity of his being, but his humanity. In the late fourteenth century, the emphasis was not so much on Christ's triumph over death as his suffering, and not so much on his role as Son of God as on his life as man among mankind. In the very final moments of this monumental work, there is a last appeal to love, the love of a son for his mother, the love of Christ for Mary (*TC* V 1868–9). The purity and goodness of earthly love, its capacity for self-sacrifice, and ability to inspire virtue, are all present in the final lines, just as they have been throughout the entire work. The love of which we are capable is far from perfect and through Troilus and Criseyde we have seen the fixations, the misunderstandings, and the failures of ordinary love, but we have also, for a while, seen the selflessness and generosity of earthly love, its ability to inspire, and its capacity to bring peace. The final lines are not, therefore, a repudiation of all that has gone before. They are instead proof of what human love is capable of being.

FURTHER READING

There are excellent notes and introduction in *Geoffrey Chaucer: Troilus and Criseyde* (2003). Ed. Barry Windeatt. Penguin Classics. London: Penguin. The poem can be read in parallel with its source in Boccaccio's *Il Filostrato* in *Geoffrey Chaucer: Troilus and Criseyde: A New Edition of 'The Book of Troilus'* (1990). Ed. B. A. Windeatt. 2nd edn. London: Longman.

For a translation of Boccaccio's *Filostrato*, see *Chaucer's Boccaccio: Sources of 'Troilus' and the Knight's and Franklin's Tales* (1980). Trans. N. R. Havely. Cambridge: D. S. Brewer. For a wide-ranging introduction to the figure of Troilus in Western literature, see *The European Tragedy of Troilus* (1989). Ed. Piero Boitani. Oxford: Clarendon Press, and for accounts of Chaucer's engagement with contemporary Italian culture and literature, see *Chaucer and the Italian Trecento* (1983). Ed. Piero Boitani. Cambridge: Cambridge University Press.

For a modern English translation of Boethius, see *Boethius: The Consolation of Philosophy* (1969). Trans. V. E. Watts. Penguin Classics. London: Penguin. A study of Chaucer's poem that explores its Boethian aspects is Ida Gordon (1970). *The Double Sorrow of Troilus: A Study of Ambiguities in 'Troilus and Criseyde'*. Oxford: Oxford University Press.

For a comprehensive introduction to critical questions in the poem, see Barry Windeatt (1992). *Troilus and Criseyde*. Oxford Guides to Chaucer. Oxford: Oxford University Press. An insightful succinct analysis can be found in A. C. Spearing (1976). *Chaucer: Troilus and Criseyde*. London: Edward Arnold. For a series of critical studies that touch illuminatingly on questions relevant to interpretation of *Troilus and Criseyde*, see A. C. Spearing (1993). *The Medieval Poet as Voyeur: Looking and Listening in Medieval Love-Narratives*. Cambridge: Cambridge University Press, together with A. C. Spearing (2005). *Textual Subjectivity: The Encoding of Subjectivity in Medieval Narratives and Lyrics*. Oxford: Oxford University Press, and also, relatedly, A. C. Spearing (2012). *Medieval Autographies: The 'I' of the Text*. Notre Dame, IN: University Press of Notre Dame.

On the subject of love, see *Writings on Love in the Middle Ages* (2006). Ed. Helen Cooney. London: Palgrave Macmillan, together with Helen Phillips, 'Love', in *A Companion to Chaucer* (2000). Ed. Peter Brown. Oxford: Blackwell, pp. 281–95, as well as Barry Windeatt, 'Love', in *A Companion to Medieval English Literature and Culture c.1350-c.1500* (2007). Ed. Peter Brown. Oxford: Blackwell, pp. 322–38, together with Corinne Saunders, 'Love and the Making of Self', in A Concise Companion to Chaucer (2006). Ed. Corinne Saunders. Oxford: Blackwell, 134–55.

Chaucer's poem has been the focus of various book-length studies. Winthrop Wetherbee (1984). *Chaucer and the Poets: An Essay on 'Troilus and Criseyde'*. Ithaca: Cornell University Press focusses on the poem's relations to classical poets and to Dante. A readable introduction to some critical issues in the poem is found in C. David Benson (1990). *Chaucer's Troilus and Criseyde*. London: Unwin Hyman, while there is a more specific focus, as implied by the title, in Thomas C. Stillinger (1992). *The Song of Troilus: Lyric Authority in the Medieval Book*. Philadelphia: University of Pennsylvania Press.

For an informative collection of essays on gender issues, try Tison Pugh and Marcia Smith Marzec, Eds. (2008). *Men and Masculinities in Chaucer's 'Troilus and Criseyde'*. Cambridge: D. S. Brewer. There are also some convenient collections of useful essays on aspects of the poem in *Essays on 'Troilus and Criseyde'* (1980). Ed. Mary Salu. Cambridge: D. S. Brewer, as also in *Chaucer's 'Troilus': Essays in Criticism* (1980). Ed. S. A. Barney. London: Scolar Press, and in addition in *Chaucer's 'Troilus and Criseyde': 'Subgit to alle poesye': Essays in Criticism* (1992). Ed. R. A. Shoaf, with the assistance of Catherine S. Cox. Binghamton NY: Medieval and Renaissance Texts and Studies.

5

THE BOOK OF THE DUCHESS

The Book of the Duchess centres upon the death of a beautiful woman, and upon the mourning of a man dressed in black. She is referred to as 'White' (*BD* 948) and is usually identified with Blanche, the first wife of John of Gaunt (see p. 7), who died, probably of the plague, in 1368–9. The home of the Man in Black is described at the end of the poem as

> A long castel with walles white,
> <u>Be</u> Seynt Johan, on a ryche hil,   by
>   (*BD* 1318–19)

John (Johan) of Gaunt was Duke of Lancaster (long castel) and Earl of Richmond (ryche hil) in Yorkshire, and these lines would appear to be a punning reference to his name. In spite of the fact that he would have two further marriages, Gaunt chose to be buried with his first wife in a double tomb. It was destroyed in the Great Fire of London, but records show that the effigies of Gaunt and Blanche were, unusually, depicted holding hands, and he held annual commemorations for her for the rest of his life. The exact occasion for this poem is unclear but, at any rate, it is a work that extends beyond one particular act of mourning and considers the themes of love and loss more widely.

The poem is a *dream vision*, a very popular form in the late Middle Ages, and one favoured by Chaucer. In addition to *The Book of the Duchess*, he wrote three other dream poems: *The House of Fame*, *The Parliament of Fowls*, and the *Prologue to the Legend of Good Women*. Dreams, of course, present all kinds of literary possibilities, but medieval dream narratives tend to follow a basic pattern. The dreamer, often unable to sleep, takes up a book or wanders outside, before succumbing to a dream in which he encounters figures of authority in a strangely transfigured landscape. He questions these figures and is led by their words towards some sense of enlightenment, relieved of the anxiety of the early part of the poem.

The dreamer in the *Book of the Duchess*, however, goes well beyond a temporary wakefulness and exists in a state of insomnia so profound that he wonders how he can carry on living. This initial declaration is immediately followed by an account of his existence in the most negative terms:

I have so many an <u>ydel</u> thought	idle
Purely for <u>defaute</u> of slep	lack
That, by my trouthe, I <u>take no kep</u>	care about
Of nothing, how hyt cometh or <u>gooth</u>,	goes
<u>Ne me nys nothyng leef nor looth</u>.	nothing is dear or undesirable to me
Al is <u>ylyche</u> good to me –	equally
Joye or sorowe, <u>wherso hyt</u> be –	wherever it
For I have felynge in nothyng,	

(*BD* 4–11)

He is not unhappy, because he does not feel enough engagement to experience emotion of any kind: nothing strikes him as desirable or undesirable. Indeed, the key word is 'nothing'. It is used three times in five lines, with the triple negativity of 'Ne me nys nothing' (literally, 'not to me is not nothing') conjuring a state close to nihilism in its purest form. The 'nothingness' arises from his 'idle thoughts', these in turn springing from his insomnia. As for the insomnia, it is due to a sickness that has assailed him for the last eight years (*BD* 37), an unspecified illness, but often thought to be lovesickness. His claim that there is only one physician who might cure him (*BD* 39–40) is a traditional metaphor for the lady 'curing' the pining youth with her love, and there is a moment later in the poem where the dreamer's rapid questioning of the Man in Black displays, perhaps, an eagerness to impose his own experience of unrequited love upon the suffering knight:

'What <u>los</u> ys that?' quod I <u>thoo</u>;   loss; then
'<u>Nyl</u> she not love yow? Ys hyt soo?   will not
Or have ye <u>oght doon amys</u>,   done something wrong
That she hath left yow? <u>Ys hyt</u> this?   is it
For Goddes love, telle me al.'
               (*BD* 1139–43)

Whatever his own situation, the dreamer is kind-hearted and full of ready sympathy. Like all dreamers in the vision tradition, he can be simple-minded and has a tendency not to grasp the full import of what is being said, or the significance of what is around him. He can also be very literal-minded. His response to the book he reads in his wakeful state – the tale of Ceyx and Alcyone – is a realisation that there are classical gods who might be willing to accept offerings in exchange for sleep, and he promises the god Morpheus a golden bedroom, with sumptuous feather bed and the finest black satin imported sheets (*BD* 248–61). It is a surprising response to a famous tale of love and loss.

THE TALE OF CEYX AND ALCYONE

The classical tale of Ceyx and Alcyone would have been well-known to Chaucer's audience. In the version by Ovid, the couple are devoted to one another, but then Ceyx is drowned in a shipwreck. The gods grant Alcyone a dream in which Ceyx tells her of his death. Distraught, Alcyone throws herself into the sea, where both of them are transformed into birds. It is a tale of marital devotion, the moral being that not even death could ever part the couple.

The tale takes up almost two hundred lines of the *Book of the Duchess* (*BD* 62–230), though Chaucer alters his source significantly in places. Notably, there are differences concerning the dream itself. In the original Ovid, there is danger for the messenger who ventures into the seductive realm of the sleep-god Morpheus, but for Chaucer's sleep-deprived narrator there is a longing description of the various snoring inhabitants and a rough awakening by trumpet for the god, who opens one bleary eye in response (*BD* 172–85). In the source, Morpheus is dispatched to imitate Ceyx in a dream. In Chaucer's version, however, he has the macabre task of inhabiting the corpse that he must retrieve from the bottom of the ocean. The instruction that the messenger is told to give him is explicit:

'Go faste into the <u>Grete Se</u>,	Great Sea (Mediterranean)
And <u>byd</u> hym that, <u>on alle thyng</u>,	command; above all
He take up <u>Seys body the kyng</u>,	the body of King Ceyx
That lyeth ful pale and <u>nothyng rody</u>.	not at all ruddy
Bid hym crepe into the body ...	
And <u>do</u> the body speke ryght soo,	make
<u>Ryght</u> as hyt was <u>woned</u> to doo'	just; accustomed
(*BD* 140–50)	

The description here is of the livid flesh of the victim of drowning. Alcyone is not going to receive a vision of her husband; she is going to be visited by his reanimated corpse, propped at the end of the bed by Morpheus as he ventriloquises the voice of Ceyx. The words, 'I am but ded' (*BD* 204) are, by this point, unnecessary. Unnecessary, too, is the instruction the corpse gives about retrieving his body from the shore at low tide, but this is the harsh and unpleasant reality of dealing with those who visit from beyond the grave. The response of Alcyone is to open her eyes quickly and dispel the visitation: 'With that hir eyen up she casteth / And saw noght' (*BD* 212–13). She does not then choose to throw herself into the waves, and there is no reunion with her husband as birds. Instead, her grief at what she has seen kills her within three days. The dead cannot be restored and would be an unappealing and inconvenient bunch if they could be. It is better to remember them as they were, as the rest of the poem will show. Of course, none of this feels particularly sinister. It is all delivered in the jog-trot rhythm of the octosyllabic couplet (see p. 20) and what might have been grotesque is lightened by comedy and moves swiftly on.

THE DREAM

Much to his own amazement, the narrator then falls asleep, sprawled across the book he has just been reading. Like the majority of dreamers in medieval poetry, he finds himself in a beautiful May landscape, the colours around him those of another world: the sky is a crystalline blue and the beams of the sun are golden (*BD* 340, 338). He is aware of the heavenly singing of birds, though the fact that these avian angels have positioned themselves on the roof 'tyles' (*BD* 300) brings them a lot closer to home. The dreamer assures us that none of them were pretending to sing, and that each one of them was doing its best (*BD* 317–18) in a manner that makes them sound more like a children's choir on its best behaviour than like an angelic host. The dreamer rhymes 'entewnes [tunes]' with 'Tewnes [Tunis]' (*BD* 309–10) in a way that shows he does not have much of a musical ear anyway. He is clearly, therefore, even from these first moments, a dreamer in the best medieval tradition: a man with certain limitations.

The narrator has, however, all the abilities of any dreamer in that he is able immediately to join in a hunt that he hears in the distance. One minute he has a horse, the next he does not; forests are there and then they are gone. The hunters are pursuing a hart, no doubt with the pun intended. This male deer, like the dreamer and like the Man in Black we are about to encounter, is utterly weary. The term used is 'embosed' (*BD* 353), an unusual and technical word from hunting when an animal has been driven to its very limits, going to ground in the woods. But the next moment, the hunt is gone, and the dreamer encounters a puppy instead. It is friendly and fawning (*BD* 389), but its significance is never explained: critics have suggested fidelity, marital devotion, healing, and even wisdom, but what is clear is that it bounds away into the darkness, where the trees tower to 40 or 50 fathoms, with branches no more than an inch apart (*BD* 422–5). The creatures of the wood, vast in number, are running, and they are running towards a man, young and bearded, who sits with his back to an oak tree.

THE MAN IN BLACK

The man instantly has much in common with the narrator. He, too, has been brought almost to the brink of death by something beyond his control, in his case the most profound sorrow. Unaware that the dreamer is listening, the man delivers a lament in which he tells us:

'I have of sorwe so gret won   abundance
That joye gete I never non,   any
Now that I see my lady bryght,   fair
Which I have loved with al my myght,
Is fro me ded and ys agoon.   gone
Allas, deth, what ayleth the,   is wrong with you
That thou noldest have taken me,   would not
Whan thou toke my lady swete,   took away
That was so fair, so fresh, so fre,   lovely; noble
So good that men may wel se
Of al goodnesse she had no mete!'   equal
                    (BD 475–86)

We had been jogging along in a metre of companionable couplets, but the knight's complaint shifts us to a more complicated rhyme scheme. We do not realise for the first five lines as we continue *aabb*, but the line in which the lady's death is declared disrupts the pattern. More than this, it disrupts the whole poem. It looks as though there might be a line missing after 'agoon', and from the early sixteenth century onwards editors have attempted to supply what they feel might be an omission, or else number the lines to include the 'missing' one (as above). However, all the manuscripts agree on the lines as they stand. It seems more likely that the lady's death *should* disrupt the Man in Black's lament, and that there is a space because that is what she has left by being 'agoon'. The lament, therefore, has 11 declared lines, the traditional number of death, and stands in isolation amidst the couplets of the rest of the poem. It acknowledges in the starkest terms, both the death of the lady and the knight's own desire for death. Death, however, will not take him, and he finds that his torment is to be 'Alway deynge and be not ded' (*BD* 588). The sense of being trapped by grief is apparent too in his declaration to the dreamer, 'For y am sorwe, and sorwe ys y' (*BD* 597). The very structure of the line locks itself in and allows no outlet for the grief that the Man in Black embodies.

THE GAME OF CHESS

The Man in Black then proceeds to an extended metaphor in which he describes his loss as a chess game against Fortune in which his queen has been taken:

'At the ches with me she gan to pleye;
With hir false <u>draughtes dyvers</u>   hostile moves
She <u>staal</u> on me and tok my <u>fers</u>.'   crept up; queen
                    (*BD* 652–4)

His adversary has the half-laughing, half-crying face found in traditional medieval depictions of Fortune (*BD* 633–4), and it emerges
that this whole section of the poem is concerned with reversals of
one kind or another. The chess board itself is a stark separation of two
colours, and the account of Fortune maintains this division, emphasising the difference between what she is and what she appears to
be: 'fylthe over-ystrawed [strewn] with floures' (*BD* 629). This is,
quite simply, what Fortune does: takes those who are happy and
destroys that happiness. The knight thinks of himself entirely in these
terms as he lists what he was and what he has become:

'... my <u>wele</u> is <u>woo</u>,   happiness; sorrow
My good ys harm, and evermoo
In wrathe ys turned my <u>pleynge</u>   joyfulness
And my delyt into <u>sorwynge</u>.'   sorrowing
                    (*BD* 603–6)

He does not wholly blame Fortune for, in her place, he would have
stolen away the queen, too, but he sees no way forward except death.
In response, the dreamer urges him to remember a motley collection
of figures from history and literature who remained calm in the face
of hostile Fortune (*BD* 717), or else who failed to remain calm and
killed themselves, or their children, having been victims of false love
(*BD* 726–39). In his literal-minded way the dreamer is still clinging
to the notion that this is about a game of chess, but the Man in Black
gently corrects him: 'Thou wost [know] ful lytel what thou menest;
/ I have lost more than thow wenest [think]' (*BD* 743–4). He then
proceeds to describe in detail exactly what he has lost.

WHITE

The description of the woman who will later be identified as 'goode
faire White' (*BD* 948) goes on for around two hundred lines. She
manages to be a combination of superlatives and perfect balance

('mesure' (*BD* 881)), and as such provides a contrast to the innate dichotomies and precarious temperament of Fortune. Set pieces describing the lady in detail were conventional in medieval love poetry, but this one is far longer than most and expands the description beyond her features to include much more of her character. The physical form described is the ideal of medieval beauty, with golden hair (*BD* 858) and ivory skin (BD 946), though with some unexpected touches for a modern reader:

'Ryght faire <u>shuldres</u> and body long	shoulders
She had, and armes, every <u>lyth</u>	limb
<u>Fattyssh</u>, <u>flesshy</u>, not gret therwith;	well-rounded; shapely
Ryght white handes, and nayles rede;	
Rounde brestes; and of good <u>brede</u>	breadth
Hyr hippes were; a streight flat bak.'	
(*BD* 952–7)	

The sum total of all of this is the declaration that her body was 'pure sewynge [perfectly conformable]' (*BD* 959), another assurance that everything about White was proportionate, from the length of her limbs to her responses towards suitors. The young men who wish to woo her are met with kindly refusal, not being sent bareheaded into the Gobi Desert (*BD* 1028) in order simply to be rejected. She scorns tricks ('knakkes' *BD* 1033) and instead a recurring word in her description is 'symple': unaffected, modest, simply true. Indeed, 'Truth' itself, we are told, chose her as his resting place, and because of this,

'Therto she hadde the moste grace	
To have stedefast <u>perseveraunce</u>	constancy
And <u>esy</u>, <u>atempre</u> <u>governaunce</u>	gentle; moderate; behaviour
That ever I knew or <u>wyste</u> yit,	encountered
So pure <u>suffraunt</u> was hir <u>wyt</u>;	patient; understanding
And reson gladly she understood;	
Hyt folowed wel she <u>koude good</u>.'	knew what was right
(*BD* 1006–12)	

This is no mere courtly lady. While it is conventional to refer to the lady's 'grace' in the context of her benign attitude towards a suitor, few authors unpack the term to explain what it means in the context of a wise, likable, and powerful woman. The detailed account of her virtues takes her well beyond the normal bounds of the formal description, capturing her perfections so completely that the dreamer feels the need to point out that all of this must be viewed as the knight's subjective response:

> 'I <u>leve</u> yow wel, that trewely   believe
> Yow thoghte that she was the beste
> And to beholde the <u>alderfayreste</u>,   fairest of all
> <u>Whoso had loked</u> hir with your eyen.'   if someone were to look at
>   (*BD* 1048–51)

The Man in Black, however, will not accept that his judgement is in any way partial. While his description of Fortune had emphasised her eternally shifting nature, he insists that White was viewed consistently by all: a woman loved and revered by all those around her. In spite of this, he wishes to emphasise that his love for her was a choice, a willed giving of himself. Having said that he 'needed' to love her, he corrects himself:

> '"Nede?" Nay, trewly, I <u>gabbe</u> now;   talk nonsense
> Noght "nede", and I wol tellen how:
> For of good wille myn herte <u>hyt wolde</u>'   wished it
>   (*BD* 1075–7)

The Man in Black loved her because he wanted to love her, and she accepted him only when she was willing to do so. It was, therefore, as the knight is keen to emphasise, a mutual love in which the perfect balance that characterised White's virtues, was extended to the perfect balance of their affection for one another, their hearts responding as one to everything around them:

> 'Oure hertes <u>wern</u> so <u>evene</u> a payre   were; evenly matched
> That never nas that oon <u>contrayre</u>   contrary
> To that other <u>for no woo</u>.   because of any unhappiness
> For sothe, <u>ylyche</u> they suffred <u>thoo</u>   alike; then
> <u>Oo</u> blysse and eke oo sorwe bothe;   one
> <u>Ylyche</u> they were bothe glad and <u>wrothe</u>;   alike; sad
> Al was us oon, withoute <u>were</u>.'   doubt
>   (*BD* 1289–95)

The unity of their love is emphasised by the repeated use of 'oo' [one], both as a word in its own right and contained within other words. Even the word for sorrow, 'woo', in this context is diminished by the fact that whatever troubles they faced were faced together as one. It is not surprising that ultimately the Man in Black should have regarded White as his 'suffisaunce' (*BD* 1038). She was simply all that he needed.

THE END OF THE DREAM

The reverie, however, is brought to an end by the dreamer, who demands to know where White is now. The question brings the knight to an abrupt halt:

'Now?' quod he, and <u>stynte anoon</u>.	stopped at once
Therwith he <u>wax</u> as ded as stoon	became
(*BD* 1299–300)	

The 'now' of the present moment leads him to her death, and to his living death. The dreamer is slow to understand and has to be guided to the realisation in the simplest terms by the knight:

'She ys ded!' 'Nay!' '<u>Yis</u>, <u>be</u> my trouthe!'	yes; by
'Is that youre los? Be God, hyt ys <u>routhe</u>!'	a pity
(*BD* 1309)	

The knight's declaration and the dreamer's startled response, 'No!', share a single line as the dreamer at last gains the same knowledge as the knight and understands that White is dead. The point of the dream has not been, however, to gain this admission from the knight. Assuming that the 'I' of the earlier lyric was, indeed, the Man in Black, then he has already declared White's death unambiguously during his complaint (*BD* 479), and it is the dreamer who has failed to understand. It is the Man in Black's clear statement of death that flanks the dreamer's unwilling 'Nay!', as the line lengthens from the steady four beats of the normal octosyllabic verse to an extended ten, the death of White having upset the natural order of things.

MEMORY

The final word of the knight in the poem is, therefore, 'trouthe', and it is this truth that the poem imparts. However, the function of the dreamer in the *Book of the Duchess* is not to help the Man in Black towards a realisation: it is to arrive at that realisation together with – or just a little bit behind – the reader. The dreamer's single-line response, that White's death is a 'routhe' [pity], has been thought inadequate by some critics. The poem does not offer any further words from the Dreamer, and the hunt immediately sounds the signal for home, for, 'al was doon ... the hert-huntyng' (*BD* 1312–13). But what is there to say beyond acknowledging a feeling of pity, for the knight and for the woman he has lost? The Man in Black's own words, his 'heart-hunting', have described the magnitude of that loss, and there is nothing more that the dreamer can add. The loss is not his, and as a mere bystander all he can do is acknowledge that the knight feels something that the dreamer very much pities. The poem might have offered consolation in the form of a promise of a life to come, but it does not. The tale of Ceyx and Alcyone has shown us that death is indeed death, and whatever happens thereafter, our loved ones will no longer be as we have known them: they cannot come back. The only consolation on offer, therefore, is the memory of White, and the beauty of the poem itself that preserves that memory. At the beginning of the work, the narrator had been afflicted by 'sorwful ymagynacioun [melancholy thoughts]' (*BD* 14) and had contemplated the 'nothingness' of his existence. However, we see in the poem that sorrowful imagination can, in fact, be used to produce something from nothing. The dreamer promises at the end of the poem to write the story of his dream, which he then presents to us as *The Book of the Duchess*. It is this work that allows White, in all her beauty and goodness, to live on. There are no words of comfort, no assurances, no supernatural encounters; there is simply the fact of loss and the consolation of memory.

THE HOUSE OF FAME

The *House of Fame*, like the *Book of the Duchess* and the *Parliament of Fowls*, is a dream poem. It differs, however, in tone from these other works, being concerned not with personal love in its various manifestations, but with matters such as reputation, truth, and authority.

BOOK I

While Chaucer's other dreamers give more of a sense of themselves as they speak of suffering and searching and how they sought comfort or inspiration in books, the narrative voice of the *House of Fame* remains at a distance, in spite of the fact that he is given the most personal of names: Geffrey (*HF* 729). Instead, the poem begins in very bookish terms with a 65-line *proem* contemplating the nature of dreams. It lists their technical categories – visions, revelations, hallucinations, and the like – and a whole heap of possible causes, from melancholy, to lovesickness, to prison life, to an imbalance of the humours. It also gives an exact date for the occurrence of the dream being narrated: the tenth of December (*HF* 63, 111). There have been many historical or astronomical theories put forward for this date, but the poem itself does not reveal a reason, which might be the important point. The *proem* is full of certainties – precise timing and precisely technical terminology – and yet it does not yield any answers. The terms are listed only for the narrator to declare his bafflement:

Why that is an <u>avision</u>	vision
And why this a <u>revelacion</u>,	revelation
Why this a <u>drem</u>, why that a sweven,	dream; vision
And noght to every man <u>lyche even</u>;	the same
Why this a <u>fantome</u>, why these <u>oracles</u>,	hallucination; revelations
I <u>not</u>;	do not know

(*HF* 7–12)

The dominant word is 'why' as a 51-line sentence tumbles breathlessly onwards, main verbs being postponed to the end of lengthy clauses ('I not'), as the narrator reaches the conclusion that he does not really know anything about dreams, in spite of a ready facility with the terminology. The same effect continues in the rambling sentences of the 'Invocation' as the narrator prays to the god of sleep (*HF* 69); to the prime mover of the universe (*HF* 81); and to 'Jesus God' (*HF* 97) – all without any apparent distinction – to bring joy to those who believe his dream, and all manner of misfortune to those who doubt. The prayer ends with a reference to the sad demise of Croesus, last King of Lydia, who did not believe his own mystical vision and consequently died on a gibbet (*HF* 104–6). This brief account of regal death is introduced with an assuring and assertive, 'Lo, with such a conclusion' (*HF* 103) as though the demise of Croesus brings all debate on the matter to a logical end, but of course it does not. What had promised initially to be an authoritative work on dreams, and therefore an authoritative work on the nature of truth itself, turns out not to be so. We have less of an idea about what the various categories of vision might be and what causes them, than we might have had at the beginning, because the dominant sense of the *proem* and invocation is one of acceptance in the midst of incomprehension. What the opening of Book I achieves is uncertainty, a feeling that is not about to be dispelled by what follows.

THE TEMPLE OF GLASS

The narrator is not like other dreamers. While they generally suffer insomnia on summer nights until some work of literature inspires slumber, this dreamer falls asleep astonishingly quickly ('wonder sone' *HF* 114) on a winter's night. He is compared to a weary pilgrim who has travelled to the shrine of St Leonard, and there may, once again, be a specific reference here, but at any rate, the effect is wholly unromantic, St Leonard being the patron saint of captives, and the exhausting pilgrimage having entailed a journey of a whole 'myles two' (*HF* 116). The dreamer instantly finds himself in a temple constructed of crystal ('glas' *HF* 120), more Gothic than classical, with pinnacles, precious stones, and myriad golden statues in niches and on stands. He knows at once that it is a temple of Venus, for Venus herself is depicted there 'in portreyture' (*HF* 131). There are, of course, different aspects of love and many different aspects of this goddess, but here she is shown, 'Naked fletynge in a see' (*HF* 133), garlanded with the red and white roses that were usually thought of as denoting erotic desire, and in the company of both Cupid and her husband, Vulcan, whose appearance would have triggered thoughts of Venus's adultery (*HF* 134–9).

On the wall, the dreamer sees a tablet of brass, inscribed with some of the best-known words from classical literature: 'I wol now synge, yif I kan,/ The armes and also the man' (*HF* 143–4). These are the opening lines of Virgil's *Aeneid*, declaiming the story of the fall of Troy and the destined adventures of the hero Aeneas, scenes from which appear on the walls of the temple in a manner that seems to conjure both words and images, static and in motion. The dreamer sees the storm that almost destroys Aeneas's fleet, and the wind blowing the hair of Venus as she tells him to journey towards the city of Carthage and Queen Dido (*HF* 230). The love story of Dido and Aeneas was one of the best known in the Middle Ages, though the dreamer coyly refrains from dwelling on the passion for which they were famous:

> What shulde I speke more queynte,   why; elaborately
> Or peyne me my wordes peynte   exert myself; to embellish
> To speke of love? Hyt wol not be;
> I kan not of that faculte.   do not have; ability
>   (*HF* 245–8)

Instead, the total, uncompromising, unrestrained surrender of Dido to Aeneas is encapsulated in one line, the alliteration of which stresses the logic that, for her, everything should be encompassed by her devotion to this man: 'Hyr lyf, hir love, hir lust, hir lord' (*HF* 258).

That Dido loved Aeneas was never in doubt. The response of Aeneas is, however, more complicated. A man with a destiny to fulfil, he was prompted by the gods to leave Dido, an act that led in turn to her suicide. Virgil makes much of the pained dedication to duty that Aeneas must embody. That other favourite classical author of the Middle Ages, Ovid, tells the same story from Dido's point of view, in turn focussing on her grief and heroism, and her betrayal by her lover. There is a shift, therefore, in Book I from the influence of one classical author to another, and Chaucer refers us explicitly to the works of both of them ('Rede Virgile in Eneydos / Or the Epistle of Ovyde', *HF* 378–9). In doing this, he makes us aware of two of the key themes of this poem: that words are largely what ultimately define us, and that the relationship between truth and words is a complicated business. What is said about people is ultimately what they become. Some will not be spoken of and will be forgotten by posterity; some will be defined by the words of others, most notably in verse. Chaucer's Dido, herself, is aware of this. Lamenting the fact that men have such divinity, 'In speche, and never a del of trouthe' (*HF* 331), her thoughts turn to the other speeches that will be made about her:

'O wel-awey that I was born!	alas
For thorgh yow is my name lorn,	reputation; lost
And alle myn actes red and songe	read; sung about
Over al thys lond, on every tonge.	
O wikke Fame! – for ther nys	malicious; is not
Nothing so swift, lo, as she is!'	
(*HF* 345–50)	

Dido's whole lament about Aeneas is built upon the falsity of his words, and her fears for the future are based on the words that will define her forever. Her speech echoes the grandeur of Virgil's claim that rumour is the swiftest of all evils, but the truth of the harm in this comes through in the imagined backbiting of those Dido feels will judge her:

" 'Loo, ryght as she hath don, now she	
Wol doo eft-sones, hardely'	again; certainly
Thus seyth the peple prively."	secretly
(*HF* 358–60)	

Dido's classical fame, her passionate grief, and her heroic action unto death in the face of abandonment, is nowhere present here. Instead, she imagines herself the focus of small-minded gossip, her love for Aeneas reduced to easy promiscuity by the local scandalmongers. In fact, everything we hear about Dido in the Temple of Glass reduces her in some way. Even her relationship with her sister, so powerful in the sources, becomes here a kind of sibling blame-shifting not encountered in the epic:

> And called on hir suster Anne,
> And gan hir to compleyne thanne,
> And seyde that she cause was
> That she first loved him, allas,
>   (HF 367–70)

What becomes clear is that the relationship between truth and words is difficult, and the exact phrasing of the inscription on the brass plate at the beginning becomes significant. The words were famous from Virgil's Latin text, but what Chaucer gives us is a translation, and like all translations it is an interpretation. What he adds to the original is exactly this sense of difficulty, for he does not say that he will simply sing of arms and the man as Virgil does; he adds the phrase 'yif I kan' (HF 143). It is a declaration of doubt at the outset.

This doubt, together with the dreamer's repeated refusals to elaborate or describe, makes sense of the final section of Book I. The post-Dido episodes of the Aeneid are passed over in a series of tableaux, and the dreamer suddenly realises that he does not know where he is or who has created any of this. He feels in need of a 'stiryng [stirring] man' (HF 478), some living soul to enlighten him, but he emerges not into the typical green garden of dreams, but instead into a desert landscape. The art of Venus's temple has been replaced by nothing at all, except sand:

> Withouten toun, or hous, or tree,
> Or bush, or grass, or <u>eryd</u> lond; ...   ploughed
> Ne no maner creature
>   (HF 484–6, 489)

The overwhelming sense is of vacancy and loneliness. The Temple of Glass, beautiful as it is, is significantly empty and lies at the heart of a wasteland. Its artistic representations in all their forms have failed to satisfy the dreamer. This knowledge prompts Geffrey to call out against 'fantome and illusion', two of the dangerous dream-types he had failed to understand at the opening of the poem. At once, he sees an eagle outlined against the sun, but larger than any normal eagle, and with golden feathers as bright as the sun itself.

BOOK II

THE EAGLE

The *proem* to Book II makes passing reference to some famous dreams, notably some in the Bible, but quickly moves back to the dream proper and to the arrival of the Eagle. Seeing 'Geffrey' out in the open ('a-roume' *HF* 540), the massive bird swoops upon him and seizes him 'with hys grymme pawes stronge' (*HF* 541), plucking him into the air, though not without noting that Geffrey is rather on the heavy side (*HF* 574). As they soar into the heavens, the dreamer begins to wonder if the eagle, traditionally the bird of Jupiter, has been sent by the king of the gods with a plan to 'stellyfye [turn into a star]' him (*HF* 586), just as he turned so many others into stars in ancient myth. However, reading his mind, the Eagle determines to set him straight. It seems that Geffrey's efforts in writing about love have come to the attention of Jupiter, and while none of this has been done well, the king of the gods appreciates that it has been done at all, given that the dreamer has no success himself as a lover and scarcely even hears about love. The Eagle paints an unflattering picture of a clerkly Geffrey working all day and all night, unaware of everything that goes on around him:

For when thy labour <u>doon</u> al ys,	done
And hast mad alle thy <u>rekenynges</u>,	calculations
In stede of reste and newe thynges	
Thou goost hom to thy hous <u>anoon</u>,	at once
And, <u>also</u> domb as any stoon,	as
Thou sittest at another book	
Tyl fully <u>dawsed</u> ys thy look;	dazed

(HF 652–8)

As recompense for this hermetical existence, it emerges that the dreamer is going to be made privy to all kinds of stories about love, more than there are grains of sand, or seeds of grain in a granary. There will be tales of new love and old, of joyful love and steadfast love, discord, and jealousy, tricks, reconciliations, and renewals. The Eagle ends with what he no doubt intended to be a rhetorical question ('I bet you can't believe it' *HF* 699), but is unexpectedly interrupted by the dreamer, their words tangled as the full rhetorical flow of the bird is met with active resistance from Geffrey:

'Unnethe maistow trowen this?'	scarcely; may you; believe
Quod he. 'Noo, helpe me God so wys,'	said
Quod I. 'Noo? Why?' quod he. 'For hyt	
Were impossible, to my wit,	understanding
Though that Fame had all the pies	magpies (i.e. chatterboxes)
In al a realme, and alle the spies,'	
(*HF* 699–704)	

How could so many stories, so many words, ever be gathered together in one place? How can such truths be assembled? Is such a thing possible? These are the doubts voiced by the dreamer.

SOUND

The Eagle responds with the enthusiastic 'O yis, yis!' (*HF* 706) of the born teacher, keen to enlighten his pupil. What this will require, the Eagle decides, is a lecture on the nature of sound itself, which he delivers with considerable learning and with a great deal of the compressed air that is the topic under scrutiny. It is a long lecture. It is, nevertheless, a fascinating collection of the beliefs that the Middle Ages held dear about sound. At its heart is the notion that everything in the universe has its proper and natural place. Before a world that concerned itself with gravity, it was thought that all things would be prompted by natural sympathies, their, 'kyndely enclynyng' (*HF* 734) to find their way home. This is why the heavy stone, no matter how far it is taken from the heavy earth, will strive to get back there if dropped; and sound and smoke, light in themselves, will attempt to mingle with the lightness of the air (*HF* 730–46). Speech, the Eagle continues, is nothing more than sound; as for sound, it,

'... ys noght but <u>eyr</u> ybroken;   air
And every speche that ys spoken,
Lowd or <u>pryvee</u>, foul or fair,   quietly
In his substaunce ys but air;'
                    (*HF* 765–8)

So, speech is broken air. The broken air, in turn, must all make its
way to the House of Fame. The Eagle is keen to do more than merely
assert this, and so continues to explain the science to Geffrey. Sound,
it emerges, must travel through the air because each disrupted airy
parcel must push into the next. Medieval science favoured a comparison with a stone that is dropped in water and causes ripples far
out into the pool, and this is the analogy that the Eagle offers:

'And ryght anoon thow shalt see wel
That <u>whel</u> wol cause another whel,   circle
And that the <u>thridde</u>, and so forth, brother,   third
Every <u>sercle</u> causynge other'   circle
                    (*HF* 793–6)

This is why even the squeaking of a mouse will make its way into
the House of Fame, for all sound will travel, like the ripples on a pool,
until it reaches its destination.

At this point, the Eagle pauses for breath and looks for some affir-
mation from Geffrey. He has been attempting to impart scientific
knowledge and would like some acknowledgement that he has done
it well. The poem has returned to its preoccupation with the ability
of words to convey truth and has pursued the question to its very
core with this disquisition on sound. The Eagle of course, is looking
for praise, not critique, and is perfectly capable of framing his own
compliments, drawing attention to what he feels has been a master-
class in unembellished truth. Having forced Geffrey into monosyllabic agreement that he has achieved his aim – the dreamer is, of
course, still dangling from the Eagle's talons during this lecture, and
his terse, 'Yis' (*HF* 864) again calls veracity into question – the Eagle
exults in his own cleverness:

'A ha,' quod he, '<u>lo</u>, <u>so</u> I can   see; how
<u>Lewedly</u> to a <u>lewed</u> man   simply; simple

Speke, and shewe hym <u>swyche skiles</u>	such arguments
That he may shake hem be the <u>biles</u>,	beaks
So <u>palpable</u> they shulden be.'	solid

(HF 865–9)

The Eagle feels that he has done very well, making the material so alive that even his slightly dim-witted protégé must be able to grasp the point and shake it by the beak if necessary, for having shaped all this in his own image it inevitably has avian form in his own mind. Geffrey is by now anxious to agree that the argument has been well made, but it is not enough to stop the Eagle. So far, the class has been on theory; the next step is 'preve [proof] by experience' (*HF* 878).

THE JOURNEY TO THE STARS

Still dangling from the Eagle's claws, the dreamer is whisked into the heavens and soars higher than anyone in history, higher even than Daedalus had done before the wings of Icarus melted (*HF* 914–24). The Eagle is keen to instruct Geffrey about any town or landmark he cares to point out, but they are soon so high that the earth seems to be no more than a pinprick below them (*HF* 907). Geffrey is treated to the story of Phaeton, who stole the chariot of the sun, but there are real wonders to encounter around him in the form of the demons of the air (*HF* 932), the Milky Way (*HF* 937) and every kind of weather – storms, snow, wind, and hail – all being formed before his eyes. The dreamer is appreciative of the Eagle's efforts, which 'gladded me ay more and more, / So feythfully to me spak he' (*HF* 962–3) and it is perhaps this that prompts a feathery reference to the philosopher Boethius:

'... A thought may <u>flee</u> so hye	fly
Wyth fetheres of Philosophye,	
To passen everych element,	
And whan he hath so fer <u>ywent</u>,	gone
Than may be seen behynde hys bak	
Cloude ...'	

(HF 973–8)

The full passage from Boethius, translated elsewhere by Chaucer, sees the narrator flying with the wings of philosophy away from the earth and seeking truth in the knowledge of God. Geffrey's aims, however, are not so lofty, either literally or metaphorically. The Eagle's philosophical feathers take the dreamer to the point where the earth is shrouded in mist behind him, but he does not want to seek any further. This is in spite of promptings from the Eagle himself, who wants Geffrey to stop musing on the astronomical works he has read and instead look at the stars around him. The dreamer is, however, resistant. He does not want to learn first-hand about the stars. He pleads that he is too old (*HF* 995) and that looking directly at the heavenly bodies would destroy his sight (*HF* 1016), but what emerges most strongly is that he simply does not want to engage with what is around him. He prefers his books. Even the coaxing of the Eagle, that many of the classical myths he likes would be enhanced by real knowledge of the stars, is not enough to entice him. The eagle, by its nature, was believed to be able to look into the sun, but the dreamer prefers his authorial filters, and for universal truths to come already packaged in words.

With that, the Eagle announces their imminent arrival at the House of Fame, and the dreamer is alerted to the 'grete swogh [wind]' (*HF* 1031) that can be heard around them. The sound is compared to that of the sea beating against the rocks in a storm, or to the rumbling of thunder. The reader is aware that the wind has been blowing in one way or another since Book I, tossing the fleet of Aeneas on the waves, or moving the hair of Venus. It blew throughout the Eagle's lecture on sound, and now it reaches its crescendo as all the voices in the world make their way upon the air to the House of Fame. Just as speech was sometimes thought in scientific treatises to shape as well as disrupt the air, so the bodies within Fame's house are shaped air. They are breaths that hold the form of those who uttered them, being 'verray hys lyknesse / That spak the word' (*HF* 1079–80). Fame's House, therefore, is populated not just by words, but by images of the forms that produced them, and in this there is a return to one of the key themes of the poem: the idea that truth is difficult to reach, shaped as it always must be by the thoughts, attitudes and, finally, words of individuals.

BOOK III

THE HOUSE OF FAME

Having been deposited by the Eagle, the dreamer begins his ascent to the House of Fame, which is positioned on top of a rocky precipice and can be reached only by an arduous climb. Other medieval and

classical texts had presented 'glory' in a similarly allegorical way: a
lofty and impressive destination, to be reached only after the most
difficult and wearying journey, for glory is not something to be
achieved easily. However, the dreamer is soon disconcerted by the
nature of the rock he is climbing. Having thought it was perhaps
'alum de glas' (*HF* 1124), a crystallised metal, he realises suddenly
that he is, in fact, clambering over ice, and that even as he touches it,
the names carved there of those seeking fame are partly 'ofthowed
[thawed]' (*HF* 1143), the outer letters melting away. It is, as he realises,
a precarious place on which to build a palace:

'This were a feble <u>fundament</u>	foundation
To bilden on a place hye.	
He <u>ought</u> him lytel <u>glorifye</u>	would; be proud
That hereon <u>bilt</u>, God so me save!'	built
(*HF* 1132–5)	

The dreamer has not yet worked out exactly where he is, but he
has reached the essential truth about the House of Fame, for it is not
concerned with 'glory' in its unproblematic sense. This is not a place
of heroic legend, but rather the slippery home of a lesser kind of
'fame' in that it encompasses renown and notoriety in all their forms,
some of which will last, and some of which will melt away even as
they are scrutinised. Later, within the House itself, the dreamer will
see the undisputed heroes of legend – Hercules and Alexander the
Great – sitting on Fame's shoulders, but these two of 'large fame' (*HF*
1412) are vastly outnumbered by the quantity of lesser tales, good
and bad, that flock to Fame's palace.

Indeed, it is crucial to remember that Fame concerns herself not
with the exploits themselves, but with the words that frame them,
and this explains the bustling assortment of characters who throng
the entrance to the House, some of them positioned in niches on
the building itself, and some milling around. This retinue consists of
harpists, bagpipers, flautists, simple shepherds with corn pipes, enter-
tainers at feasts, tumblers, jugglers, and magicians (*HF* 1197–281),
essentially all those who preserve the fame of others through their
songs and tales; and once through the door, there is an onslaught of
heralds, concerned to promote the fame of those who feature in their
stories.

The response of the dreamer is characteristically bookish. Faced with the multitudinous colours, coats of arms, and symbols of the heralds, he imagines a reference book 'Twenty foot thykke' (*HF* 1335) to document them all; and his description of the jewelled walls of the palace itself is also displaced by a reference to a treatise on gems that would elucidate them (*HF* 1352). The effect is of a great, tumbling babble of noise that the dreamer is attempting to order in his usual way: distancing himself from the experience and inserting written authority in its place. It is no surprise, therefore, to find that the great hall of this palace is supported by pillars on which stand the classical poets and great historians of the past, all supporting the fame of their subjects upon their shoulders, and yet not without doubt being expressed about their venerable words. Even Homer, the most ancient among them, is accused of bias and 'Feynynge [lies] in hys poetries' (*HF* 1478). In the end, the carefully described pillars of poetry are dismissed with a memorable simile that compares them to the untidy rooks' nests that can be seen at the very tops of bare winter trees:

The halle was al ful, <u>ywys</u>,	indeed
Of <u>hem</u> that writen olde <u>gestes</u>	those; deeds
As ben on treës <u>rokes</u> nestes;	rooks
But hit a ful <u>confus matere</u>	confusing business
Were alle the gestes for to here	
That they of write, or <u>how they highte</u>.	the declarations they made

(HF 1514–19)

Lofty they may be, but the words of the authors, like the twiggy nests of the rooks, are a tangled and confusing business. The profusion of voices here cannot lead to simple truth. Instead, the narrator is overwhelmed by what he hears, and the noise grows as a new group arrives, their murmuring like the sound of a hive as the bees swarm (*HF* 1522–3).

FAME

The latest arrivals are a diverse group of rich and poor, all of whom pray to Fame for her favour. As for Fame herself, she is described as a 'femynyne creature' (*HF* 1365), sitting on a throne of red carbuncle, a precious stone believed to resist engraving or any attempts to impose human design upon it. Certainly, Fame herself is difficult to define, her shape and size shifting and changing even as she sits on her throne:

For <u>alther-first</u>, <u>soth</u> for to seye,	first of all; truly
Me thoughte that she was so <u>lyte</u>	small
That the lengthe <u>of a cubite</u>	from elbow to tip of middle finger
Was <u>lengere</u> than she semed be.	longer
But thus sone in a whyle she	
Hir <u>tho</u> so <u>wonderliche streighte</u>	then; wondrously stretched out
That with hir <u>fet</u> she <u>erthe reighte</u>,	feet; touched the earth
And with hir hed she touched hevene,	

(HF 1368–75)

It is the nature of fame that it should wax and wane with miraculous speed; that it should be at once almost nothing and all important. It catapults some to the heavens and ignores the achievements of others, defying merit in the process. Fame, simply, defies all rules (including those of physics), and all natural laws. She might have the wavy golden hair of the medieval lady, but she also has as many eyes as a bird has feathers or, more ominously, as the four beasts of the Apocalypse possess (HF 1381–5). As for her ears and her tongue, these are as numerous as animal hairs, for Fame hears everything and has thousands of tongues with which to pass the words on, her speed signalled by her feathered feet (HF 1388–92). She is, ultimately, more monster than goddess and, like her sister Fortune, capricious in the extreme (HF 1547–8).

THE SUPPLICANTS

While all those rushing towards Fame in the vanguard have deserved good renown, she grants it indiscriminately to some and not to others. Worse, she then rewards other supplicants who have committed bad deeds by having them lauded as good. Worst of all, she calls upon Slander to defame some of those who have never done anything in their lives except good, and she ensures that they will be remembered as villains. She is approached by the good, the evil, and by those who have done nothing at all. Some of them want fame, others oblivion, but Fame disposes of them entirely at her own whim, granting them renown – or not – as she chooses. When asked why she has failed to act justly, her answer is simple: "For me lyst [wanted] hyt noght' (*HF* 1564). Much of Book III is taken up with arranging the supplicants into categories of this kind, and in the process, we can detect the dreamer's customary desire for order. Those who 'don't give a leek' for fame (*HF* 1708) but have it inflicted upon them anyway, are separated from those who have never deserved renown, but seek to have it 'glued' to them nevertheless (*HF* 1761). But Fame is nothing if not inconsistent, and the very next group, equally undeserving, and asking for exactly the same rewards, are dispatched as 'masty [sluggish] swyn' (*HF* 1777) and seen off like the fabled cat that would like to have the fish but refuses to get its claws wet (*HF* 1783–5). There are even those who desire fame so much that they would rather be remembered as fools, than not be remembered at all (*HF* 1852–6). In the end, there are nine different groups, but none of this classifying reveals any particular insight, it only establishes beyond doubt the capricious nature of Fame. The effect is reminiscent of the poem's opening section on the nature of dreams, for we have gone through the motions of knowledge, but without any progress in terms of true understanding. The dreamer has clawed at his own head in frustration (*HF* 1702) and refuses to tell a shadowy new guide his name, protesting that he does not want his name preserved for posterity. What he wants, he insists, is news:

Somme newe tydynges for to <u>lere</u>,	learn
Somme newe thinges, <u>y not</u> what,	I don't know
Tydynges, <u>other</u> this or that,	either
(*HF* 1886–8)	

His insistence grows with the repetition, and his new guide understands the distinction between the words with which the supplicants announce their deeds in the House of Fame, and the words that arrive bearing fresh 'news'. Such words do not, however, come straight to Fame's house: they arrive instead at the house of Rumour.

THE HOUSE OF TWIGS

The noise and confusion of Fame's house is surpassed by this new edifice, the earlier comparison to the noise of swarming bees being supplanted by the roar of the boulder released from the catapult (*HF*

1933–4). The sound is coming from a strange house constructed of twigs, the kind shaped to make cages or baskets. The noise of the wind – its 'swough' – that has been heard throughout the poem is still present, and in addition, the wicker house is full of 'gygges [squeakings]' and 'chirkynges [creakings]' (*HF* 1941–3), for it is endlessly moving, swirling around, 'as swyft as thought' (*HF* 1924). Its twiggy structure is similar to the rooks' nests mentioned in Fame's hall, and the effect is similarly one of myriad strands woven together to make a whole. However, it is a more ingenious structure than the simply tangled nests of history. The labyrinthine twists and turns of rumour are reflected in a building so intricate that it surpasses that of Daedalus, master of the maze himself, so 'queyntelych [elaborately]' (*HF* 1920–3) is it made. It has as many doors as there are leaves on a tree to allow the rumours in, and thousands of other holes through which the rumours leak out again. As is fitting for a house that specialises in 'rounynges [whispering]' and 'jangles [gossip]', it has more than its fair share of corners (*HF* 1959–60). It is, in essence, a vast cage (*HF* 1985), 60 miles in length and, as we would expect of a house of rumour, built of the flimsiest material, and yet surprisingly enduring (*HF* 1979–81). The breathless arrival of all kinds of gossip and news is reflected in a 16-line catalogue of the kinds of material that arrive at its many doors:

Of <u>werres</u>, of <u>pes</u>, of mariages,	wars; peace
Of reste, of labour, of <u>viages</u>,	voyages
Of <u>abood</u>, of deeth, of lyf,	staying
Of love, of hate, acord, of stryf …	
(*HF* 1961–4)	

As the repetitive structure indicates, all of it, good or bad, is given the same treatment by the rumour mongers, all tidings being treated the same.

Getting inside the house of Fame had not been difficult, for fame is potentially available to all, regardless of merit. It is, however, more difficult to get to the heart of rumours, and Geffrey is unable to find his way in to rumour's house of twigs. At this point, the Eagle reappears and launches into an explanation (25 lines without a breath), which essentially tells the dreamer that the house simply moves too quickly for anyone to enter it, but that Jove will nevertheless deliver on his promise of 'tidings' (*HF* 2000–25). The Eagle, therefore, flies Geffrey in through a window and deposits him in a room packed with whispering, chattering people, the stock expressions of gossip crammed into fast-paced lines:

> 'Thus hath he sayd,' and 'Thus he doth,'
> 'Thus shal hit be,' 'Thus herde y seye,'   it must be like this;
>   I heard it said
> 'That shal be founde,' 'That dar I leye'   wager
>   (*HF* 2052–4)

Fame's retinue had consisted of minstrels and tellers of tales; but the house of rumour is more readily served by those who travel: shipmen, pilgrims, couriers and messengers (*HF* 2122–8). However, news is not simply passed from one to the next. Each recipient magnifies what he has been told, eagerly embellishing as he passes it on, 'encresing ever moo' (*HF* 2077). In such a situation, it is difficult to separate truth from lies, and Geffrey watches as 'A lesyng [lie] and a sad soth sawe [reliable, true story]' (*HF* 2089) collide at a window, both attempting to escape at the same moment. Unable to extricate themselves, they swear an oath as brothers and, 'fals and soth [true] compouned [compounded]', they enter the world as 'oo [one] tydynge' (*HF* 2108–9). There is, therefore, no easy distinction to be made between false and true. Rumour specialises in stories with at least a grain of truth, albeit compounded with lies, or magnified beyond recognition. Fame's house had at least allowed for some separation of motives, and for distinction to be made between deserving and undeserving, whether or not the treatment of each was ultimately just. In the House of Rumour, however, there are no such distinctions, truth and lies being interwoven like the wicker in the cage.

AUTHORITY

The final moment comes when noise erupts in the corner given over to 'love-tydynges' (*HF* 2143), those at the back of the crowd jumping up, clambering over one another, and treading on each other's heels in order to see. The focus of their attention is 'A man of gret auctorite …' (*HF* 2158). At last, the dreamer, promised tales of love by the Eagle back in Book II, looks set to have his reward. However, this is where the poem ends, breaking off abruptly as Geffrey catches sight of the man. Some critics are persuaded that the poem is simply unfinished as it stands, while others argue that we have it in its final form, and that there is a point to it suddenly coming to an end when it does. Certainly, it seems fitting that a poem that has focussed so much on the difficulties of literary 'authority', should end with that very word, but that it should break off before anything can be learned and before we even know the identity of the man, a man that we should note only 'semed' (*HF* 2157) to have such authority in the first place.

The poem began with uncertainty in the midst of apparent certainty and ends in much the same way. While it was the convention in medieval dream poems that the dreamer should learn something along the way, Geffrey has been presented instead only with the certainty that such truths are difficult in themselves. The very words that are used to convey truth are shaped by those who create them, and truth, in its turn, is shaped, too. It is this complicated relationship that lies at the heart of the dream, as the dreamer encounters first the famous tale of Dido and Aeneas, setting its authorities against each other, then moves to the concept of fame itself and the ungovernable and unpredictable effect that words have on lives. Finally, the dreamer observes rumour and the uneasy relationship of truth and lies there, too. But even this is to use words to impose order and authority on a text that frequently seems to resist it with its noise and tumult. The overwhelming sense is often one of confusion, of hot air, of truth that cannot be extricated from lies. The dreamer rejects the Eagle's encouragement to see things for himself and retreats to texts, preferring the filter of words, with all that it implies.

FURTHER READING

There is much essential information and guidance on reading in this edition of the poem: *The House of Fame* (2013). Ed. Nicholas Havely. 2nd edn. Toronto: Pontifical Institute for Medieval Studies. The poem has been the subject of a number of book-length studies, from J. A. W. Bennett (1968). *Chaucer's Book of Fame*. Oxford: Oxford University Press to the influential and independent interpretation in Sheila Delany (1972). *Chaucer's 'House of Fame': The Poetics of Skeptical Fideism*. Chicago: University of Chicago Press, together with the invaluable account of tradition and context in Piero Boitani (1984). *Chaucer and the Imaginary World of Fame*. Cambridge: D. S. Brewer, and more recently a collection of essays in *Chaucer and Fame: Reputation and Reception* (2015). Ed. Isabel Davis and Catherine Nall. Cambridge: D. S. Brewer. For an interesting contemporary analysis, see Ruth Evans, 'Chaucer in Cyberspace: Medieval Technologies of Memory and *The House of Fame*', in *Studies in the Age of Chaucer*, 23 (2000), 43–69.

On Dido, see Marilynn Desmond (1994). *Reading Dido: Gender, Textuality, and the Medieval Aeneid*. Minneapolis: University of Minnesota Press. For discussion of the poem's scientific background, see Alexander N. Gabrovsky (2015). *Chaucer the Alchemist: Physics, Mutability and the Medieval Imagination*. New York: Palgrave. See also Helen Cooper, 'The Four Last Things in Dante and Chaucer: Hugolino and the House of Rumour', in *New Medieval Literatures* 3 (1999), 39–66.

THE PARLIAMENT OF FOWLS

The Parliament of Fowls opens with one of the best-known lines from Chaucer's work: 'The lyf so short, the craft so long to lerne' (*PF* 1). In the original Latin it had meant essentially that life passes quickly and is gone before we have time truly to master any part of it. However, Chaucer has a very specific kind of 'craft' in mind:

Th'<u>assay</u> so hard, so sharp the conquerynge,	attempt
The <u>dredful</u> joye alwey that <u>slit</u> so <u>yerne</u>:	fearful; slides away; eagerly
<u>Al this mene I by</u> Love, that my <u>felynge</u>	by this I mean; consciousness
<u>Astonyeth</u> with his wonderful <u>werkynge</u>	stuns; work
(*PF* 2–5)	

He is thinking of love: a joy that is also full of fear, and so wondrous that it stuns the consciousness that attempts to grasp it even as it slips away. Not that the narrator has had first-hand experience of such love, he would have us understand. In place of the deed (*PF* 8), he has experienced the exploits of Love – a lord famed for his miracles and his cruelty – in books, and while there has been no first-hand experience, there have been very many books.

THE DREAM OF SCIPIO

One very old volume in particular has captured his imagination, to the extent that it becomes an artefact in the poem ('Chapitres sevene it hadde' *PF* 32). Instead of an oblique reference to an old story, the narrator refers us specifically to 'Tullyus of the Drem of Scipioun [Cicero's Dream of Scipio]' (*PF* 31), the most authoritative work on dreams in the Middle Ages. Written by the Roman orator, Cicero, it was equipped with a moral commentary in the Middle Ages and became one of the most popular books of the medieval period. It is not, however, an obvious source for information about the 'myrakles and … crewel yre [anger]' (*PF* 11) of a personified 'Love'. It is the account of a vision in which the dreamer ascends to a 'sterry place' (*PF* 43) – the very 'Galaxye' (*PF* 56) itself – and surveys the whole universe (see p. 9). From his vantage point he understands how insignificant the earth is in comparison to the vastness of the heavens, and is brought by his guide to realise that the things of this world are both deceptive and transitory:

Than <u>bad</u> he hym, <u>syn</u> erthe was so <u>lyte</u>,	urged; since; little
And <u>dissevable</u> and ful of <u>harde grace</u>,	deceptive; ill fortune
That he ne shulde hym in the world delyte.	
Thanne tolde he hym, in <u>certeyn yeres space</u>	a certain period of time
That every sterre shulde come into his place	
Ther it was first, and al shulde <u>out of mynde</u>	be forgotten
That in this world <u>is don of</u> al mankynde.	has been done by

(PF 64–70)

It is the fate of the earth and of everything in it that it must come to an end. The whole moving, turning cosmos will ultimately return to its starting point, and all human striving will simply be forgotten. The virtuous will achieve heavenly peace, having realised that they are immortal, and having worked in their lifetime for the 'commune profit' (*PF* 47, 75) a repeated phrase that encompasses dedication to the common good and a placing of others before self. As for the sinful, they will 'whirle aboute' (*PF* 80) the earth in pain until many worlds have passed. In the end, though, their wicked deeds, too, will be forgiven, and they will be allowed to come to rest in heavenly bliss.

The contempt for the world that is so much a part of the Latin source is retained by Chaucer, but eventual salvation for all is his addition to the classical work. The 'harde grace [ill-fortune]' (*PF* 65) of earthly life is to be replaced by God's 'grace [mercy]' (*PF* 84), and all will finally be saved. It is a traditional Christian message in its rejection of earthly values, its emphasis upon working for the good of others, and in its belief that salvation is possible for all who want it. What is surprising, therefore, is that it fails to satisfy the narrator. He goes to bed in a spirit of 'busy hevynesse' (*PF* 89), the intense weight of sadness bearing down on him, and explained by the fact that:

> For bothe I hadde thyng which that I <u>nolde</u>,   did not want
> And <u>ek</u> I <u>ne hadde</u> that thyng that I <u>wolde</u>.   also; did not have; wanted
> (*PF* 90–1)

This is a clear statement about being dissatisfied, not just because he does not have what he wants, but also because he does not want what he has. The reason for this depressed state of mind is not clear, however, though it arises after a day of reading the *Dream of Scipio*, and it seems likely that while the book has provided him with a great deal, none of it was precisely what he was searching for. The poem had opened by declaring love to be a difficult craft to learn, and while a Christianised Scipio allows for both love of the state and a merciful, heavenly love, neither engages with the kind of awe-inspiring, bittersweet, miraculous, and terrible force that a personified Love wields in the opening stanzas. The almost mercantile, thinly spread tone of 'common profit' does not reach quite as far as brotherly love, and certainly not as far as 'Love' as the narrator has conceived of it. For such love, he must abandon this book and enter the world of dreams instead.

THE DREAMER

The narrator is an unlikely investigator into the ways of love, and an uncharacteristic dreamer. Unlike many other literary dreamers, he does not suddenly fall asleep upon a bank of flowers or in a wood but, more prosaically, in his own bed, no longer having enough daylight to read by, and exhausted by his scholarly efforts (*PF* 87–8). He feels the need to give some rational justification for his dream, not as a vision, or as divine inspiration, but as the manifestation of a preoccupied mind:

The <u>wery</u> huntere, slepynge in his bed,	weary
To wode <u>ayeyn</u> his mynde <u>goth</u> anon;	again; goes
The juge dremeth how his <u>plees been sped</u>;	cases have fared
The cartere dremeth how his cart is gon;	

(PF 99–102)

He is a most sensible dreamer and, while he cannot say for certain that a day reading about Scipio Africanus has caused this ancient figure to appear in his dream, the implication is there. He is measured in his responses, inclined towards uncertainty or indecision as he makes his way through the landscape of his dream ('nyste whether me was bet [I did not know whether it was better] …' PF 152) rather than the dogged incomprehension of many medieval dreamers (see p. 120).

Neither a lover nor a fighter, he is more of a spectator, as his guide acknowledges:

'For many a man that may nat <u>stonde a pul</u>	withstand a fall
Yet liketh hym at <u>wrastlyng</u> for to be,	wrestling
And <u>demen</u> yit wher he do bet or he.'	judge

(PF 164–6)

The metaphor places him at two removes from the experience of love: not a participant, not even a spectator at the right event, but rather a dreamer encased in a metaphor that emphasises his lack of engagement. His guide, the venerable Scipio, calls him 'dul' (PF 162), in the sense of lacking sensation, in the same way that a sick man, he says, cannot discern what is bitter or sweet (PF 160–1). It is an interesting assessment of the dreamer – caught between extremes but experiencing neither – and it chimes with his own sense of his state of mind earlier in the poem as he had contemplated love, not entirely knowing 'wher that I flete [float] or synke' (PF 7). Uncertain as to whether he is floating or sinking, he exists in the in-between.

To a certain extent this is true of all dreamers, entering, but not *of*, a dream-world – but it is particularly true of the dreamer in this poem. Repeatedly, he frames his experience in terms of moving untouched between polar opposites, but nowhere more obviously than in his initial reaction to his dream landscape. Undecided as to whether or not to enter or leave, he describes himself as if suspended between two magnets, powerless between them:

Right as betwixen <u>adamauntes</u> two   magnets
Of <u>evene myght</u>, a pece of yren set   equal power
Ne hath no myght to meve <u>to ne fro</u> –   backwards or forwards
               (PF 148–50)

It is a simile that encapsulates the dreamer and is also symbolic of the love that interests him: a state of unresolved opposites and an experience of helpless immobility.

THE GARDEN OF LOVE

Within two lines of the dream beginning, the narrator finds himself at the entrance to a park, the gate of which bears two, contradictory, inscriptions. The first is a joyful message, painted in gold, promising fulfilment and the heart's well-being:

'<u>Thorgh</u> me men gon into that blysful place   through
Of hertes hele and dedly woundes cure;
Thorgh me men gon unto the welle of grace,
<u>There</u> grene and <u>lusty</u> May shal evere endure.   where; pleasant
This is the wey to al good aventure.
Be glad, thow redere, and thy sorwe <u>of-caste</u>;   cast off
Al open am I – passe in, and <u>sped thee faste</u>!'   prosper
               (PF 127–33)

On the other side, in black letters, is a warning of suffering and death:

"Thorgh me men gon," than spak that other
   side,
"Unto the mortal strokes of the spere
Of which Disdayn and <u>Daunger</u> is the <u>gyde</u>,   Standoffishness; guide
Ther nevere tre shal fruyt ne leves bere.
This strem yow ledeth to the sorweful <u>were</u>   weir
<u>There</u> as the fish in prysoun is al drye;   where
<u>Th'eschewing</u> is only the remedye!"   the avoidance
               (PF 134–40)

It is not entirely clear from the first inscription that its subject is romantic love, but the appearance of Disdain and Standoffishness in the second leaves no room for doubt. Theirs is the territory of rejected advances, their realm sterile and deadly, the only hope being (and here the line misses a beat to emphasise the point) to avoid the lure of love in the first place. However, contradictory as these inscriptions are in their message, their form maintains an essential similarity, each beginning in the same way ('Through me'), and each paralleling the other: deadly wounds of love are cured in one, while mortal strokes prevail in the second; the first is all May-time fecundity, the other a barren landscape. The point of this is to make it clear that the two states are potentially part of the one experience. The dreamer is not being asked to choose a gate: there is only one gate and one path. To embark on the journey towards love, therefore, is to accept that both states are possible.

The dreamer's dithering on the threshold is brought to an end by a 'shof [shove]' (*PF* 154) from Scipio, and he finds himself in a typical dream-landscape: a springtime world of vivid greenness, temperate climate, and constant daylight. Nothing ages here, or grows sick, and this, together with its natural fecundity, gives the garden the feel of an earthly Paradise, but one or two details disrupt this seeming perfection. The first is a catalogue of trees, the uses of which allow a world beyond the garden to intrude. Such lists are common in epic poetry, but the effect here is of the 'emeraude' (*PF* 175) canopy of the dream forest being felled for lumber:

The byldere ok, and ek the hardy asshe;	oak for building
The piler elm, the cofre unto carayne;	pillar; coffin for corpses
The boxtre pipere, holm to whippes lashe;	boxwood for pipes; holly
The saylynge fyr; the cipresse, deth to playne ...	fir for ships; cypress for lamenting death
The olive of pes, and eke the dronke vyne;	
The victor palm, the laurer to devyne.	laurel for prophecy

(PF 176–82)

Admittedly, there is music, wine and victory here, but there is also the lash of the whip, the lament for the dead, and coffins for corpses. As the inscriptions on the gate had promised, the garden begets sorrow as well as joy.

THE TEMPLE OF BRASS

Beneath one of these trees, the dreamer then spies Cupid, making arrows together with his daughter, Will. This marks the beginning of an allegory of love, where various aspects of initial attraction are personified as female figures. That Will should be present with the arrow-touting Cupid is symbolic of the fact that love is a choice. The darts might be made by the winged god, but it is Will who arranges them as she pleases (*PF* 211–17). The dreamer is then aware, as well he might be, of Pleasure, Pretty Clothes, Lust, and Fine Manners, all keeping company together. As for 'Craft', that cunning quality in love that will twist anything to achieve its ends, she is, unsurprisingly, 'disfigurat' (*PF* 222). There are other figures around, such as Delight, Flattery, and Bribery, and a mysterious three, whose 'names shul not here be told' (*PF* 229), but the dreamer's attention is taken by a solidly unshakeable temple made of 'bras', equated in the Middle Ages with copper, and thought of as the metal of Venus. Here, worryingly, Peace and Patience have been left outside, the Temple of Brass being no place for either of them (*PF* 239–43).

Instead, Jealousy is within, prompting sighs as hot as fire to ignite the altars. The atmosphere is sweltering, a thousand sweet smells emanating in the heat, the dreamer's eyes gradually adjusting to the darkness. A diaphanous Venus reclines on a golden couch, attended, appropriately, by Riches (*PF* 260–73), but first the dreamer encounters Priapus, god of fertility, suggestively 'with hys sceptre in honde' (*PF* 256). It is a temple of sexual desire, in which Patience is abandoned, Peace forsaken, and an encounter with Priapus leads to Venus herself. The walls, therefore, are decorated with the broken bows of those who ultimately surrendered virginity and, on the other side, the images of those who died for their passion, among them Cleopatra, Dido, Helen of Troy, and even Chaucer's own Troilus. There are no half-hearted lovers depicted here, for the Temple of Brass is a shrine to all-consuming desire, to morbid infatuation, and to lust.

NATURE

Seeking 'solace' (*PF* 297) from the passionate heat of the Temple, the dreamer returns to the fresh greenness of the garden and encounters another goddess. This is Nature, surpassing the beauty of any other creature in the same way that the light of the summer sun outshines that of the stars (*PF* 299–301), but the dreamer does not describe her in detail. Instead, there is another surprisingly bookish reference, for we are told that she looked exactly as Alanus de Insulis had described her in *The Complaint of Nature* (*PF* 316–18). This reference to a twelfth-century theological work replaces the expected formal description of Nature here, though the work was so well-known to medieval audiences that they would have instantly conjured a picture of a woman clothed in a robe that depicted the natural world in all its glory. Chaucer goes one step further, for his Nature is enveloped not by images of creatures, but by the creatures themselves, a vast number of birds surrounding her. Indeed, there are so many that both the dreamer and his guide seem to disappear among them, and this is perhaps the point. The authority of *The Dream of Scipio*, with its message of contempt for the world, has been replaced by another authority, *The Complaint of Nature*, in which everything in the universe is 'knyt' (*PF* 381) and held together by love, for Nature is the deputy ('vicaire' *PF* 379) of God himself. As we have seen, however, it is the way of this poem to set up unresolved dichotomies, and the goings-on of nature that follow are to be regarded more as another facet than an answer.

THE BIRDS

The birds, like the earlier description of the trees, are characterised by their chief attribute, and, like the earlier catalogue, allow for death and destruction in this pastoral world. The peacock might have the feathers of an angel, the turtle-dove a true heart (*PF* 355–6), but this is not Paradise, and for every avian positive there are many negatives: rapacious goshawks, jealous swans, ominous owls, lecherous sparrows, destructive drakes, treacherous lapwings, avenging storks. Even the swallow, elsewhere in literature the embodiment of summer joy, is here characterised as the 'murderer' of bees (*PF* 353).

This avian mass is assembled on St Valentine's day (*PF* 386), the day on which it was popularly believed that the birds chose their mates. There is, however, no spirit of abandon in this. Nature is a firm believer in rank and rules, and the choosing of partners is to be done in line with her 'ryghtful ordenaunce [orderly arrangement]' (*PF* 390). This is a Nature who believes very much in the laws of nature, and to that end, she intends to proceed through the various ranks of birds, beginning with the noblest, the birds of prey and, among them, the eagle, as the most exalted of bird-kind:

"The <u>tersel</u> egle, as that ye knowe wel,	tercel (male)
The <u>foul</u> royal, above yow in <u>degre</u>,	bird; rank
The wyse and <u>worthi</u>, <u>secre</u>, trewe as <u>stel</u>,	noble; discreet; steel
Which I have formed, as ye may wel se,	
In every part <u>as it best liketh me</u> –	as I think best
It nedeth not his <u>shap</u> yow to <u>devyse</u> –	form; imagine
He shal first <u>chese</u> and speken in his <u>gyse</u>."	choose; usual manner
(*PF* 393–9)	

There is no doubting Nature's approval of the male eagle, and she already has, resting on her hand, his ideal mate in the form of a female eagle, the 'moste benygne and the goodlieste' (*PF* 375) of all her creatures, whose beak she kisses as a sign of her favour. It would seem to be a natural match, and the tercel lives up to Nature's expectations by giving an eloquent speech worthy of any lover in the courtly tradition:

<u>Besekynge hire of</u> merci and of grace,	begging her for
As she that is my lady sovereyne;	
Or let me <u>deye</u> <u>present</u> in this place.	die; soon
For certes, longe may I nat lyve in payne,	
For in myn herte is <u>korven</u> every veyne.	cut
Havynge reward only to my trouthe,	
My deere herte, have on my wo som <u>routhe</u>.	pity
(*PF* 421–7)	

He presents as a supplicant, begging only for mercy, offering his life or his death as it pleases his 'lady', and asking only that his 'trouthe', that all-encompassing knightly virtue, should be taken into account. The Garden of Love is not, however, Noah's Ark, and there is more than one suitor for the wing of the formel eagle. Two more tercels present themselves, lower in rank than the first, but eagles nonetheless, one of them claiming to have loved her far longer (*PF* 453–5), and the other claiming a greater depth to his love (*PF* 479–80). Bird love has suddenly become complicated, as it emerges that there are three viable suitors among the tercel eagles and a mute and blushing object of their desires.

THE PARLIAMENT

The other birds, sensing a likely delay to their own mating, erupt in a cacophony of "Kek kek! kokkow! quek quek!" (*PF* 499) and have to be told to hold their tongues by Nature who, like any good teacher or civil servant, 'alwey hadde an ere / To murmur of the lewednesse [ignorance] behynde' (*PF* 519–20). She settles them down and orders their bickering and grumbling by asking each group of birds to select a representative to convey their views. What follows is a typical medieval *demande d'amour* in which the merits of the various suitors are considered by the group, each putting forward its own verdict on the 'love question' being considered. Still proceeding according to rank, therefore, (after all, Dame Nature is still in charge), the falcon, on behalf of the birds of prey, withdraws an initial suggestion of mortal combat and offers the opinion instead that, based on blood-line and nobility, the choice should in fact be a very easy one for the female eagle to make (*PF* 533–53). The goose, on behalf of the waterfowl, is of the view that there are plenty more fish in the sea, and that if love is not reciprocated then another mate can easily be found (*PF* 561–7). The grain-eating birds put forward the turtledove, who argues that the only way to love is until death, and that a lifetime of unrequited love should be the fate of two of the tercelets. This earns a scornful, 'You have to be joking!' (*PF* 589) from the duck, who is in turn reprimanded by the falcon for views that belong in the 'donghil' (*PF* 597). The cuckoo gives the final verdict on behalf of the worm-eaters, the lowest of bird-kind and furthest from the concerns of eagles. As such, the cuckoo simply does not care what the eagles do and is content for them to remain solitary all their lives, providing he can get on with choosing his own mate (*PF* 603–9). This results in a very rude speech from the ostensibly noble merlin ('wormes corupcioun!' *PF* 614) until Nature decides that she has had enough of them all and calls for silence.

Herding birds, it seems, is rather like herding cats and, while Nature is willing for them to make an attempt at wise council, she wryly observes that none of this has taken the birds any further forward (*PF* 619). She concludes, therefore, that the formel eagle herself should choose her mate, though being a medieval Nature of a law-enforcing variety, she gives a strong steer as to what she thinks the decision ought to be:

> 'If I were Resoun, thanne wolde I
> <u>Conseyle</u> yow the royal tercel take,   advise
> As seyde the <u>tercelet</u> ful skylfully,   falcon
> As for the <u>gentilleste</u> and most worthi,   most noble
> Which I have <u>wrought</u> so wel to my plesaunce   made
> That to yow hit oughte to been a <u>suffisaunce</u>.'   enough
>   (PF 632–7)

It is not a command as such, but it is an eloquent speech that draws attention to the similar view of those of rank, in the form of the falcon. It distinguishes the first eagle as chief amongst her creations and a source of pleasure, and, therefore, surely good enough for anyone. Such would certainly be the rational view. However, amongst all the allegorical figures we encountered in the Garden of Love, we did not come across Reason. It is not a virtue that is traditionally prized by lovers, so it is not a surprise, therefore, that the female eagle does not seize upon this carefully weighed advice as the solution to her dilemma. With a timorous voice, she asks instead for a year's respite, after which, she promises, she will make her own choice. Her request is granted; the other birds choose their mates; and the poem concludes with a song to welcome in the summer.

SUSPENDED ANIMATION

That both the parliament of birds and the formel eagle should have failed to make a decision should not come as a surprise. It is merely another example of the suspended state that has existed throughout the poem. After the rejection of worldly things advised by Scipio, Nature's garden had seemed to be a far more likely place for the dreamer to learn about earthly love. However, the perspective offered here is also limited. The Temple of Brass is nothing more than a shrine to sexual frustration and gratification, and the whole of the avian world is engaged in the activity of finding a mate. They do so far more prettily than Priapus in the temple, and the final image is of lovingly entwined pairs, where,

> ... ech of hem gan other in wynges take,
> And with here nekkes ech gan other <u>wynde</u>,   entwine
> Thankynge alwey the noble goddesse of <u>kynde</u>.   nature
>   (PF 670–2)

But this remains the love of ducks and geese, where a mate is easily found, or easily replaced. Human love is more complicated, as its parody with the eagles has shown, and any hint of its difficulties, nuances, and contradictions in the natural world simply brings 'kynde' to a halt. The festivities of St Valentine's Day cease as soon as the eagles consider themselves as courtly lovers and present conflicting claims, excluding themselves from the simple solutions that are available to their lesser brethren. All that can be done, therefore, is to move the problem aside and leave it for another year, allowing the natural world to get on with its own kind of loving. As such, the poem does not offer any kind of solution for the dreamer. The joyful singing of the birds awakens him, and he takes himself back to his books. The beauty of the universe shown to him by *The Dream of Scipio*, and the call for a love that seeks the common good had failed to satisfy him. The natural love inspired by *The Complaint of Nature*, with its sexual desire and frustrations, and its avian couplings had likewise failed to deliver the answers he wants. There are, however, more books, and the final lines of the poem make it clear how this investigator into the ways of love intends to spend his time:

I <u>wok</u>, and othere bokes tok me to,	awoke
To reede upon, and <u>yit</u> I rede alwey.	still
I hope, <u>ywis</u>, to rede <u>so</u> som day	indeed; in such a way
That I shal <u>mete</u> som thyng for to fare	encounter
The <u>bet</u>, and thus to rede I nyl nat <u>spare</u>.	better; stop
(*PF* 695–9)	

His incessant reading is signalled by the appearance of the word four times in the last five lines, bringing the poem to an end with this urgent scholarly activity. The opening lines had warned us that life is short and that the craft of love takes a long time to learn. The poem has shown us, however, that the narrator does not intend to derive his learning from experience. His world is the world of books, and if one volume fails to satisfy him then there are others to which he can turn and turn again as required. If nothing else, he is aware that there are no easy answers.

FURTHER READING

Very useful information may be found in the introduction and appendices of this edition of the poem: *Geoffrey Chaucer: The Parlement of Foulys* (1972). Ed. D. S.

Brewer. Manchester: Manchester University Press, as also in the edition: *Dream Visions and Other Poems* (2007). Ed. Kathryn L. Lynch. New York: Norton.

For a booklength account of the poem in its contexts, see J. A. W. Bennett (1957). *The Parlement of Foules: An Interpretation*. Oxford: Clarendon Press.

For an argument that the suitors represent historical persons, including Richard II, see Larry D. Benson, 'The Occasion of "The Parliament of Fowls"', in Ed. Larry D. Benson and Siegfried Wenzel (1982). *The Wisdom of Poetry*. Kalamazoo, MI: Western Michigan University Press, 123–44. On the contexts of the *Parliament* as a Valentine poem, see Henry Ansgar Kelly (1986). *Chaucer and the Cult of Saint Valentine*. Leiden: Brill. On Chaucer's representations of gardens, see Laura L. Howes (1997). *Chaucer's Gardens and the Language of Convention*. Gainesville: University Press of Florida.

For a translation of Macrobius's commentary on the sixth book of Cicero's *De Republica*, or 'Dream of Scipio', see William Harris Stahl, Trans. (1952). *Commentary on the Dream of Scipio*. New York: Columbia University Press.

For a translation of Alan de Lille's *De Planctu Naturae*, to which the Parliament refers, see James J. Sheridan, Trans. (1980). *The Plaint of Nature*. Toronto: Pontifical Institute of Mediaeval Studies.

On concepts of nature in medieval literature, see George D. Economou (1972). *The Goddess Natura in Medieval Literature*. Harvard: Harvard University Press, together with Hugh White (2000). *Nature, Sex, and Goodness in Medieval Literary Tradition*. Oxford: Oxford University Press. For an interpretation of love in the poem, see Helen Cooney, '*The Parlement of Foules: A Theodicy of Love*', *Chaucer Review* 32 (1998), 339–76.

For analysis of astronomical references in the poem, see J. D. North (1988). *Chaucer's Universe*. Oxford: Oxford University Press, 326–66.

THE LEGEND OF GOOD WOMEN

The Legend of Good Women gathers together the great women of ancient literature and shifts the focus of their stories. Usually, they are the supporting actresses in tales about great men, but in this work the spotlight is supposedly on them: a celebration of their steadfast love in the face of adversity. That, at least, is the task that Chaucer the dreamer is given by an angry God of Love. The poem opens with a prologue in which the author is condemned for his previous writings about love and is sentenced to tell the stories of 'good' women instead, which he does in a sequence of short legends. What emerges is a fascinating and complex study of story-telling and truth, as the spotlight is turned instead on the women who are usually simply the collateral damage of classical myth.

DAISY WORSHIPPING IN THE PROLOGUE

The month is May, the meadow is green, and there are daisies everywhere. Chaucer, the narrator, is a daisy worshipper, a man dedicated to what he calls the 'flower of flowers' (*LGW* F.53), spending his day in floral contemplation and his night in an 'herber [arbour]', a grassy chamber, liberally strewn with blossoms (*LGW* F.203–7). Sleep eventually claims him, and he finds himself in a dream landscape very similar to the one in which he has spent his day: the meadow is green, there are daisies everywhere, and he roams around as he had done in the waking world.

The dreamer is not, however, alone in this dream landscape, for he instantly encounters the God of Love holding the hand of a woman who appears to be a living and breathing daisy, dressed in green with a golden hairnet and a crown of pearly white petals (*LGW* F.214–20). The God of Love wears silk embroidered with green leaves and red roses, and he is crowned with a sun (*LGW* F.226–30). He is clearly no ordinary Cupid. He fixes the dreamer with a look that makes his blood run cold, demanding that the kneeling dreamer remove himself from the silent throng of women who surround his daisy queen. The god is direct as well as stern: 'Yt were better worthy, trewely,/ A worm to neghen ner [draw near] my flour than thow.' (*LGW* F.317–8). It quickly emerges that Chaucer the dreamer is considered worse than a worm because of his writings on love, specifically his *Troilus and Criseyde* and his translation of the *Romance of the Rose*, neither of which, the god feels, has shown love in a good light. The god threatens Chaucer with cruel torture – assuming, that is, that he is allowed to live.

At this point, however, the daisy queen intervenes. She reminds the irascible God of Love of the behaviour required of gods or, perhaps, of the behaviour required of them had they ever been perfect, for this daisy is as skilful in argument as she is beautiful. None of her arguments, however, flatter Chaucer the dreamer. He is a mere fly, she says, buzzing around the head of a kingly lion, deserving no more attention than the swat of a noble tail (*LGW* F.391–4); he might be an author, but he clearly does not understand what he writes, or perhaps he is simply weak-willed, coerced into writing these works (*LGW* F.366–8). At any rate, she says, he has served the god well with his poetic 'makynge' (*LGW* F.413) elsewhere. The god capitulates at once, full of praise for this 'charitable and trewe' woman (*LGW* F.493). Like any good lawyer, she then silences her client when the dreamer decides he has things to say about his own work in his own defence:

> And she answerde, 'Lat be thyn arguynge,
> For Love ne wol nat <u>countrepleted</u> be   contradicted
> In ryght ne wrong; and lerne that at me!
>   (*LGW* F.475–7)

Her advice is to take the sentence and run, or rather write, for the sentence is to create a 'gloryous legende' of *good* women.

THE DAISY QUEEN

In the course of *The Legend of Good Women*'s Prologue, this clever, beautiful, daisy woman is identified. She is, it emerges, Alceste, famed in ancient Greek legend as a woman who died in place of her husband. She is known, therefore, as the embodiment of self-sacrificing love. Rescued from the Underworld by Hercules, she comes to be thought of in the Middle Ages as a female Christ figure, dying willingly for others and being resurrected from the dead. While transformation into flowers is common in ancient myth, the association of Alceste with the daisy appears to be Chaucer's own invention, but it connects her again to Christ. The detailed description in the Prologue of the daisy closing its petals as darkness comes and opening them again in the morning in response to the rising sun, evokes death and rebirth:

And whan the sonne gynneth for to <u>weste</u>,	move to the west
Than closeth it, and draweth it to reste,	
So sore it is <u>afered</u> of the nyght,	afraid
Til on the morwe that it is dayes lyght.	
(LGW G.51–4)	

The daisy is the day's eye, like the sun itself, the source of life. The humble daisy finds itself exalted in the Middle Ages, not just as the focus of a whole collection of courtly French poetry, but as the flower that was believed to have grown at the foot of the Cross, the red marks on some daisies being believed to have originated in the blood shed by Christ. Even holding daisies was thought to be a medieval cure-all. In turn, the daisy Alceste is a defence and a comfort to the dreamer:

For <u>ne hadde confort been</u> of hire presence,	had it not been for the comfort
I hadde be ded, withouten any defence.	
(LGW G.181–2)	

It is not surprising, therefore, that Alceste should be a skilful mediator. The God of Love, in praising her as 'charytable' (*LGW* F.444), is making a large claim for her, for this is an important kind of medieval love. It is the kind of love that thinks of the well-being of others, that is, by its very nature, generous. Its Latin name is *caritas* and it gives us the modern word 'charity', but for the Middle Ages it is a term that goes well beyond benevolent giving and encompasses all unselfish love. She is, it must be said, better than the company she keeps.

THE GOD OF LOVE

The God of Love himself is a volatile character. He is quick to condemn Chaucer, and the overall sense of his presence is one of burning intensity. His complexion dazzles so much that the dreamer cannot look upon him, and in his hands he clutches two red-hot arrows (*LGW* G.163–7). He declares the dreamer to be his 'mortal fo' (*LGW* G.248) and launches into a tirade about both Chaucer's work and about his inability to select stories of good women from the 'sixty' books he owns (*LGW* G.273) – a vast number of volumes for any individual in the Middle Ages. The god declares that there are a hundred stories about good women for every single story about a bad one. Unfortunately, the authors he proceeds to name have a very specific kind of 'goodness' in mind:

'For to <u>hyre</u> love were they so trewe	their
That, rathere than they wolde take a newe,	
They chose to be ded in <u>sondry wyse</u>,	various ways
And <u>deiden</u>, as the story wol <u>devyse</u>;	died; tell
And some were <u>brend</u>, and some were cut the <u>hals</u>	burned; neck
And some <u>dreynt</u> for they wolden not be fals;'	drowned
(*LGW* G.288–93)	

These are all dead women, admittedly dead in a variety of ways, but nevertheless being 'true' to love has brought about their end. For the god, however, the reality of death, in the sense of what it means for the women, is immaterial: what matters is the symbolic value of their deaths, their devotion to love, and to the God of Love's laws. Like an amatory accountant, he is concerned only with the bottom line. This is why he has reduced more than eight thousand lines of *Troilus and Criseyde* to the simple notion that it shows 'How that Crisseyde Troylus forsok' (*LGW* G.265).

READING AND TELLING TALES

Much of the Prologue is concerned with the difficulty of interpreting literary texts. In addition to the reductive literary habits of the God of Love, there is the dreamer's own musings on what we can believe when it comes to reading. His conclusion that we might as well believe the books in the absence of evidence to the contrary (*LGW* G.27–8) is far from powerful, and it sets the tone for a work in which the written word is destabilised. The punishment inflicted upon the dreamer by Alceste has at its heart the same preoccupations. She demands, on behalf of the God of Love, that Chaucer should spend his time,

'In makynge of a gloryous legende	
Of goode women, maydenes and wyves,	
That were trewe in lovynge al <u>here</u> lyves;	their
And telle of false men that <u>hem</u> betrayen,	them
That al <u>here</u> lyf ne don <u>nat</u> but <u>assayen</u>	their; nothing; try to discover
How manye wemen they may <u>don a shame</u>;	dishonour
For in youre world that is now <u>holden game</u>.'	considered fun
(*LGW* G.473–80)	

On the one hand, it is a very suitable punishment: Chaucer will rectify the situation by telling the other side of the story, essentially following the logic of the Wife of Bath's 'Who peynted the leon?' on a grand scale (see p. 52). However, where the Wife of Bath had made no attempt to hide the faults of either side, the task here is more partisan. There is a clear division between 'goode women' and 'false men'. Indeed, these are men who apparently spend all their time engaged in dishonouring women for fun. As for the use of the word 'legende', it is in itself a loaded term, reserved for the life stories of saints. It is, therefore, not the healing punishment that we might have expected from Alceste: a balm to soothe the differences between men and women and clear the way for a higher kind of love. She is instead setting up a literary world of saintly female lovers and wickedly false men. Perhaps, as some critics have suggested, this was going to be an educative process in itself: the God of Love was going to discover that we need to be careful what we wish for, and a collection of stories about 'good' women might be no more to his romantic taste than the works of Chaucer that he had already condemned.

However, *The Legend of Good Women* remains unfinished, and we cannot speculate about how it might have ended. Chaucer's famous 'Retraction' at the end of the *Canterbury Tales* mentions a book of 'twenty-five ladies' (*CT* X 1086–7), so it appears that the plan for the *Legend* may have been considerably larger than the ten tales that have come down to us. In addition, the God of Love demands that the collection should culminate in the tale of Alceste herself as a, 'calandier [model] … Of goodnesse, for she taughte of fyn lovynge' (*LGW* G.533–4). That she should provide a blueprint for goodness is natural, given what we know of her, but the justification that hers was 'fyn lovynge' – courtly love – is reductive. She chose to die in place of her husband and descended into Hell. This is a long way from the delicate games of pity and mercy that constitute courtly love (see p. 95). Alceste, like every woman in the *Legend*, is a famous name, and the currency of the tales is suicide, rape, betrayal, and abandonment. The God of Love sets the tone for all of this when he chooses for the dreamer the subject of the first tale: Cleopatra, Queen of Egypt.

THE LEGEND OF CLEOPATRA

The story of Cleopatra was well known in the Middle Ages, and it is not wholly surprising that she should be the nominee of the God of Love. She was famous for her passion, known for her sexual liberality (Dante places her among the lustful in the second circle of Hell), and her suicide by serpent was the stuff of legend. She was, in essence, a famous lover, whose full story encompasses adultery, murder, and incest. In the face of this, the narrator is tentative. Indeed, for almost three-quarters of the tale, he would seem to prefer not to speak of Cleopatra at all. The opening lines are very telling:

After the deth of <u>Tholome</u> the kyng,	Ptolemy
That al Egipt hadde in his governyng,	
<u>Regned</u> his queene Cleopataras;	reigned
(*LGW* 580–2)	

It would appear that it is impossible to launch into the story of Cleopatra without first placing her in the context of male rule. In fact, Cleopatra's own reign is summarised in this one line, as the narrator turns his attention instead to Anthony:

He was, of persone and of gentillesse,   in terms of his body and manners
And of discrecioun and hardynesse,   judgment; bravery
Worthi to any wyght that liven may;   as good as any man
And she was fayr as is the rose in May.
                              (*LGW* 610–13)

Anthony is praised for all things, while Cleopatra is a one-line cliché of beauty. She does not even get a description of her own, her 'May' being a mere repetition of the 'may' that had made Anthony the equal of any man on earth. The echo is, however, symptomatic of a relationship in which she has vowed to duplicate not just his actions, but his fate:

'And in myself this covenaunt made I tho,   promise; then
That ryght swich as ye felten, wel or wo,   whatever happened to you
As fer forth as it in my power lay,   much
Unreprovable unto my wyfhod ay,   forever irreproachable as a wife
The same wolde I fele, lyf or deth.'
                              (*LGW* 688–92)

However, it takes the narrator a while to get to this point. Faced with the task of describing the couple's wedding feast, he decides that he would rather not 'overload the boat' (*LGW* 621) in terms of description, and that he can, therefore, omit the festivities. Almost as though he has been inspired by his own metaphor, he then turns his attention instead to the sea battle that proves to be the downfall of Anthony and Cleopatra. This is a subject that captures his imagination, and he launches into a virtuoso account of medieval warfare (in his enthusiasm, the narrator has forgotten that this is a tale of Ancient Egypt), seen through sea-going eyes as a 'grete gonne' goes off, grappling hooks are used to draw the enemy vessels alongside, riggings are cut, and peas are scattered to make the decks treacherous (*LGW* 635–49). It is one of the most detailed and technical battle scenes in all of Chaucer's work, but it is not what the dreamer has been commissioned to produce. It is as if he only dares to focus on the dangerously sexual Cleopatra once Anthony is safely dead, by his own hand. Until that point, the viewer's eye pans over her, picking out a purple sail instead, or the furiously churning oars (*LGW* 654–5). Her adulterous body can only be viewed once the opportunity for transgression has been removed, and she is able to become a model for female suicidal 'trouthe' (*LGW* 668).

The final focus is, therefore, upon the tomb, or more specifically, the tomb and the pit, that Chaucer has invented for Cleopatra's end. Her final queenly act is to order a 'shryne' (*LGW* 672) to be constructed using all the precious stones of Egypt. But it is to be the final resting place only of Anthony, whose body is embalmed and laid among the spices. The word 'shryne' is used three times, for this is not a mere tomb, we must understand. The word is used in the Middle Ages in the context of saints and holy relics. Anthony's body is, therefore, an object of adoration for Cleopatra, and she does not intend to lay her own body next to his. Instead, she digs a pit and fills it with snakes, orchestrating her death, 'with good cheere' (*LGW* 700). She makes herself the sacrificial offering at his shrine and in so doing purifies one of the most famous female bodies in history. Medieval images rarely failed to depict a naked Cleopatra, but there is no erotic charge in the naked body that here descends into the earth:

> And with that word, naked, with ful good herte,
> Among the serpents in the pit she <u>sterte</u>,   went
> And there she <u>ches</u> to have hire buryinge.   chose
> > (*LGW* 696–8)

'Sterte' is a verb of vigorous or decisive movement. This is the death she chooses. But there is nevertheless no sense of triumph. Cleopatra has proved her fidelity to the point of suicide, but she is alone in the earth. It is the kind of sacrifice that accomplishes nothing, not even a romantic notion of union in death.

THE LEGEND OF HYPSIPYLE AND MEDEA

In creating the double legend of Hypsipyle and Medea, Chaucer is able to follow the fortunes of Jason as he wreaks havoc in the lives of several women, moving through the ancient world like a small but deadly poison. We are left in no doubt that Jason, hero of the Argonauts and captor of the Golden Fleece, is to be regarded as a villain. The narrator vents his indignation in a series of exclamations:

Yif that I live, thy name shal be shove	if; widely known
In English that thy sekte shal be knowe!	your sect (i.e. 'men like you')
Have at thee, Jason! Now thyn horn is	take this; you've been found
blowe!	out

(LGW 1381–3)

Jason is described throughout in terms of consuming women. He is a bottomless pit of appetite (*LGW* 1582–6), a devourer (*LGW* 1581), the fox in the henhouse:

For evere as tendre a capoun et the fox,	capon; ate
Thow he be fals and hath the foul betrayed,	though; bird
As shal the good-man that therfore hath payed.	for it

(LGW 1389–91)

The difficulty with this metaphor, however, is that while Jason might be condemned as a fox, the fate of women is to be devoured no matter what: if not by the thief in the night, then by the 'good-man' who has somehow 'payed' for the privilege.

This sense of women as male prey is reinforced by the behaviour of the other men in the legend. Jason is accompanied by an oafish Hercules, who does much of Jason's wooing for him; a none-too-bright best friend who makes nonsensical declarations:

'As wolde God that I hadde yive	I wish to; given
My blod and flesh, so that I myghte live,	
With the nones that he hadde owher a wif'	on the condition; anywhere

(LGW 1538–40)

This makes just as little sense in translation ('I wish to God that I had given my blood and flesh, provided I still might live, if only he had a wife!'), and is uttered in monosyllabic or repetitive tones ('for swich a lusty lyf / She shulde lede with this lusty knyght!' *LGW* 1541–2). The father of Medea is more subtle than Hercules, but nevertheless offers his daughter up to Jason:

He made hire don to Jason companye	keep Jason company
At mete, and sitte by hym in the halle.	dinner

(LGW 1601–2)

It would be easy to miss the quietly coercive 'made', but the sense in this legend of a world controlled by men is very strong.

The real difficulty of the tale, however, comes in the form of the women. Jason's first wife, Hypsipyle, is traditionally regarded as a 'good' woman, and Chaucer emphasises this by having her come across the Argonauts when she is doing her daily reconnaissance of the beaches in search of shipwrecked sailors. It is simply her nature to help everyone (*LGW* 1477) and she is easily duped by Hercules's praise of Jason. Medea, however, is a woman with a more difficult history. In classical sources she is a sorceress, a powerful and pro-active force, sometimes accused of bewitching Jason, and certainly instrumental in the deaths of his enemies. She retains only a little of her autonomy and power here. Not a mere 'innocent' like Hypsipyle (*LGW* 1546), Medea negotiates marriage in return for the information Jason needs to obtain the Golden Fleece, outlining the dangers, the solutions, and her own indispensability to the enterprise:

Tho gan this Medea to hym declare	
The peril of this <u>cas</u> <u>from poynt to poynt</u>,	business; from beginning to end
And of his batayle, and in what <u>disjoynt</u>	jeopardy
He <u>mote</u> stonde, of which no creature	must
<u>Save only she ne myghte his lyf assure</u>	could save his life except her
(*LGW* 1629–34)	

There is no witchcraft here. Medea is making a business arrange-ment, sealed with a wedding night, and even though the narrator refers to her 'enchauntement' (*LGW* 1650), the sorceress has been reduced to a rather pragmatic wife. Indeed, within a few lines she is no longer even that, for Jason takes a third wife and abandons Medea as he had abandoned Hypsipyle:

For as a traytour he is from hire <u>go</u>,	gone
And with hire <u>lafte</u> his yonge children two,	left
And falsly hath betraysed hire, allas,	
As evere in love a <u>chef</u> traytour he was;	principal
(*LGW* 1656–9)	

Jason is a traitor; this we know. However, in the middle of this condemnation, there is a glimpse of something truly disturbing, something that a medieval audience would have been awaiting from the beginning. It is the mention of the children. Medea had a talent for murder: a taste for the theatrical and an ability to build suspense. The classical sources tell us that when she eloped with Jason, she murdered her brother and scattered the pieces of his body behind her in order to slow down their pursuers; she duped loving daughters into murdering their own father in a three-day magic trick; and she killed Jason's third wife with the gift of a crown and robe that ate into the bride's flesh and made her die in torment. All of this is as nothing, however, compared to the fact that she slaughters her own children as an act of vengeance against Jason. The narrator steers the audience away from the horrors that await the little boys and focusses instead on Medea's letter of recrimination to the man who has abandoned her. The audience is aware, however, of what is to come.

The God of Love had demanded counter-narratives, a retelling of the stories that traditionally condemned women. He also, in his own inability to understand the complexity of the works he condemns, is living proof that any narrative is open to other interpretations. Except perhaps this one. Traitorous acts, adultery, betrayal are the flip side of fidelity to purpose, the triumph of true love, the pursuit of ultimate truth: it simply depends on who is telling the story. But the murder of the children cannot be finessed in this way. Medea can be rehabilitated only up to the point that she kills her sons. The dreamer knows that this is the part of the story he cannot drag out into the light and, yet, like touching a painful tooth, he cannot leave it alone. Chaucer therefore uses the gentlest statement of fact to unleash the horror that lies at the unchangeable heart of Medea's tale. He leaves the children painfully exposed in the midst of his condemnation of Jason, waiting for their mother to finish her lament that she will never again see her husband's yellow hair (*LGW* 1672).

THE LEGEND OF LUCRECE

Not all of the women in the *Legend* have the image problems of Cleopatra or Medea. Topping any medieval list of 'good' women would have been Lucrece, the Roman matron raped by Tarquin, who killed herself rather than bring 'dishonour' upon her husband. It is a horrible tale, but the one that ancient and medieval authors most frequently reached for when searching for examples of female virtue. That being the case, the reader might have expected a triumphalist account of self-sacrifice, but what Chaucer gives us is a far more complex and disturbing tale.

It is the boasting of Lucrece's own husband that starts the tragic process. In an idle moment during a siege, Tarquin, son of the king, invites the men to praise their wives and decide among themselves whose wife is best. The young Collatinus, not content with this, declares that description is nothing in comparison with the real thing, and invites Tarquin to come and view his wife. The plan is that Lucrece should be caught unawares, so the men sneak into the house like criminals:

The husbonde knew the <u>estris</u> wel and fyn,	layout of the house
And <u>prively</u> into the hous they gon,	secretly
Nor at the <u>yate</u> porter <u>nas there</u> non,	gate; there was
And at the chambre-dore they abyde.	
This noble wif sat by hire beddes side	
<u>Dischevele</u>, for no malyce she ne <u>thoughte</u>;	hair unbound; suspected

(*LGW* 1715–20)

The intimate nature of this moment, with the unsuspecting Lucrece in her bedroom, her hair hanging loose and the reader viewing her from the doorway with the furtive men, is already a violation before Tarquin states his intent. She will be 'dischevele' again after the rape (1829), emphasising that the crime starts here with this illicit gaze upon her.

The horror of the rape that eventually follows is intensified by the detail of confused experience as Lucrece is awakened by a 'presse', an unfamiliar weight, in her bed (*LGW* 1787). Tarquin has the point of a sword aimed at her heart, and her panic is shown in the text's rapid succession of questions:

What shal she <u>seyn</u>? Hire wit is al ago ...	say
To whom shal she compleyne or make mone?	
What, shal she fyghte with an <u>hardy</u> knight? ...	strong
What, shal she crye, or how shal she <u>asterte</u>	escape
<u>That</u> hath hire by the throte with <u>swerd</u> at herte?	the man who; sword

(*LGW* 1797–1803)

The free indirect style of her thought brings us close to her state of mind, but we are propelled outwards again the next minute as Lucrece herself loses consciousness (*LGW* 1816).

The deadly faint is Chaucer's own addition to the story, and its effect is to distance Lucrece from the unfelt violation of her body. Her reaction afterwards will be, therefore, not to the memory of the rape, but to the knowledge of the rape. It is not her private horror that appals her, but the fact, and she shares that fact with everyone she knows: sending for her friends, her father and mother, and her husband all together. The narrator commends her as 'so wyfly [womanly] and so trewe' (*LGW* 1843) and his report of what follows contains all that we might have expected in terms of wanting to save her husband's Roman reputation, the reassurance of friends, the absolving of all blame, the assurance of forgiveness. But the effect of this last word on Lucrece is startling, and we hear her own voice issue her final words:

> 'Be as be may,' quod she, 'of forgyvyng,
> I wol not have noo <u>forgyft</u> for nothing.'   forgiveness
> (*LGW* 1852–3)

The clumsy assurance of her well-meaning relatives and friends is challenged. She does not want forgiveness; she has done nothing. She would, therefore, prefer to cancel out her life, and does so. Few suicide speeches can have begun with the phrase, 'Be that as it may', but these are the words of rather prim contradiction that signal the end of Lucrece, as she catches up a knife and stabs herself. As she falls, her final thought is to rearrange her clothing, so that not even a foot is exposed:

> And as she fel <u>adoun</u>, she <u>kaste hir lok</u>,   down; glanced around
> And of hir clothes yet she <u>hede tok</u>.   took heed
> For in hir fallynge yet she had a care,
> <u>Lest that hir fet</u> or suche thyng lay bare;   in case her feet
> (*LGW* 1856–9)

It is clear that Lucrece is not a Cleopatra or a Medea. She does not strip for the grave; she does not wreak havoc on those who have done her wrong. She is simply a Roman woman, whose concerns had been those of her household and of her own person. If the narrative voice somehow belittles her in this moment, it is perhaps only because Chaucer wants to show us the ultimate tragedy of Lucrece: that there is no safe place, no sanctuary for the bodies of women. Tarquin is the only monster in the tale, but he is not the only one to violate Lucrece. The narrator-dreamer draws attention to her body, even as she tries to cover it in death; he imagines horrors that people might perpetrate on her unconscious form even as she swoons to block out the real horror (*LGW* 1817–18), and when she is dead, Brutus subjects her to further exposure, telling her story 'openly' and ordering that she be carried 'openly' on a bier through Rome, 'that men may see and here' (*LGW* 1865–7). The intention may be to overthrow the Tarquins, but every man in Rome still gazes upon Lucrece. To be the focus of forgiveness, lasciviousness, or horror is not what she wants, but Lucrece realises that she cannot control what other people do to her. Ultimately, the only defence she has is to detach herself from consciousness, as her body did during the rape, and as she does finally in her suicide. The narrative voice is, as usual, unequal to the task of understanding his subject and, as always, the remarks he makes are sententious and inappropriate, but it no longer matters: Lucrece is no longer there.

The remaining legends, of Dido, Ariadne, and the rest, are similarly tales of female suffering. With the one exception of Thisbe, they are all betrayed, abandoned, or worse, by the men they have loved, and the end of each tale bequeaths us either at least one distraught woman or, more usually, a lone female corpse. Each tale is different in the detail, and those details can be heart-breakingly vivid – Ariadne kissing her departed lover's footprints in the sand (*LGW* 2208–9); Hypermnestra, ice-cold with fear (*LGW* 2683) – but the end result is always a woman literally or metaphorically bleeding. The critics have been unsure what Chaucer meant to achieve with this blood bath, and reactions range from hostility towards what the critics take to be a satire against women, to a wholehearted belief that the tales promote female 'goodness'. The task that the dreamer was given in the Prologue sounds simple but is, in fact, an immensely difficult one, for how can someone describe something as complicated as love, with a starting point that demands 'good' women and 'false' men? The simple, daisy-worshipping dreamer is dispatched into a minefield of classical stories and does his best to follow his orders. Sometimes he more or less succeeds, and at other times he very much fails. In the process, the tone pitches from idealism to tragedy, to unexpected humour. No matter what the circumstances, no matter what the mess, his job is to label the women as 'trewe in lovynge' (*LGW* G.475) and move on. Behind this, however, are complicated ideas about perspectives in storytelling, and particularly about the men entrusted with telling those stories. Like the lifeless Lucrece, viewed from all angles, these women have been filtered through the gaze of countless men before they reach the dreamer. He is only the latest to appropriate their lives and attempt to shape them to his will, and if he fails, and he surely does fail, then that failure is Chaucer's ultimate success.

FURTHER READING

For an informative edition of the Prologue and of the Legend of Dido, with introductions and notes, see *Chaucer's Dream Poetry* (1997). Ed. Helen Phillips and Nick Havely. Harlow: Longman.

For translations of an immensely influential classical model in Ovid's *Heroides*, imaginary letters by famous abandoned women to the men who variously seduced and betrayed them, see Ovid, *Heroides, Amores* (1977). Trans. G. Showerman, rev. G. P. Goold. Loeb Classical Library. Cambridge, MA: Harvard University Press.

For a translation of Boccaccio's *De Claris Mulieribus* (Concerning Famous Women), a pioneering collection of biographies exclusively of women (ca. 1355–9), see *Giovanni Boccaccio, Famous Women* (2001). Trans. V. Brown. I Tatti Renaissance Library. Cambridge, MA: Harvard University Press.

Chaucer's *Legend of Good Women* has been the focus of a number of book-length studies, of which a recent example is Carolyn P. Collette (2014). *Rethinking Chaucer's* Legend of Good Women. Woodbridge, Suffolk: York Medieval Press, along with an informative collection of essays in *The Legend of Good Women: Context and Reception* (2006). Ed. Carolyn P. Collette. Cambridge: D. S. Brewer. For a succinct introduction, see Julia Boffey and A. S. G. Edwards, 'The *Legend of Good Women*', in Jill Mann and Piero Boitani, Eds. (2003). *The Cambridge Companion to Chaucer*. 2nd edn. Cambridge: Cambridge University Press, together with James Simpson, 'Ethics and Interpretation: Reading Wills in Chaucer's *Legend of Good Women*', *Studies in the Age of Chaucer*, 20 (1998), 73–100.

Also valuable and stimulating are Carolyn Dinshaw (1989). *Chaucer's Sexual Poetics*. Madison: University of Wisconsin Press. Ch. 2 'The naked text in English to declare', and Sheila Delany (1994). *The Naked Text: Chaucer's 'Legend of Good Women'*. Berkeley: University of California Press, together with F. Perceval (1998). *Chaucer's Legendary Good Women*. Cambridge: Cambridge University Press, and in addition Lisa J. Kiser (1983). *Telling Classical Tales: Chaucer and 'The Legend of Good Women'*. Ithaca, NY: Cornell University Press.

BIBLIOGRAPHY

This bibliography is organised thematically. Many sections are in two parts, with introductory essays followed by fuller studies. The introductory essays are mostly to be found in the volumes listed in the 'Guides and companions' section. Reference to these works is in the form of editor name(s) and date: for example, 'Boitani and Mann 2003'.

GUIDES AND COMPANIONS

Boitani, Piero, and Mann, Jill, eds. (2003). *The Cambridge Companion to Chaucer*, 2nd edn. Cambridge: Cambridge University Press.

Brown, Peter, ed. (2007). *A Companion to Medieval English Literature and Culture c.1350–c.1500*. Oxford: Blackwell.

———. (2019). *A New Companion to Chaucer*. Oxford: Blackwell.

Corrie, Marilyn, ed. (2009). *A Concise Companion to Middle English Literature*. Oxford: Wiley-Blackwell.

Ellis, Steve, ed. (2005). *Chaucer: An Oxford Guide*. Oxford: Oxford University Press.

Fein, Susanna, and Raybin, Daniel B., eds. (2010). *Chaucer: Contemporary Approaches*. Philadelphia: University of Pennsylvania Press.

Galloway, Andrew, ed. (2011). *The Cambridge Companion to Medieval English Culture*. Cambridge: Cambridge University Press.

Gray, Douglas, ed. (2003). *The Oxford Companion to Chaucer*. Oxford: Oxford University Press.

Lerer, Seth, ed. (2006). *The Yale Companion to Chaucer*. New Haven: Yale University Press.

Saunders, Corinne, ed. (2006). *A Concise Companion to Chaucer*. Oxford: Blackwell.

———. (2010). *A Companion to Medieval Poetry*. Oxford: Blackwell.

Scanlon, Larry, ed. (2009). *The Cambridge Companion to Medieval English Literature 1100–1500*. Cambridge: Cambridge University Press.

Strohm, Paul, ed. (2009). *Middle English*. Oxford: Oxford University Press.
Turner, Marion, ed. (2013). *A Handbook of Middle English Studies*. Oxford: Blackwell.

INTRODUCTIONS

Brewer, Derek (1998). *A New Introduction to Chaucer*, 2nd edn. London: Longman.
Brown, Peter (2011). *Geoffrey Chaucer*. Oxford: Oxford University Press.
Minnis, Alastair (2014). *The Cambridge Companion to Chaucer*. Cambridge: Cambridge University Press.
Wallace, David (2017). *Geoffrey Chaucer: A New Introduction*. Oxford: Oxford University Press.

WRITING AND READING IN A MANUSCRIPT CULTURE

Boffey, Julia, 'From manuscript to modern text', in Brown 2007.
————, 'Manuscript and print: books, readers and writers', in Saunders 2010.
Boffey, Julia, and Edwards, A. S. G., 'Manuscripts and audience', in Saunders 2006.
Gillespie, Alexandra, 'Production and dissemination', in Corrie 2009.
————, 'Books', in Strohm 2009.
————, 'Manuscript', in Turner 2013.
Wakelin, Daniel, 'Manuscripts and modern editions', in Corrie 2009.
Gillespie, Alexandra, and Wakelin, Daniel, eds. (2011). *The Production of Books in Medieval England, 1350–1500*. Cambridge: Cambridge University Press.
Hanna, Ralph (2013). *Introducing English Medieval Book History: Manuscripts, Their Producers and Their Readers*. Liverpool: Liverpool University Press.
Kerby-Fulton, Kathryn, Hilmo, Maidie, and Olson, Linda (2013). *Opening Up Middle English Manuscripts: Literary and Visual Approaches*. Ithaca, NY: Cornell University Press.
Turville-Petre, Thorlac (2007) *Reading Middle English Literature*. Oxford: Blackwell, chapter 2, 'Texts and manuscripts'.

AUDIENCES AND READING

Boffey, Julia, and Edwards, A. S. G., 'Manuscripts and audience', in Saunders 2006.
Coleman, Joyce, 'Aurality', in Strohm 2009.
————, 'Audience', in Turner 2010.
Green, Richard Firth, 'Textual production and textual communities', in Scanlon 2009.
Hanna, Ralph, 'Middle English manuscripts and readers', in Saunders 2010.
Horobin, Simon, 'Chaucer's audiences: manuscripts and scribes', in Fein and Raybin 2010.

Coleman, Joyce (1996). *Public Reading and the Reading Public in Late Medieval England and France*. Cambridge: Cambridge University Press.
Lawton, David (1985). *Chaucer's Narrators*. Cambridge: D. S. Brewer

AUTHORS AND AUTHORITY

Bose, Mishtooni, 'Religious Authority and Dissent', in Brown 2007.
Galloway, Andrew, 'Auctorite', in Brown 2019.
Gillespie, Vincent, 'Authorship', in Turner 2013.
Griffiths, Jane, 'The Author', in Corrie 2009.
Nuttall, Jenni, 'Patronage', in Brown 2019.
Steiner, Emily, 'Authority', in Strohm 2009.
Yeager, R. F., 'Books and Authority', in Corrie 2009.

GENRES: KINDS AND MODES OF LITERATURE

Burrow, J. A., '*The Canterbury Tales*: romance', in Boitani and Mann 2003.
Eckhardt, Caroline D., 'Genre', in Brown 2019.
Ferster, Judith, 'Genre in and of the *Canterbury Tales*', in Saunders 2006.
Hiatt, Alfred, 'Genre without system', in Strohm 2009.
Kendrick, Laura, 'Comedy', in Brown 2019.
Orlemanski, Julie, 'Genre', in Turner 2013.
Pearsall, Derek, '*The Canterbury Tales*: comedy', in Boitani and Mann 2003.
Spearing, A. C., '*The Canterbury Tales*: exemplum and fable', Boitani and Mann 2003.
Cooper, Helen (1983). *The Structure of the Canterbury Tales*. London: Duckworth, chapter 3, 'An encyclopaedia of kinds'.
Crane, Susan (1994). *Gender and Romance in Chaucer's Canterbury Tales*. Princeton, NJ: Princeton University Press.
Davenport, W. A. (1988). *Chaucer: Complaint and Narrative*. Cambridge: D. S. Brewer.
Kelly, Henry Ansgar (1997). *Chaucerian Tragedy*. Cambridge: D. S. Brewer.

FORM AND STYLE

Cannon, Christopher, 'Chaucer's style', in Boitani and Mann 2003.
———, 'Form', in Strohm 2009.
Copeland, Rita, 'Chaucer and Rhetoric', in Lerer 2006.
Windeatt, Barry, 'Literary structures', in Boitani and Mann 2003.
Benson, C. David (1986). *Chaucer's Drama of Style: Poetic Variety and Contrast in the Canterbury Tales*. Chapel Hill: University of North Carolina Press.
Holton, Amanda (2008). *The Sources of Chaucer's Poetics*. Aldershot: Ashgate.

Payne, Robert O. (1963). *The Key of Remembrance: A Study of Chaucer's Poetics*. New Haven, CT: Yale University Press.

TRANSLATION

Batt, Catherine, 'Translation and society', in Brown 2007.

Cooper, Helen, 'Translation and adaptation', in Corrie 2009.

Ellis, Roger, 'Translation', in Brown 2019.

Warren, Michelle R., 'Translation', in Strohm 2009.

Windeatt, Barry (2008). 'Chaucer as translator', in Roger Ellis, ed., *The Oxford History of Literary Translation in English*, vol. 2. Oxford: Oxford University Press, pp. 137–48.

CHAUCER AND THE CLASSICAL PAST

Baswell, Christopher, 'England's antiquities: Middle English literature and the classical past', in Brown 2007.

Cooper, Helen, 'The classical background', in Ellis 2005.

Fyler, John M., 'Pagan survivals', in Brown 2019.

Galloway, Andrew, 'The past', in Corrie 2009.

Fumo, Jamie C. (2010). *The Legacy of Apollo: Antiquity, Authority, and Chaucerian Poetics*. Toronto: Toronto University Press.

Minnis, Alastair (1982). *Chaucer and Pagan Antiquity*. Cambridge: D. S. Brewer.

CHAUCER AS AN ENGLISH WRITER

Lavezzo, Kathy, 'England', in Fein and Raybin 2010.

Scase, Wendy, 'The English background', in Ellis 2005.

Smith, D. Vance, 'Chaucer as an English writer', in Lerer 2006.

Davenport, W. A. (1998). *Chaucer and His English Contemporaries*. Basingstoke: Macmillan.

Lavezzo, Kathy, ed. (2004). *Imagining a Medieval English Nation*. Minneapolis: University of Minnesota Press.

CHAUCER'S ENGLAND AND EUROPE

Butterfield, Ardis, 'Nationhood', in Ellis 2005.

Hanrahan, Michael, 'Flemings', in Brown 2019.

Lavezzo, Kathy, 'Nation', in Turner 2013.

———, 'Ethnicity', in Brown 2019.

Simpson, James, 'Chaucer as a European Writer', in Lerer 2006.

Thomas, Alfred, 'Bohemia', in Brown 2019.

Turner, Marion (2019). *Chaucer: A European Life*. Princeton, NJ: Princeton University Press.

CHAUCER'S FRENCH BACKGROUND

Butterfield, Ardis, 'Chaucer's French inheritance', in Boitani and Mann 2003.

———, 'England and France', in Brown 2007.

———, 'France', in Fein and Raybin 2010.

Hanly, Michael, 'France', in Brown 2019.

Phillips, Helen, 'The French background', in Ellis 2005.

Butterfield, Ardis (2009). *The Familiar Enemy: Chaucer, Language, and Nation in the Hundred Years War*. Oxford: Oxford University Press.

Nolan, Barbara (1992). *Chaucer and the Tradition of the Roman Antique*. Cambridge: Cambridge University Press.

Wimsatt, James I. (1991). *Chaucer and His French Contemporaries: Natural Music in the Fourteenth Century*. Toronto: Toronto University Press.

CHAUCER'S ITALIAN BACKGROUND

Edwards, Robert R., 'Italy', in Fein and Raybin 2010.

Havely, Nick, 'The Italian background', in Ellis 2005.

Havely, Nick, 'Britain and Italy: Trade, travel, translation', in Brown 2007.

Wallace, David, 'Chaucer's Italian inheritance', in Boitani and Mann 2003.

Wallace, David, 'Italy', in Brown 2019.

Boitani, Piero, ed. (1983). *Chaucer and the Italian Trecento*. Cambridge: Cambridge University Press.

Clarke, K. P. (2011). *Chaucer and Italian Textuality*. Oxford: Oxford University Press.

Edwards, Robert R. (2002) *Chaucer and Boccaccio: Antiquity and Modernity*. London: Palgrave.

Ginsberg, Warren (2002). *Chaucer's Italian Tradition*. Ann Arbor: University of Michigan Press.

Wallace, David (1997). *Chaucerian Polity: Absolutist Lineages and Associational Forms in England and Italy*. Stanford: Stanford University Press.

CHAUCER AND LONDON

Benson, C. David, 'London', in Ellis 2005.

Brown, Peter Guy, 'London', in Brown 2019.

Turner, Marion, 'Politics and London life', in Saunders 2006.

Barron, Caroline (2004). *London in the Later Middle Ages: Government and People 1200–1500*. Oxford: Oxford University Press.

Butterfield, Ardis, ed. (2006). *Chaucer and the City*. Woodbridge, Suffolk: Boydell & Brewer.

Turner, Marion (2006). *Chaucerian Conflict: Languages of Antagonism in Late Fourteenth-Century London*. Oxford: Oxford University Press.

Wallace, David (1992). 'Chaucer and the Absent City', in Barbara Hanawalt, ed., *Chaucer's England: Literature in Historical Context*. Minneapolis: University of Minnesota Press.

COURT CULTURE AND CHIVALRY

Brewer, Derek, and Windeatt, Barry, 'Chivalry', in Brown 2019.

Kaeuper, Richard W. and Bohna, M., 'War and chivalry', in Brown 2007.

Sherman, Mark, 'Chivalry', in Ellis 2005.

Windeatt, Barry, 'Courtly writing', in Saunders 2006.

———, 'Courtiers and courtly poetry', in Saunders 2010.

Burnley, David (1998). *Courtliness and Literature in Medieval England*. Harlow: Longman.

Green, Richard F. (1980). *Poets and Princepleasers: Literature and the English Court in the Late Middle Ages*. Toronto: Toronto University Press.

Kaeuper, Richard W. (1999). *Chivalry and Violence in Medieval Europe*. Oxford: Oxford University Press.

Keen, Maurice H. (1984). *Chivalry*. New Haven: Yale University Press.

Scattergood, V. J., and Sherborne, J. W., eds. (1983). *English Court Culture in the Later Middle Ages*. London: Duckworth.

LOVE AND MARRIAGE

Cartlidge, Neil, 'Marriage, sexuality and the family', in Saunders 2006.

O'Donoghue, Bernard, 'Love and marriage', in Ellis 2005.

Phillips, Helen, 'Love', in Brown 2019.

Windeatt, Barry, 'Love', in Brown 2007.

Hume, Cathy (2012). *Chaucer and the Cultures of Love and Marriage*. Cambridge: D. S. Brewer.

Kelly, Henry Ansgar (1975). *Love and Marriage in the Age of Chaucer*. Ithaca, NY: Cornell University Press.

Schultz, James A. (2006). *Courtly Love, the Love of Courtliness, and the History of Sexuality*. Chicago: Chicago University Press.

GENDER AND SEXUALITIES

Blamires, Alcuin, 'Sexuality', in Ellis 2005.

Burger, Glen, and Kruger, Steven F., 'Sexuality', in Turner 2013.

McDonald, Nicola, 'Gender', in Turner 2013.

Beidler, Peter G., ed. (1998). *Masculinities in Chaucer: Approaches to Maleness in the Canterbury Tales and Troilus and Criseyde*. Cambridge: D. S. Brewer.

Blamires, Alcuin (2006). *Chaucer, Ethics and Gender*. Oxford: Oxford University Press.

Burger, Glenn (2003). *Chaucer's Queer Nation*. Minneapolis: University of Minnesota Press.

Crocker, Holly A. (2007). *Chaucer's Visions of Manhood*. New York: Palgrave Macmillan.

Davies, Isabel (2007). *Writing Masculinity in the Later Middle Ages*. Cambridge: Cambridge University Press.

Dinshaw, Carolyn (1989). *Chaucer's Sexual Poetics*. Madison: University of Wisconsin Press.

——— (1999). *Getting Medieval: Sexualities and Communities, Pre- and Postmodern*. Durham: Duke University Press.

Hansen, Elaine Tuttle (1992). *Chaucer and the Fictions of Gender*. Berkeley: University of California Press.

Mann, Jill (2001). *Feminizing Chaucer*, 2nd edn. Cambridge: D. S. Brewer.

Martin, Priscilla (1996). *Chaucer's Women: Nuns, Wives and Amazons*. Basingstoke: Macmillan.

Phillips, Kim M. (2003). *Medieval Maidens: Young Women and Gender in England, 1270–1540*. Manchester: Manchester University Press.

Zeikovitz, R. F. (2003). *Homoeroticism and Chivalry: Discourses of Male Same-Sex Desire in the Fourteenth Century*. New York: Palgrave Macmillan.

FEELING, PERCEPTION, IDENTITY, SELFHOOD

Ganim, John M., 'Identity and subjecthood', in Ellis 2005.

Lawton, David, 'Public interiorities', in Turner 2013.

McNamer, Sarah, 'Feeling', in Strohm 2009.

———, 'Emotion', in Brown 2019.

Miller, Mark, 'Subjectivity and ideology in the *Canterbury Tales*', in Brown 2007.

Staley, Lynn, 'Personal identity', in Brown 2019.

Turner, Marion, 'The senses', in Brown 2019.

Windeatt, Barry, 'Chaucer's tears', *Critical Survey*, 30 (2018), 74–93.

Crane, Susan (2002). *The Performance of Self: Ritual, Clothing and Identity during the Hundred Years War*. Philadelphia: University of Pennsylvania Press.

Spearing, A. C. (2005). *Textual Subjectivity: The Encoding of Subjectivity in Medieval Narratives and Lyrics*. Oxford: Oxford University Press.

——— (2013). *Medieval Autographies: The 'I' of the Text*. Notre Dame: University of Notre Dame Press.

SOCIAL STRUCTURES

Davis, Isabel, 'Class', in Turner 2013.

Rigby, S. H., 'Society and politics', in Ellis 2005.

————, 'Ideology', in Brown 2019.

Smith, D. Vance, 'Institutions', in Strohm 2009.

Strohm, Paul, 'The social and literary scene in England', in Boitani and Mann 2003.

Swanson, Robert, 'Social Structures', in Brown 2019.

Barbara Hanawalt, ed. (1992). *Chaucer's England: Literature in Historical Context*. Minneapolis: University of Minnesota Press.

Mann, Jill (1973). *Chaucer and Medieval Estates Satire*. Cambridge: Cambridge University Press.

Rigby, S. H. (1996). *Chaucer in Context: Society, Allegory, Gender*. Manchester: Manchester University Press.

STRUCTURES OF BELIEF

Edden, Valerie, 'The Bible', in Ellis 2005.

Gillespie, Vincent, 'Vernacular theology', in Strohm 2009.

Hirsh, John C., 'Christianity and the Church', in Saunders 2006.

Holsinger, Bruce, 'Liturgy', in Strohm 2009.

Perry, Ryan, 'The sins', in Brown 2019.

Rhodes, J. 'Religion', in Ellis 2005.

Sobecki, Sebastian, 'Pilgrimage and travel', in Brown 2019.

Watson, Nicholas, 'Religion', in Brown 2019.

Aers, David (2000). *Faith, Ethics and Church: Writing in England 1360–1409*. Cambridge: D. S. Brewer.

Benson, C. David, and Robertson, Elizabeth, eds. (1990). *Chaucer's Religious Tales*. Cambridge: D. S. Brewer.

Cole, Andrew (2008). *Literature and Heresy in the Age of Chaucer*. Cambridge: Cambridge University Press.

Ellis, Roger (1986). *Patterns of Religious Narrative in the Canterbury Tales*. London: Croom Helm.

Phillips, Helen, ed. (2010). *Chaucer and Religion*. Cambridge: D. S. Brewer.

Swanson, R. N., trans. (1993). *Catholic England: Faith, Religion and Observance before the Reformation*. Manchester: Manchester University Press.

SCIENCE AND PHILOSOPHY

Taarvitsainen, Irma, and Landert, Daniela, 'Science', in Brown 2019.

Tasioulas, J. A., 'Science', in Ellis 2005.

Utz, Richard, 'Philosophy', in Ellis 2005.

Voigts, Linda Ehrsam, 'Bodies', in Brown 2019.

Carey, Hilary (1992). *Courting Disaster: Astrology at the English Court and University in the Later Middle Ages*. Basingstoke: Macmillan.

Curry, Walter Clyde (1960). *Chaucer and the Mediaeval Sciences*, rev. edn. London: Allen & Unwin.

Gabrovsky, Alexander N. (2015). *Chaucer the Alchemist: Physics, Mutability and the Medieval Imagination*. New York: Palgrave.

Lynch, Kathryn L. (2000). *Chaucer's Philosophical Visions*. Cambridge: D. S. Brewer.

Manzalaoui, M. (1974). 'Chaucer and science', in Derek Brewer, ed., *Geoffrey Chaucer: Writers and Their Background*. London: Bell, pp. 224–61.

Miller, Mark (2004). *Philosophical Chaucer*. Cambridge: Cambridge University Press.

North, J. D. (1988). *Chaucer's Universe*. Oxford: Oxford University Press.

Wood, Chauncey (1970). *Chaucer and the Country of the Stars: Poetic Uses of Astrological Imagery*. Princeton, NJ: Princeton University Press.

VISUALITY

Brantley, Jessica, 'Vision, image, text', in Strohm 2009.

———, 'Material culture', in Turner 2013.

Brown, Peter, 'Images', in Brown 2007.

Kendrick, Laura, 'Visual texts in post-Conquest England', in Galloway 2011.

Nolan, Maura, 'Aesthetics', in Turner 2013.

Stanbury, Sarah, 'Visualizing', in Brown 2019.

Windeatt, Barry, 'Signs and symbols', in Corrie 2009.

Brown, Peter (2007). *Chaucer and the Making of Optical Space*. Oxford: Lang.

Fein, Susanna, and Raybin, David B., eds. (2016). *Chaucer: Visual Approaches*. Philadelphia: University of Pennsylvania Press.

Knapp, Peggy A. (2008). *Chaucerian Aesthetics*. New York: Palgrave Macmillan.

Kolve, V. A. (1984). *Chaucer and the Imagery of Narrative: The First Five Canterbury Tales*. Stanford: Stanford University Press.

——— (2009). *Telling Images: Chaucer and the Imagery of Narrative, II*. Stanford: Stanford University Press.

THEORETICAL APPROACHES, MEDIEVAL AND MODERN

Ashton, Gail, 'Feminisms', in Ellis 2005.

Burger, Glenn, 'Queer theory', in Ellis 2005.

Cohen, Jeffrey J., 'Postcolonialism', in Ellis 2005.

Federico, Sylvia, 'New Historicism', in Ellis 2005.

Ganim, John M., 'Postcolonialism', in Turner 2010.

Ingham, Patricia Clare, 'Psychoanalytical criticism', in Ellis 2005.

Windeatt, Barry, 'Postmodernism', in Ellis 2005.

Zeeman, Nicolette, 'Imaginative Theory', in Strohm 2009.

Cohen, Jeffrey J., ed. (2000). *The Postcolonial Middle Ages*. New York: Palgrave Macmillan.

Johnson, Eleanor (2013). *Practicing Literary Theory in the Middle Ages*. Chicago: Chicago University Press.

Fradenburg, L. O. Aranye (2002). *Sacrifice Your Love: Psychoanalysis, Historicism, Chaucer*. Minneapolis: University of Minnesota Press.

Minnis, Alastair (2010). *Medieval Theory of Authorship: Scholastic Literary Attitudes in the Later Middle Ages*, 2nd edn. Philadelphia: University of Pennsylvania Press.

Minnis, A. J., and Scott, A. B., eds. (1988). *Medieval Literary Theory and Criticism c.1100–c.1375. The Commentary Tradition*. Oxford: Oxford University Press.

Minnis, Alastair, and Johnson, Ian, eds. (2005). *The Cambridge History of Literary Criticism, vol. 2: The Middle Ages*. Cambridge: Cambridge University Press.

CHAUCER'S AFTERLIVES: READINGS AND RESPONSES

Brewer, Derek, ed. (1978). *Chaucer: The Critical Heritage*, 2 vols. London: Routledge and Kegan Paul.

Ellis, Steve (2000). *Chaucer at Large: The Poet in the Modern Imagination*. Minneapolis: University of Minnesota Press.

Lerer, Seth (1993). *Chaucer and His Readers: Imagining the Author in Late-Medieval England*. Princeton, NJ: Princeton University Press.

Meyer-Lee, Robert J. (2007). *Poets and Power from Chaucer to Wyatt*. Cambridge: Cambridge University Press.

Morse, Ruth, and Windeatt, Barry, eds. (1990). *Chaucer Traditions: Studies in Honour of Derek Brewer*. Cambridge: Cambridge University Press.

Prendergast, Thomas A. (2004). *Chaucer's Dead Body: From Corpse to Corpus*. London: Routledge.

Richmond, Velma Bourgeois (2004). *Chaucer as Children's Literature: Retellings from the Victorian and Edwardian Eras*. Jefferson, NC: McFarland.

Trigg, Stephanie (2001). *Congenial Souls: Reading Chaucer from Medieval to Postmodern*. Minneapolis: University of Minnesota Press.

INDEX